Financial Economy

This book examines how contemporary financial economy evolved as the predominant economic system, and why unabated accumulation of financial capital takes place in such systems. It reviews the mechanics of accumulation of wealth by tracing the historical roots of financial capital. Traversing the evolutions of capitalist systems since the 1850s till recent times, *Financial Economy* provides a lucid and logical explanation of the phenomenon. It uses a new methodology based on economic circuit of stocks and flows following the early ideas of the French economists of the 18th century and the contemporary Circuit school. It provides an alternative framework for studying economic systems design, keeping aside the orthodox neoclassical analysis of equilibrium market exchange. Further, it highlights the global financial circuit, the state of the current digitalised economy with electronic money transfers, consumer's decision-making and expected future earnings, and questions the relevance of some fundamental concepts of economics as well as economic policies. Using a notion of sequential economy, it also shows how present economic activities are treading upon the future.

This book will interest students and researchers of advanced macroeconomics, political economy, heterodox economics, economic history, and evolutionary economics. The historical account of the evolutions of capital, interest, and corporate structures will also be of interest to general readers.

Smita Roy Trivedi is Assistant Professor at the National Institute of Bank Management (NIBM) in India. She has a PhD in economics from the University of Kalyani, West Bengal, India, where she has worked as UGC research fellow. With specialisation in financial economics and banking, she is currently involved in teaching, training, research, and consultancy in the areas of international banking, financing of international trade, and technical analysis of financial markets. Her research interests include financialisation, central bank intervention, and bank profitability. Her most recent publications have been featured in *Economic Papers: A Journal of Applied Economics and Policy* (2016) and *Asia-Pacific Financial Markets* (2016).

Sutanu Bhattacharya is Professor of Economics at the University of Kalyani, West Bengal, India, and has been engaged in teaching and research since 1978. Along with a PhD in economics, he has professional qualifications as a cost and management accountant and an operational researcher. He specialises in financial economics, business accounting and corporate finance, operational research, econometrics, history of economics, and economics of education. In addition, he has work experience in the fields of corporate finance and educational administration. He has published widely, and has worked as a covenanted staff member in the Finance Division, Chloride India Ltd. and as Joint Secretary, University Grants Commission, India.

Financial Economy
Evolutions at the
Edge of Crises

Smita Roy Trivedi and
Sutanu Bhattacharya

Routledge
Taylor & Francis Group

LONDON AND NEW YORK

First published 2018
by Routledge
2 Park Square, Milton Park, Abingdon, Oxon OX14 4RN

and by Routledge
605 Third Avenue, New York, NY 10017

First issued in paperback 2020

Routledge is an imprint of the Taylor & Francis Group, an informa business

British Library Cataloguing-in-Publication Data
A catalogue record for this book is available from the British Library

Library of Congress Cataloging-in-Publication Data
A catalog record for this book has been requested

ISBN 13: 978-0-367-73516-6 (pbk)
ISBN 13: 978-1-138-22845-0 (hbk)

Typeset in Sabon
by Apex CoVantage, LLC

Contents

List of figures   vii
List of tables   viii
Preface   ix
List of abbreviations   xii

1 Introduction   1

2 Paradoxes of crisis and growth: the landscape   10

3 The twin concepts of capital: historical roots   30

4 Financial breeding: legitimisation of interest on money   43

5 Critique of neoclassical economics and revival of the idea of circuit analysis   62

6 The circuit construct: nascent corporate production economy   82

7 Rudimentary formulation of the circuit   101

8 Matured corporate accumulation: the creditisation phase   124

9 The financial circuit: leveraging the growth   143

10 Concluding note: the present as the future   162

Appendix: Notes on some financial aspects   171
Bibliography   190
Index   207

Figures

6.1 Nascent corporate production circuit, 1850–1930   94
6.2 Central part of the corporate production circuit   95
8.1 Matured corporate economic circuit: creditisation
    phase since the 1940s   133
9.1 The real and financial circuit   153

Tables

2.1 World growth rates of GDP by region   12
2.2 World per capita GDP growth rates by region   12
2.3 Savings rates as percentage of GDP in select countries   18
2.4 Household debt as percentage of net disposable
     income in select countries   19
2.5 Forbes Global 2000 – top companies' assets   20
2.6 Forbes Global 2000 – top companies' revenue   20
2.7 Growth rates of gross capital formation in select
     countries, 1976–2015   25
7.1a Items of initial money stocks and transfers   105
7.1b Items of circuit flows   105
7.1c Items of economic outcomes   106
7.2 Household sector's stock balance sheet   110
7.3 Household sector's flow account   110
7.4 Corporate production sector's stock balance sheet   111
7.5 Corporate production sector's flow account   112
7.6 Banking sector's stock balance sheet   113
7.7 Banking sector's flow account   114
A.1 Rentier income share in GDP in India, 1981–2016   187
A.2 Manufacturing sector and rentier incomes as
     percentage of GDP in India, 1981–2016   188

Preface

The present as the future:
If we are all dead in the longer run,
We don't survive in the present either.

After the global financial crisis of 2008 we have become concerned about the economic future that lies ahead. The concern is to know what is happening and how it is happening in respect of our economic existence. A reflection of this concern is also found in economic studies. A large volume of studies has now emerged giving descriptions of the events and the courses of development of the crisis of 2008. The discussions we find in economic literature are often too technical and address one aspect or another in bits and pieces. Consequently, we lose sight of the forest for the trees – our focus on what is happening on the whole gets blurred in a large volume of literature and so the question, why is it happening, goes completely out of focus.

What do we see on the whole in the current economic landscape? We see the corporate sector, or more specifically the large global corporations, continuously accumulating its wealth at an alarming rate while the household sector and the national governments are slipping into more and more accumulated debts. This is a now a global phenomenon.

At the background we see a growing financial economy over the last few decades with almost all monetary transactions now linked to an intricate global financial network. And it is growing even when our production sector stagnates. How has this become possible? More alarming is the fact that most of our financial savings is now linked to this global financial web and may evaporate overnight in financial crises originating anywhere in the web. Any major financial default or bankruptcy may spread like a wildfire in this web. We used to have faith in our national governments as the rescuer of the last resort, but here is also a big question mark, now put by the recent sovereign debt crisis in Europe. With an uncomfortable feeling at the back of our mind, we ask ourselves – is this the world we created and how?

The economic systems are not something given to us; they evolve through the economic constructs or institutions we create. The economic system we live in today has come through several economic evolutions that started with the Age of Capital in the 1850s in the West. It traversed a long way through repeated crises and the consequent evolutions out of necessity to obviate the crises. To understand what is happening and why it is happening now in the economic arena we need to trace the economic evolutions – why and how we created this world.

We discuss here broadly three phases of evolution – the nascent corporate production system (1850–1930), the matured corporate production with creditisation (1945–70) and, finally, the financial economy since the 1990s. Each of these phases evolved in the context of one crisis or another in the existing system. Probing the fundamental nature of the economic systems and their crises in these three phases, we may get some answer to our questions.

This book does not deal with the technical details of different financial commodities and operations in various financial markets. It focuses rather on the organisational evolution of the financial economy and its implications. Moreover, we rarely get any clear idea in respect of our questions from the conventional economic theories. Therefore, before tracing out the economic evolutions, we have examined at some length the conventional economic ideas and methodologies to locate the conceptual ambiguities that prevail at the foundation of mainstream economic analyses, for which they are unable to answer our questions. A paradigm shift in economic studies is now required. We propose an alternative – the economic circuit methodology – for studying the organisational evolutions in economic systems through the crises.

This book is just an attempt to explain, overall, what has so far happened and what is now happening around us. It does not try to predict what will happen next – another economic evolution in a new direction, a structural transformation in our current economic systems, or a hopeless economic devastation. We await the answer to come in the future.

This book has been built on the contributions of celebrated economic thinkers – from the French physiocrats to Karl Marx, Michal Kalecki, and J. M. Keynes, and, finally, the modern circuit theorists – to whom the authors acknowledge a profound intellectual debt. Prof.

Sutanu Bhattacharya acknowledges Prof. Amiya Kumar Bagchi and Prof. Sunanda Sen, who have encouraged him to question, deliberate, and reflect. Further, he remembers his parents, who taught him how to think. He expresses his indebtedness to his colleague Prof. Byasdeb Dasgupta, with whom he has shared some of the ideas, and above all to his students, who have given him indirect inputs to conceptualise and develop the idea.

Dr Smita Roy Trivedi acknowledges her deep intellectual debt to her mentor (and co-author), Prof. Sutanu Bhattacharya for the conception and development of the theoretical construct and its implications. The continued support of her family – Ashmi Trivedi (daughter), Akshoy Trivedi (spouse), R. N. Roy and Subhra Roy (parents) – are beyond words to express. She sincerely acknowledges the enthusiastic encouragement given by her colleagues and the director, NIBM.

Abbreviations

ABS	Asset backed securities
BIS	Bank of International Settlements
BRIC	Brazil, Russia, India, and China
CBO	Collateralised bond obligation
CBOT	Chicago Board of Trade
CDO	Collateralised debt obligation
CDS	Credit default swap
CEO	Chief executive officer
CFTC	Commodity Futures Trading Commission
CLO	Collateralised loan obligation
CME	Chicago Mercantile Exchange
CSO	Central Statistical Organisation
DCL	Degree of combined leverage
DFL	Degree of financial leverage
DOL	Degree of operating leverage
DPS	Dividend per share
E&D	Equity and debt
EBIT	Earnings before interest and tax
EMS	European monetary system
EPS	Earnings per share
EU-15	The European Union countries consisting of Austria, Belgium, Denmark, Finland, France, Germany, Greece, Ireland, Italy, Luxembourg, the Netherlands, Portugal, Spain, Sweden, the United Kingdom
FIH	Financial instability hypothesis
FX	Foreign exchange
GCF	Gross capital formation
GDI	Gross domestic investment
GDP	Gross domestic product
GNP	Gross national product

HNI	High net worth individual
IBRD	International Bank for Reconstruction and Development
ICT	Information and communication technology
IET	Interest equalisation tax
IMF	International Monetary Fund
LDC	Less developed country
M&A	Merger and acquisition
MBS	Mortgage backed securities
NAS	National Accounts Statistics
O&M	Organisation and method
OECD	Organisation for Economic Cooperation and Development
OPEC	Organisation of the Petroleum Exporting Countries
OTC	Over the counter
SDR	Special drawing rights
SEC	Securities and Exchange Commission
SIV	Structured investment vehicle
SPV	Special purpose vehicle
TMC	Theory of monetary circuit
TNC	Transnational corporation
UNDP	United Nations Development Programmes
USSR	Union of Soviet Socialist Republics
WTO	World Trade Organisation

1   Introduction

The principal aim of this book is to examine how the contemporary financial economy evolved as the predominant economic system, and why unabated accumulation of financial capital takes place in it. The book intends to explain the mechanics of accumulation of financial capital in economic systems by tracing out the historical roots of financial evolutions at the edge of crises. The secondary aim is, keeping aside the orthodox neoclassical analysis of equilibrium market exchange, to bring into focus an alternative framework for studying economic systems designs in terms of economic stocks and flows, following the circuit analysis of the French physiocrats. In a nutshell, the objective of this study is threefold – tracing out the evolutions of capitalism through crises in the historical contexts, developing for this an alternative methodology of economic circuits, and establishing logically the accumulation of wealth as a systemic phenomenon in capitalist systems.

The rationale behind this book could be seen in the context of the historical crises and the turning points of the capitalist economy. The economic scenario in the last few decades has seen sweeping changes in the financial sector. The investments and production capital in the real sector is stagnating, but a continued growth of financial capital has been taking place almost in the form of an explosion. Another paradoxical feature is that alongside this phenomenal growth in financial assets and increasing dominance of the financial sector, we see recurrence of financial crises in the system.

There are several other paradoxical features of contemporary economic growth, like the service sector growth paradox, productivity paradox, which remain unexplained in the conventional analytical framework of economics. A striking fact is that never in the recorded economic history before the industrial revolution has such high economic growth and accumulation of wealth alongside widening inequality been seen. The huge financial wealth of the top global corporations and high net worth individuals (HNIs) has now dwarfed many national economies. In a recent study, Piketty has highlighted the growing accumulation and concentration of wealth and inequality as global phenomena. Analysing a large volume of data he has sketched out the evolution of inequality since the beginning of the industrial revolution in Western European society (Piketty 2014). Our question, vis-à-vis Piketty's study, is how to give a logical explanation for this statistical phenomenon.

In this context, an 'inquiry into the nature and causes of the wealth' creation in economic systems needs a review. But how do we make this review? Neoclassical economics does not provide a satisfactory framework for understanding the creation and accumulation of wealth in economic systems as it is beyond the scope of the equilibrium market exchange framework. The circuit approach of studying economic systems in terms of economic stocks and flows, as developed in this book, gives an alternative methodology for probing the structural foundation of economic systems and seeing how wealth and debt in various forms of stocks can accumulate through various circuit flows.

The central theme of the book is tracing out the evolutionary stages of Western capitalism. We mark three stages of evolution. First, we see the nascent stage with corporate industrial production in the West after the industrial revolution (1850–1930) with some scant replications of corporate production systems in the colonies. Second is the matured stage of the corporate production economy of the West with creditisation of money (1945–70). At this stage, corporate production systems also evolved in other national economies, especially in the newly independent developing countries. The final stage we mark as the current stage of financialisation and globalisation since the 1990s, now creating a single global economic circuit.

We must mention that the evolutions which we are considering here are the organisational evolutions that emerge out of the necessity created by the crises in economic systems. The source of the crises is the continuous accumulation of financial capital in the systems. This view of organisational evolution is clearly in contrast with what Marx pointed out as 'forces of production', what Weber pointed out as the 'protestant ethics and the spirits' of capitalism, and what Schumpeter tried to highlight as technological 'innovations'. Our focus is on the organisation of capitalism, which evolved in the West and established its global supremacy. We call this organisation an economic circuit. The continuous accumulation of financial capital in economic circuit causes crises and leads to its subsequent organisational evolutions.

The central point in this evolutionary process is what the current theory of monetary circuit calls the 'paradox of profits'. Profits generate through buying cheaper and selling dearer. This is evident in all trading activities, whether on goods or on financial commodities that we see in recent times. In industrial production activities, this simple fact got somewhat camouflaged in what the classical and neoclassical economics call value addition by the manufacturing process. But the fact remains – money to be received through sale of the goods produced must be more than the money paid out as its cost of production. A justification for this may be given as 'value addition', but in effect it is also buying cheaper and selling dearer.

The paradox of profits is quite simple. Profits could be realised by one individual in a process of buying cheaper and selling dearer, but there would be an equal amount of loss to those who sold cheaper or bought dearer. Therefore, in an economy as a whole, aggregating the gains or losses of all individuals, there are no profits. Yet, profits are not only the facts of reality, but also reflect accumulated wealth in economic systems. How do we then resolve this riddle?

Economic studies have lived with many paradoxes. We begin with a brief look at some of the paradoxical phenomena in our present economic landscape. From the narration of these paradoxes in Chapter 2 we get a clue – possibly the continuous accumulation of financial capital in economic systems could be a key factor behind these apparently paradoxical phenomena. This leads to a deeper question – how financial capital evolves and accumulates in economic systems? In Chapter 3 we probe the historical roots of the evolution of financial capital, as distinct from physical (production) capital. At the foundation of our analysis we need conceptual clarity in using these two terms. We make an attempt to trace out the evolution of the concepts and connotations of the term 'capital' in economic literature with reference to the ideas of financial and physical capital. Without a clear demarcation between physical capital as a means of production and financial capital as financial resources, the concept of capital remains elusive.

Traditionally, classical and neoclassical economic studies have considered capital in its physical dimensions only – the capital goods as the produced means of production. Only recently financial capital as a separate entity has come into focus in the studies of financial economics. However, the concept of financial capital is still somewhat amorphous, without a clear definition demarking as well as relating it with production capital in an overall analytical framework.

Intertwined with the evolution of capital as a monetary fund, interest on money evolved as another key economic entity. However, its legitimisation as an economic phenomenon took some time and so, in the early economic literature, the concepts of capital and interest were used in various contexts with varied connotations. In Chapter 4 we trace out the advent of the phenomenon of interest in human history, its evolutions in different forms and, later on, the recognition of money interest in economic literature. The implications of interest rate are of fundamental importance in this study. It links the future with the present, presuming an everlasting growth in the future over the present, without which a positive interest rate cannot be sustained. Therefore, it gives a way of discounting the future to the present, and thus acts as an instrument of creating financial claims in the present, treading upon the future. Further, by our economic construct, firms charge, on one hand, interest on the debt finance and, on the other, depreciations on the physical assets created out of it. The dynamic implications of this economic construct of charging twice for capital (in two forms) for the economy in aggregate have not been examined in economic studies. Yet, it is a clear source of accumulation of financial capital by the firms and thereby creating a mismatch in the longer run between the further debt financing required by the firms for physical capital and the finance that would be available with the banks through repayments of loans with interest by the firms.

Accumulation of financial capital as a stock can only be traced out properly in terms of stock-flow relations in economic systems. Unfortunately, this cannot be done with the aid of the neoclassical methodological framework of equilibrium market exchange. In Chapter 5 we point out why neoclassical economics disappoint us in this respect and propose an alternative methodology of circuit theory of viewing economic systems in terms of economic flows and stocks. As the background of this circuit methodology we trace out its historical roots in the French physiocrats' circuit formulations, and then in its recent revival in the theory of monetary circuit. The current theory of monetary circuit reveals an important fact – there cannot be monetary profits within a closed economic circuit. The circuit theorists mark this as the 'paradox of profit' and have tried to resolve this paradox in many ways. However, that money profit cannot arise in a closed circuit is the theoretical underpinning of our study – an economic circuit must earn monetary profits through monetary flows from outside and for that matter it must be an open circuit. So here, we construct not a pure closed monetary circuit, but an open economic circuit with flows of production, trade, and finance, as well as creation of their corresponding stocks. We must mention that in this circuit methodology we consider the actual flows and stocks of economic entities. The neoclassical abstract concepts of demand and supply reflecting the desires, say consumption demand or investment demand, of the economic agents do not fit into the circuit methodology.

Using the circuit approach of stock-flow relations we examine the evolution and operation of the corporate economic circuit and its accumulation of financial capital in three stages of evolution – the nascent corporate production circuit in the West (1850–1930); the matured corporate production circuit of the West (1945–70) with similar circuits operating in the national economies of the developing world; and then a single global corporate financial circuit now shaping since the 1990s. We discuss the circuit operations and implications as well as the crises leading to the next turn of evolution in these three phases in Chapters 6 through 9.

The nascent corporate production circuit began in Western Europe in the 1850s. This is marked as the beginning of the 'Age of Capital' (Hobsbawm 1975). In Chapter 6 we give briefly a historical account of the organisational evolution of company as a business entity – from the earlier joint stock companies to the formation of limited liability companies. Then we develop the chart of the nascent economic circuit with corporate production and discuss its operations through the flows and the creations of stocks. The circuit operated with the Gold Standard money and achieved its golden era of realising money profit and accumulation of financial capital through colonial trade with the rest of the world. But soon it reached its limits. The Gold Standard money that ensured a 'golden era' turned into the 'golden fetters', as Keynes had famously expressed it, and came the crisis of the 1930s. Facing this crisis, the corporate production circuit needed an organisational evolution.

Before going into discussing the next stage of evolution, in Chapter 7 we have made some detailed analysis of the operations of economic circuit at the nascent stage with the help of its rudimentary formulations. The sectoral accounts of the flows and the formation of the stocks in the balance sheets are presented here. Since the rudimentary production circuit remains at the foundation of capitalist economic systems, the internal dynamics and economic growth (endogenous and exogenous) of the rudimentary economic circuit are examined here at some length.

The organisational evolution that became a necessity to remove the 'golden fetters' and to recover from the depression of the 1930s took place in the next stage. This organisational evolution was reflected in three forms – institution of central banks and endogenous credit money creation by banks; government fiscal systems incorporating

Keynesianism; and Bretton Woods arrangements of international monetary systems. In Chapter 8 we begin with a brief account of these institutional changes in the mid-1940s as the background of the organisational evolution of the matured corporate production circuit in the West. This economic circuit was replicated also in the developing countries. So we had several country-specific circuits at this stage. However, it was the economic circuit of the developed West that attained maturity. We have examined here the chart and the operations of economic circuits with credit money and foreign trade with the rest of the world. The matured corporate industrial production economy of the West continued to grow through its net exports to the rest of the world with the consequent incidence of growing balance of payment and fiscal deficits there. For the developed economies of the West, the period 1945–65 was the golden period of economic growth with apparently unhindered accumulation of financial capital through creditisation and trade. However, it did not last long. Another crisis was again brewing since the early 1970s with stagnating demand in the real sector and declining labour productivity. We conclude this chapter with analysing the cause of this new crisis and the consequent necessity for another organisational evolution.

However, this organisational evolution did not come easily. During the period 1970–90, the world economic systems were in some turmoil. Afterwards, the organisational evolutions of this stage came to adapt to the information and communication technology (ICT) revolution that started in the mid-1980s. The ICT revolution neither generated from within the economic systems nor should be interpreted simply as innovations in production technology to be reflected in raising productivity. We discuss in Chapter 2 that some economic studies have tried empirically to find its reflections in productivity and got paradoxical results, known as the Solow paradox (Triplett 1999).

The ICT revolution has created a new environment for business. It has made possible, on one hand, instantaneous financial transactions or virtual money flow through account or claim transfers across the world and, on the other hand, globalisation of economic activities through business process outsourcing. Thus, it has given birth to a global financial web. To adapt to this change, the earlier economic circuits with corporate production of goods and services have undergone a complex organisational evolution. Now a single global economic circuit has emerged, in place of the earlier country-centric economic circuits.

In Chapter 9 we examine the operation and implications of the global economic circuit. The organisational evolutions at its background are quite complex – there is now a new generation of financial commodities like derivatives and structured securities created by financial architecture; the process of securitisation creating special purpose vehicles (SPVs); new financial markets – future and option trading exchanges – and their regulatory bodies; new entities like hedge funds, private equity funds, or foreign institutional investments; and corporations and conglomerates dealing in diversified financials, their global networks, and their operations through the corporate havens. Besides these, we see changes in the role of the banks and governments and the coming legislation of new rules and regulations for companies and banking, as well as changes in government tax and subsidy polices. There are also changes in the business accounting norms and practices, like allowing marking to market of the financial assets and off-balance sheet transactions. A reasonable discussion on all these would require almost a book. We therefore keep a brief discussion on some of these aspects in the Appendix, so as not to lose sight of the forest for the trees.

We begin Chapter 9 with a discussion on leveraging as an important operational aspect of the financial economy and then present the chart of the global economic circuit combining the real and financial circuits as the final stage of evolution in our study. We mention, first, that the global circuit is now a single economic circuit which is engulfing the earlier country-specific circuits. This is the essence of economic globalisation. Within the global circuit the earlier paradigms of country-specific concerns – like foreign and domestic countries and their interdependent production and trade structures, outsourcing by one country to another and its implications for them, etc. – really do not make much sense any longer, although these are traditionally some important areas of economic studies. However, these issues exist as globalisation is not complete yet. The global circuit has not yet engulfed the entire world of economic activities. There are still some local economic activities with financial transactions and savings which are not directly linked to the global circuit. So the global circuit still has an avenue to expand by linking these activities through financialisation. We see its reflections in the financialisations that are now taking place in the developing countries, particularly in the so-called emerging ones. In this context we have examined and kept in the Appendix a note on financialisation in the Indian economy as reflected in growing rentier income shares in India's gross domestic product (GDP).

The second aspect of the global circuit is of particular significance. Within itself the global circuit appears to be a closed single circuit. It may be seen in the chart that we have kept no link to outside the circuit. Therefore, as happens in all closed economic circuits, there should be the paradox of profits, since every gain must be accompanied by an equal amount of loss within the circuit. Nevertheless, we make an important point here that the global financial circuit, although a single one, is not a closed circuit. It has its opening to the future, now created by securitisation, through which it treads upon the future economic activities and brings them to the present for inflating the current financial transactions and profits. This is, in fact, leveraging banked upon debt financing. In all debts the debtors bear the liability to be met in the future, which are the claims of the creditors on the future. In other words, debts mean the debtors have sold their future to the creditors. In addition, by securitisation of financial assets as the store of such claims, the creditors get the opportunity to give further loans and thereby leverage their claims on the future.

It may sound unacceptable if we say that in the financial economy it is now the future that determines the present. Our common understanding is the other way around – from our present activities emerges the future. But the financial economy has reversed it. When the future is expected to grow, one can take loans to be repaid in the future out of the growing earnings and use it in inflating the consumption or investment activities at present.

We have examined the operational implications of the global economic circuit. The most important ones are: the growing concentration of wealth and income of giant corporations and HNIs; rising capital intensity in spite of growing unemployment; stagnating growth of production in the real sector and shifting production towards high-end products shrinking the production of wage goods or basic items of consumption; and, above all, the growing indebtedness of the governments and the households (excluding HNIs).

Because of the nature of its economic construct it is inevitable that the global economic circuit can now operate only through accumulation of the corporate sector's and HNIs' wealth or net worth on one hand and the matching accumulation of government and household net debts on the other. We have commented that, theoretically, if it were possible to calculate and construct a balance sheet of the global financial economy, the four stocks would have been balanced – the net government debt and household debts (excluding HNIs) as liabilities and the net worth of the corporate sector and the HNIs as assets.

How long can these assets and liabilities keep on accumulating and what would be its repercussions? A value judgement of this phenomenon and the questions of prediction are not in the objectives of this book. However, we must point out the vulnerability of this system.

The digitalised global financial web with digitalised virtual money has a highly fragile intricate network beyond any control of any government or their international agencies. Any default or bankruptcy arising at any corner may spread like a wildfire. In the crisis of 2008 we had just a glimpse of it, which could be tackled by bail-out packages of the governments. However, now there are signs of sovereign debt crisis also – even the governments may become bankrupt in more severe crisis. What would happen then – who would bail out whom?

Piketty (2014) has suggested imposing a progressive global tax on capital or wealth and far higher marginal tax rates on top incomes. In his view, development of new forms of property and democratic control of capital are now needed. Piketty's recommendations are quite bold but may be a little unrealistic. Would the national governments and their international agencies be able to implement this? Our experience so far – though on a different plane in reaching a consensus through several summits on reducing the global greenhouse gas emissions – does not give an encouraging answer.

What would happen then? Could our future have everlasting economic growth? This is exactly what our economic present requires. Our present now lives, not simply in the present, but on the future. The future must therefore grow. If it fails to grow then an unabated erosion of financial capital would start taking place in the system.

We conclude this book with an uncomfortable note – the present as the future. Will there be another economic evolution in a new direction, or a structural transformation at the foundation of our current economic systems, or a situation hopelessly entangled in an economic devastation? We apprehend that the evolutions in capitalist economic systems are reaching the final stage with the global financial circuit – the end of its evolutionary path. Therefore, to avoid economic devastation we focus on some structural transformations, which may appear to be somewhat revolutionary. Would it be possible? The future will say.

2 Paradoxes of crisis and growth

The landscape

In the last few years there have been some dramatic changes in the global financial and economic landscape. The year 2008–09 saw the world facing the worst possible recession since the Great Depression of the 1930s. Financial institutions in the United States and Europe were on the verge of collapse. They had to be salvaged by huge injections of emergency credit or takeovers either by the governments or by other financial institutions. A massive liquidity injection by central banks and a loose monetary policy stance around the world somewhat scaled down the impact but could not avert the crisis. Alongside this, in the stock markets and commodity markets, prices remained volatile ever since. Inter-bank lending remained constrained in the developed countries, banks cut lending to the corporate and smaller firms, and the credit crisis escalated to a general financial crisis. Then the sovereign debt crisis in Europe came in 2011. It had put the governments of some of the European nations on the verge of collapse.

The impact of the global recession of 2008–09 is widespread, prolonged, and devastating. According to the World Bank (2017) data, global output growth plummeted from 4.25 percent in 2007 to 1.8 percent in 2008 and recorded a negative growth of -1.7 percent in 2009. Recovery thereafter has been uncertain, jerky, and uneven: it plummeted from 4.3 percent in 2010 to 2.7 percent in 2015. The United Nations Report (2009: 3) suggested that about 125 million people had been pushed into extreme poverty following the rise in food prices since 2006. The World Bank Global Economic Prospects (2010) feared that the crisis would leave an additional sixty-four million people in poverty by 2010 relative to a no-crisis scenario. OECD (2016) data shows, income inequality in Organisation for Economic Cooperation and Development (OECD) nations have worsened in the post-crises period. The developing nations saw the move towards Millennium

Goals slackening and income inequality worsening (Ötker-Robe and Maria Podpiera 2013). Alongside the accumulation of global poverty, there has been accumulation of enormous wealth in the hand of a few transnational corporate giants.

For a considerable period of time, there had been an apprehension of some crises for the reason that growing imbalances in a system could not be sustained for long. These imbalances were reflected in some specific developments in world economy in the last three decades. A prior indication of the present crisis could have been seen in these developments. However, they were marked in mainstream economic literature just as paradoxes. Economic studies have lived with many paradoxes. Therefore, considering these as a few more paradoxes, several isolated studies have focused on one aspect or another of them. As the developments are being marked as paradoxes, not general phenomena, the need for a general theoretical framework to probe these developments deeper has been bypassed.

A list of the paradoxical developments in the contemporary economic scenario would be quite long. Some of these may be mentioned as: growth and productivity paradox; stagnating real sector and jobless growth; declining household savings and rising indebtedness; accumulation of corporate wealth; rising inequality and poverty; increasing instability and frequency of financial crises; and, above all, growing financial economy and financialisation. We will present only a brief outline of the issues. The discussion here is developed further on an earlier version of a study by Roy (2011).

Growth and productivity paradoxes

High growth rates and productivity in the post-World War II decades characterised what is oft called the 'golden age of modern capitalism' in the advanced countries. However, there have been some confusing developments in respect of both the growth rates and productivity since the 1970s. In respect of growth rates, some declining trends have been noticed. It is estimated that the growth rate of world GDP fell from an average 4.91 percent to 3.01 percent from 1950–73 to 1973–2001, and the per capita GDP growth rate fell from 2.93 percent to 1.33 percent over the same time period. Except for a few Asian countries this alarming fall in growth rates is noted in most of the advanced countries of the world (Maddison 2001: 125–26).

As shown in Tables 2.1 and 2.2, growth rates of both GDP and per capita GDP have fallen in the post-1970s period consistently in all the major regions, with the exception of Asia (excluding Japan). Data from World Bank (2017) presented in Table 2.1 shows that, post-2009, recovery has been uneven. Generally, there is a deceleration in growth rates recorded in the post-crises period. Even for South Asia, East Asia, and the Pacific, which have driven the recovery process, growth rates fell during 2010–12 to 2013–15.

Table 2.2 shows GDP per capita registered a similar decline post 2009. The per capita growth rates in different regions show highly skewed income distribution. While South Asia, East Asia, and the Pacific have registered some respectable per capita growth rates, the rest of the regions have recorded much lower per capita growth rates.

Table 2.1 World growth rates of GDP by region

(Annual percents)

Region	1990	2000	2007–09	2010–12	2013–15
Sub-Saharan Africa	2.40	3.62	5.10	4.48	4.12
South Asia	5.42	4.08	6.52	6.97	6.79
North America	1.74	4.20	–0.38	2.17	2.19
East Asia and Pacific	5.50	4.88	3.78	5.44	4.31
Euro area	3.58	3.87	–0.35	0.91	0.98
Europe and Central Asia	2.31	4.32	0.06	1.65	1.34
Middle East and North Africa	11.33	5.62	4.25	3.99	2.92
World	2.94	4.39	1.46	3.29	2.66

Source: Calculated from World Bank data (2017)

Table 2.2 World per capita GDP growth rates by region

(Annual percents)

Region	1990	2000	2007–09	2010–12	2013–15
Sub–Saharan Africa	–0.44	0.94	2.28	1.66	1.34
South Asia	3.13	2.17	4.94	5.47	5.36
North America	0.56	3.07	–1.32	1.34	1.38
East Asia and Pacific	3.94	3.89	3.08	4.75	3.62
Euro area	3.09	3.52	–0.80	0.83	0.66
Europe and Central Asia	1.79	4.21	–0.33	1.29	0.86
Middle East and North Africa	7.56	3.60	2.03	1.91	1.02
World	1.19	3.03	0.23	2.07	1.45

Source: Calculated from World Bank data (2017)

Maddison has further pointed out that since the 'golden age' the difference in the growth performance of different regions of the world has been all the more pronounced (*Ibid.*: 23). In Western Europe and Japan, per capita growth rates in the post-1970s period have registered a marked deterioration. One-third of the world population in the countries of Africa, Eastern Europe, and Latin America, as well as in parts of Asia, have experienced a stark fall in incomes. In Africa there has been no advancement in per capita income in the past quarter century. In Eastern Europe and in the countries under the former Union of Soviet Socialist Republics (USSR) the average per capita income in 1998 has fallen to about three-quarters of that in 1973. Similarly, in Latin America and in many Asian countries, income gains have been a fraction of what they were in the 'golden age'. However, in the 'resurgent Asia' (consisting of fifteen countries, namely China, India, Singapore, Hong Kong, Taiwan, South Korea, Malaysia, Thailand, Pakistan, Sri Lanka, Philippines, Indonesia, Bangladesh, Burma, and Nepal) the growth rates and per capita incomes have registered a phenomenal rise since the 1970s. But at the same time, they have been constantly marred by some crisis or other since the late 1990s (Maddison 2006: 142–46).

The two economic giants, China and India, have managed to achieve high growth rates in the last decade but the reduction of poverty and lessening of income inequality have been far from impressive. The most impressive growth rates for China came in the period from 1973 to 1993, whereas foreign trade and foreign investment has increased only after the 1990s (Bardhan 2010: 6), suggesting that the impressive growth in the period 1973–93 is more attributable to internal factors rather than globalisation. For India, the rate of decline of poverty did not accelerate in the post-reform period (1993–2005). In fact, for both China and India, the nations currently seen as the emerging economies, inequality, and consequent social discontent are seething below the surface. As Bardhan says:

> those who envisage 'billions of new capitalists' in China and India do not realise that hundreds of millions of poor people in both countries are currently scrounging a living from tiny family enterprises of extremely low productivity, and they don't have access to credit, marketing, and infrastructure or the basic skills and education and risk-bearing capacity that can make a capitalist enterprise possible.
>
> (*Ibid.*: 7)

Alongside this growth profile, the productivity trends have also been found declining. The fall in productivity levels has been most pronounced in the developed nations, as pointed out in several studies (Nordhaus 1982, 2004; Cullison 1989; Gordon 1995; Wolff 1997; Kozicki 1997). These studies have shown that compared to the preceding 'Fordist' era there has been a fall in both labour and total factor productivity levels in OECD countries. In the United States the annual growth rate of labour productivity fell from 1.8 percent in 1958–67 to 0.9 percent in 1967–77, and further to 0.7 percent in 1977–87 (Wolff *Ibid.*: 8). Total Factor Productivity (TFP) growth also fell from 1.5 percent in 1958–67 to 0.3 percent in 1967–77, and showed no signs of recovery during 1977–87. The same trend has been noted in all the major OECD nations (Cullison *Ibid.*: 11).

Apparently, fall in growth and productivity has been somewhat unacceptable as a general phenomenon. So, a search for reversal of the trend has been made. Some studies have contended that there has been a revival of productivity and growth rates in the United States in the late 1990s and early 21st century (Nordhaus 2004: 16–17; Gordon 2002; Bosworth and Triplett 2007: 3–4). However, while productivity improved in the United States in the 1990s, the productivity gains in the 'New Economy' of the early 1990s has not been permanent and has gone away after 2000 (Gordon 2002: 5). Further, the European nations have lagged behind in productivity standards (O'Mahony and Van Ark 2003; Timmer, O'Mahony and Van Ark 2003). The average GDP growth rate for the EU-15 countries of the European Union has remained constant at 2.2 percent, and the labour productivity growth fell from 2.4 percent in 1980–95 to 1.4 percent in 1995–2004 (Timmer et al. *Ibid.*: 7).

The sectoral profiles of growth and productivity performances have revealed a further paradox, known as the paradox of service sector growth. Evidence suggests that the service sector productivity tends to lag behind the productivity of the manufacturing sector. Yet, the service sector has been registering higher growth rate than the manufacturing sector. This paradoxical development since the 1970s is noted in several countries around the world, especially in the developed economies (Kozicki *Ibid.*: 36–7; Wolff *Ibid.*: 8–10; Maclean 1997: 3–9:, Baumol 2001: 3–28).

Next, on studying the impact of the ICT revolution on the productivity performance, another paradox has been revealed. The ICT revolution has drastically altered the production processes and operations around the world. Yet, no positive impact of it on the productivity performances has been seen, especially in the US economy. It is pointed out that the price of new computers in the United States has fallen sharply after 1974, implying rapid technological advancement. However, the growth in labour productivity has remained stagnant in spite of the rise in ICT investments. Moreover, ICT investments have increased sharply after 1974, but the labour productivity growth has fallen to about 0.8 percent from 2 percent per annum after 1974 (Greenwood 1997: 3). There has not been any empirical evidence of positive contribution of ICT to productivity, which Solow has famously pointed out as, 'You can see the computer age everywhere but in productivity statistics' (Solow 1987). This has been labelled the Solow paradox.

Studying the decline in the growth rates of GDP would be much more complex than a study of falling productivity. Moreover, falling productivity, as evidenced, could be the reason for the decline in GDP growth rates. Therefore, the focus shifted mostly to the study of productivity decline. The decline in productivity has been more or less a general phenomenon worldwide. Yet, most of the studies, lacking a general theory, have searched for its probable causes in some country-specific empirical investigations. Several probable causes of the slowdown in productivity have been put forward. For example, for the United States, these include the oil price shocks, depletion of investment opportunities, inflation, and macroeconomic policy (Nordhaus 1982: 140–50). However, there is no consensus in this regard. Economic literature has remained little satisfied with the probable reasons, as pointed out in different studies, and the productivity slowdown remained 'paradoxical' even after three decades of analysis, with new studies continually trying to pin-point the actual causes of the slowdown (Dowrick 1995; Gordon 1995; Kozicki 1997; Nordhaus 2004).

The productivity slowdown in the United States for the periods from 1948–63 to 1973–80 is estimated by Nordhaus as 2.5 percentage points (Nordhaus 1982: 138–40). Out of the trend slowdown of 2.2 percentage points, one percentage point remains 'unexplained', which indeed is too high to be comfortable. He contends that the 'unexplained' part in the US productivity slowdown could be due to the depletion of investment opportunities and the competition or 'catch-up' by Japan and Germany (Nordhaus *Ibid.*: 149–51).

In a revised estimate, Nordhaus has put one-third of the slowdown in the US productivity to measurement errors and specific problems in individual industries, and pointed out the energy crisis as the most important factor for the slowdown (Nordhaus 2004: 19–20). However, the energy crisis was a fact of the 1970s, while the productivity slowdown, even by most conservative estimates, continued in the 1990s. Therefore, the oil price shocks can hardly be a valid factor for the more recent slowdown. Nordhaus has claimed a rebound of productivity after 1995. But it has been shown that for the United States, the productivity gains in the 'new economy' after 1995 were short-lived and were gone by 2000 (Gordon 2002). Thus, no consensus could be reached in respect of the 'best guess' sources of productivity slowdown, as estimated by Nordhaus.

There are also attempts in some studies to explain one paradoxical phenomenon by another. The paradox of overall productivity decline could naturally be a reflection of service sector growth. Since the service sector productivity lags behind that of the goods sector, as the size of the service sector increases, productivity growth for the economy as a whole falls (Baumol 1967). So, one would argue that it is the service sector growth that is responsible for the overall productivity decline. Following this line of argument some studies have shown that it is in the service sector that the productivity decline in the US economy is concentrated (Kozicki 1997: 36–43; Wolff 1997: 8–10; Maclean 1997). But the question, what drives the service sector to grow in spite of its lower productivity – that is, the service sector growth paradox – has remained an insoluble riddle.

Some country-specific explanations have been attempted; for example, for the US economy, the lagging computerisation of service industries, outsourcing, measurement issues, and differences in competitive pressures (Kozicki 1997: 37). Another argument is that a structural shift in the labour market operations in the United States has reduced the real wages at the bottom half of income distribution, which has its feedback effect on lower productivity and consequently slower growth. The sources of these structural shift are weak unions, decline in the share of employment in industries where unions are strong, decline in the real minimum wage, and substantial immigration, both legal and illegal (Gordon 1995: 165).

The 'Solow paradox' has kept on baffling the economists. One could guess that the adoption of any new technological know-how takes time, as does the diffusion of knowledge, and so the computer's productive potentials are not yet fully realised (Greenwood 1997: 1–4). However, given the sharp fall in prices of computers, quick replacements of pre-computer age devices, and application of computers in almost all the widest possible fields, this seems to be an unlikely cause. There is another argument that rapid technological change may be the cause of declining productivity as the breathtaking 'rate of obsolescence' has caused discard of technology earlier than needed (Triplett 1999: 324–25). Further, to explain the service sector growth paradox, data measurement problems are also highlighted. Griliches has noted that more than 70 percent of the private sector computer investments is concentrated in areas like wholesale and retail trade, finance, insurance, and real estate, where output is difficult to measure (cited in Triplett 1999: 318).

Stagnating real sector and jobless growth

Stagnation in real wages and falling employment have been marked during the period 1970–90 (Eatwell and Taylor 2000; Panchmukhi 2000; Crotty 2000). The unemployment rate in OECD countries increased from 3.2 percent in 1960–73 to 5 percent in 1973–79, further to 7.2 percent in 1979–89, and fell marginally to 7.1 percent in 1989–95. There is also evidence that the real wage rate growth in nineteen developed countries (not including the United States), after rising rapidly through the early 1970s, declined by 1.2 percent a year in 1979–89 and further to 0.7 percent a year in 1989–96 (Crotty 2000: 6, 29). Moreover, the unprecedented technological progress following the ICT revolution has been accompanied by a widening wage inequality (Greenwood 1997: 3). The post-1970 period is characterised as 'jobless growth' in view of the stark fall in employment in industrialised countries (Panchmukhi 2000: 16).

Another disquieting feature of the present growth has been the deindustrialisation in developed economies. In the most advanced twenty-three economies, employment in the manufacturing sector fell from about 28 percent of the workforce in 1970 to 18 percent in 1994. In the United States, the share of manufacturing sector employment declined massively from 28 percent in 1965 to 16 percent in 1994. In Japan manufacturing sector employment went down from 27 percent of total employment in 1973 to about 23 percent in 1994. In EU-15 countries the share of manufacturing sector employment was at a comparatively high level of more than 30 percent in 1970, but then fell sharply to only 20 percent by 1994 (Rowthorn and Ramaswamy 1997: 2).

The real sector investment has also declined sharply after the 1970s. Some calculations have been made of the annual rate of growth of the world real gross domestic investment (GDI) based on World Bank data. The rate of growth was found to stay at 7.0 percent from 1966 to 1973. It then fell sharply to 2.2 percent from 1974 to 1979, rose modestly to 2.8 percent from 1980 to 1989, and then fell again to 2.7 percent from 1990 through 1996. Side by side, it has been found that the average annual growth rate of real gross capital formation (GCF) for

OECD countries fell from 6.3 percent in 1960–73 to 1.5 percent in 1973–79. It improved somewhat to 2.4 percent in 1979–89 but fell again to 1.5 percent in 1989–95 (Crotty 2000: 6).

Here we highlight the stagnation in real wages, fall in employment in the manufacturing sector indicating 'jobless growth' as well as rise in unemployment rates, and fall in GDI and GCF in the advanced countries of the West over the period 1970–90 as a backdrop of the financial growth to be seen later, after the 1990s. It is not our purpose at the moment to examine what has caused these paradoxical developments.

Declining household savings and rising indebtedness

In OECD countries the household savings rates have been declining. They were declining for the Euro area, the United States, and Japan over the 1990s and early 2000s (Harvey 2005). We have examined the trend even after, in the post-2009 period, from OECD data (2017). Table 2.3 shows the household saving rates as percentage of GDP for selected countries over the period 1976–2015. As may be seen, the household savings rates fell drastically over this period for these countries.

Side by side, household debts have also increased to record levels in a number of OECD countries (Girouard, Kennedy and André 2006: 6; Stockhammer 2008: 6–8). Here also, calculating the trend form OECD data (2017), we find the trend continues in the post-2009 period. Table 2.4 shows the high level of household debt as a percentage of net disposable income (NDI) for select countries. For the US economy, there has been a fall in savings rate coupled with a rapid

Table 2.3 Savings rates as percentage of GDP in select countries

(Annual average)						
Year	*US*	*France*	*UK*	*Japan*	*Australia*	*Canada*
1976–80	8.3	9.8	5.3	16.0	10.4	6.7
1981–85	6.2	4.8	3.3	13.7	8.1	5.0
1986–90	4.6	6.7	3.1	14.2	7.2	4.6
1991–95	3.3	5.6	2.0	11.9	3.4	0.7
1996–2000	6.1	7.6	3.8	9.1	4.9	5.5
2001–05	3.0	6.7	2.8	5.8	5.0	7.9
2006–10	0.4	4.5	0.8	3.6	6.7	6.5
2011–15	2.3	2.0	−0.2	1.5	6.8	4.6

Source: Calculated from OECD data (2017)

Table 2.4 Household debt as percentage of net disposable income in select countries

(Annual average)

Year	US	France	UK	Japan	Australia	Canada
1995–2000	109	77	121	138	124	117
2001–05	136	92	164	133	169	145
2006–10	123	105	155	127	195	168
2011–15	113	107	151	133	201	174

Source: Calculated from OECD data (2017)

increase in both household wealth and indebtedness since the 1970s (Van Treeck 2009: 474).

The rapid increase in household debts coupled with household wealth, as evidenced in the United States, is an interesting finding. It has some important bearings for our study in the final chapters of this book. About the apparent anomaly of rising wealth with rising debts we would mention here that it could be resolved if we separate out the HNIs included in the household sector, which we would propose in this study.

Accumulation of corporate wealth

In a seminal work Piketty has made a detailed study of the accumulation and concentration of wealth as global phenomena (Piketty 2014). Analysing voluminous statistical data over a long period, Piketty's study has shown the country-specific distribution of wealth. In our study, as will be seen in the final chapters, we will segregate and assign a key role to the corporate sector behind this global accumulation and concentration of wealth. So, we present here how perplexing is the enormous accumulation and concentration of income and wealth by the corporate sector in the current economic landscape.

In 2010 the Forbes Global 2000 companies accounted for $30 trillion in revenues, $1.4 trillion in profits, and $124 trillion in assets. In the year 2011 they accounted for $32 trillion in revenues, $2.4 trillion in profits, and $138 trillion in assets. All metrics are up from 2010 with profits growing the most, rising 67 percent (Forbes 2011).

In Tables 2.5 and 2.6 we present the assets and revenue of the ten biggest corporate giants of 2011 over a period of five years, 2007–11. They clearly show that the assets and revenue of these corporate giants have continued to increase from 2007, even during and in spite of the financial downturn of 2008–09.

Table 2.5 Forbes Global 2000 – top companies' assets

(Billion US$)

Company	2007	2008	2009	2010	2011
JP Morgan Chase	1351.52	1562.20	2175.05	2031.99	2117.60
HSBC	1860.76	2349.00	2570.45	2355.83	2467.90
General Electric	697.24	795.30	797.77	781.82	751.20
Exxon Mobil	223.95	242.10	228.05	233.32	302.50
Royal Dutch Shell	232.31	266.20	278.44	287.64	317.20
Petro China	96.42	111.70	145.14	174.95	251.30
ICBC	800.04	961.65	1188.08	1428.46	1723.50
Berkshire Hathaway	248.44	273.2	267.40	297.12	372.20
Petrobras-Petróleo Brasil	95.61	129.98	120.68	198.26	313.20
Citigroup	1884.32	2187.63	1938.47	1856.65	1913.90
Total	4909.05	7675.21	5785.20	9646.04	10530.50
Average	490.91	767.52	578.52	964.60	1053.05

Source: Compiled from Forbes Global 2000 (2006–11)

Table 2.6 Forbes Global 2000 – top companies' revenue

(Billion US$)

Company	2007	2008	2009	2010	2011
JP Morgan Chase	99.30	116.40	101.49	115.63	115.50
HSBC	121.51	146.50	142.05	103.74	103.30
General Electric	163.39	172.70	182.52	156.78	156.20
Exxon Mobil	335.09	358.60	425.70	275.56	341.60
Royal Dutch Shell	318.85	355.80	458.36	278.19	369.10
Petro China	68.43	88.24	114.32	157.22	222.30
ICBC	31.98	37.48	53.60	71.86	69.20
Berkshire Hathaway	98.54	118.30	107.79	112.49	136.20
Petrobras-Petróleo Brasil	74.12	87.52	92.08	104.81	121.30
Citigroup	146.56	159.23	106.66	108.07	111.50
Total	1147.82	1244.69	1441.79	1484.35	1746.20
Average	114.78	124.47	144.18	148.44	174.62

Source: Compiled from Forbes Global 2000 (2006–11)

When we compare the average revenue income of these top ten companies with the GDP of the countries, we see many of the countries in the lower- and middle-income group come below the average revenue of the ten companies. These corporate giants have dwarfed many of the national economies. They are evolved through a process of continuous mergers and acquisitions and a large part of their financial transactions are routed through numerous corporate havens. They are the 'super entity' in the global network of transnational corporations (TNCs), which we will discuss later in a following section in this chapter. This is a perplexing development indeed. How and why in economic systems such accumulation and concentration can take place should no more be left unaddressed in the discipline of economics.

Rising inequality and poverty

Besides the study by Piketty (2014) on accumulation and concentration of wealth in the global scenario, several earlier studies have also confirmed that inequality is growing with disparities increasing between the rich and the poor in individual countries (Milanovic 2011; OECD 2008: Pieterse 2002). The Human Development Report (2011) confirms that income inequality has worsened in most of the countries and regions. There is a striking increase in the income share of the wealthiest groups in much of Europe, North America, Australia, and New Zealand. From 1990 to 2005 the within-country income inequality, measured by the Atkinson inequality, increased 23.3 percent in countries with a very high Human Development Index (Bagnoli, Goeschl and Kovacs 2008: 46). The inequality worsened over the last two decades in more than three-quarters of OECD countries and in many emerging economies. In China, India, and South Africa also, income has become more concentrated among the top earners (UNDP 2011: 28–30).

Worsening income inequality has offset the improvements in health and education. With human capital now being scarcer than machines, widespread education is generally emphasised. However, access to education for all is difficult to be achieved, unless a society has a relatively even income distribution. Spread of education not only demands relatively even income distribution but, in a virtuous circle, reproduces it, as it reduces income gaps between skilled and unskilled labour (Milanovic *Ibid.*; UNDP *Ibid.*: 28).

The inequality in wage distribution has also been noticed to be increasing, favouring the white-collar wages. The wage inequality in the US economy (measured by top percentile wage shares) has been increasing since the 1970s. The top 1 percent share increased from 5 percent to 7.5 percent from 1970 to 1984. From 1986 to 1988 the top wage earners' share increased more sharply, with the top 1 percent share jumping from 7.5 percent to 9.5 percent. From 1988 to 1994, top wage earners' share remained somewhat constant, but increased again from 1994 to 1998, with the top 1 percent wage share increasing from 9 percent to 11 percent (Piketty and Saez 2003: 31–2).

Alongside income inequality, global poverty has been a major concern in recent times. It is anticipated that in the absence of a well-functioning social security system, economic crisis could lead to a significant rise in poverty in a number of countries. Prices of primary commodity have increased faster between 2003 and 2008 than in the previous decade. High food prices have increased the number of people living in extreme poverty by about 130–150 million. Within the countries, the largest poverty impacts have been among the urban populations, who have not been benefited from the increased earnings by the same degree as the rural population (IMF 2009: 95–6).

Increasing instability and frequency of financial crises

The economic landscape stands more puzzling when we consider the frequency of crisis that has affected the world since the 1970s. The trend that began with the collapse of the par value system in the early 1970s was followed by the oil price crisis. In the 1980s there were the Latin American debt crisis, the Chilean crisis, and the persisting savings and loan crisis in the United States. Then in the 1990s came the EMS (European Monetary System) crisis of 1992–93 and the tequila crisis of 1994–95 in Mexico. A string of crises continued with the South East Asian crisis of 1997, the Brazilian crisis of 1998–99, the 'Dot-com Bubble' crash in 2000, and the sub-prime crisis of 2007–08 in the United States, culminating in the global recession of 2008–09. That the frequency of financial crises has increased in the current era has been pointed out in some studies (Bordo et al. 2001; Panchmukhi 2000). The new international financial order that has emerged since the 1980s is not only characterised by an enormous volume of trading in financial assets, but also a financial system that has become more and more susceptible to financial fragility (Eatwell and Taylor 2000: 5–6).

Growing financial economy and financialisation

The most important development in the current economic landscape is perhaps the emergence of financial capital in newer dimensions and a growing financial economy revolving around it. With the emergence of a new generation of financial commodities and securitisation, financial markets have developed at unprecedented levels. The developments and operations in the financial economy are quite complex. There we find issues relating to investors' decision-making in terms of future risk and returns in financial assets as well as relating to corporate finance in the context of time, uncertainty, options, and information involved in financial decision-making. The complex decision-making process could not be addressed with the standard analytical tools of textbook economics. Therefore, to address them, a new branch of economic studies called financial economics has emerged in the last two decades. At the aggregate level there are several reflections of a growing financial economy, which appear to be paradoxical. Some of the major trends seen in the financial economy are the tremendous growth of financial markets and trading on financial commodities, rise in financial profits and rentier income shares, financial growth and real sector slowdown, and the varied impacts of financialisation.

It is difficult to define what financialisation is, just as it is difficult to arrive at a unique definition of globalisation. There could be multiple dimensions of the process of financialisation, as may be reflected in its various impacts. In a subsequent sub-section we will briefly mention some of these reflections as the impact of financialisation.

Growth of financial markets and commodities

Growing financial markets with trading on financial commodities has been noticed since the 1980s. Between 1982 and 1993 the stock market capitalisation grew by an annual average of 15 percent from $2 trillion to $10 trillion (Demirguc-Kunt and Levine 1995: 1). Similar growth has been seen in the emerging stock markets. There the stock market capitalisation increased from 3 percent to 14 percent in the same period. Moreover, there has been increasing globalisation of the financial markets, with international bank lending increasing from $265 billion in 1975 to $4.2 trillion in 1995 (Schmidt 2002: 17).

Private capital flows, which were insignificant in the 1960s, have increased significantly by 1997 in net new issues of international loans and bonds. Further, there has been a rise of a new class of institutional investment funds since the early 1980s, which includes mainly the pension funds, mutual funds, private equity, and hedge funds. Between 1981 and 1990, the US institutional investors realised a rise in total assets from $2 trillion to $6.5 trillion. The increase in assets of the UK institutional investors during the same period was from 130 billion pounds to 550 billion pounds (Goldstein et al. 1993: 2).

Even more surprising is the growth of the new-generation financial commodities. The Bank of International Settlements (2009) statistics show that there has been an astounding growth of the amounts outstanding on over-the-counter (OTC) derivatives since the late 1990s. In 1992, the notional amount of global OTC derivatives was $25 trillion, which reached $72 trillion in mid-1998; by mid-2001 it was

$98 trillion and in mid-2006 it became $370 trillion. Credit default swaps (CDSs) increased from $180 billion in 1996 to $2 trillion in 2002 and further to $20 trillion in 2006. Again, OTC interest rate derivatives increased from $70 trillion in 2000 to $262 trillion in 2006 (Crotty 2007: 31–2). The present age has been aptly named the 'Golden Age of Finance' (Crotty *Ibid.*: 4).

Beside the OTC derivatives there has been growing markets for other types, called the exchange traded derivatives. As early as the 1970s investments on exchange traded futures contract were found to be on the rise in the Chicago Board of Trade (CBOT). Trading on another type of such contract was recorded in CBOT in 1973, called the options. The largest exchanges in which futures contracts are now traded are the CBOT and the Chicago Mercantile Exchange (CME). As regulatory authorities the Commodity Futures Trading Commission (CFTC) was established in the United States in 1974, followed by the formation of the National Futures Association in 1982. Other bodies, like the Securities and Exchange Commission (SEC), were also established. We now see similar exchanges and regulatory bodies in almost all the developed and developing countries (Hull 2001).

The unprecedented growth of trading on financial commodities underlines the tremendous financial accumulation process in the current economic systems. This growth has come despite the stagnation in the real sector, which makes it all the more significant. Finance today has far surpassed the need of the real sector and assumed an extraordinary growth process of its own.

Rise in financial profits and rentier income shares

A peculiar characteristic of the post-1970 growth process, first noticed in the United States, is the coexistence of high financial sector profits in spite of intense finance market competitions. This appears to follow Volcker's paradox (Crotty 2007: 2). The US financial markets have been under intense competition with the removal of restrictions on foreign capital flows by governments worldwide, the repeal of the Glass–Steagall Act in 1999 in the United States, and the ICT revolution transforming financial transactions. However, the financial profits have reached a historically high level in spite of it (Crotty 2007: 3–6). This is another paradoxical development in the current era.

As such we do not have an explanation for this phenomenon – competition should have eliminated supernormal profits as per textbook economic theories. Crotty has tried to indicate three possible reasons for the persistence of financial profits in the United States despite rising competition. These are the exponential growth of financial products; the rise of concentration in most wholesale, retail, and global financial markets; and rise in risk-taking by firms. However, he has also argued that the last few decades have been characterised by the rise of 'core-spective' firms who do not engage in active price competition that may significantly lessen profits. They have also been able to achieve high margins by selling the bulk of their financial products OTC rather than on exchanges, thus insulating the profit margin from competition (Crotty 2007: 5–6).

A closely related development in this context has been the rise in the rentier incomes shares. They increased dramatically in many countries between the first two decades and the second two decades from 1960–2000 (Power, Epstein and Abrena 2003: 70).

Financial growth and the real sector slowdown

Increasing financial investments by non-financial businesses over the last two decades have resulted in a slowdown of physical asset accumulation. In the major economies of the West (Germany, France, the United Kingdom, and the United States), the investment–profit ratio has been showing a clear declining trend (Stockhammer 2004). Again, the gross fixed capital formation as percentage of GDP has been falling in major industrialised countries since the late 1970s (Navarro, Schmitt and Astudillo 2004: 150). As seen in Table 2.7, investment, as expressed in rate of growth of gross fixed capital formation, was dwindling in these countries over the period 1973 to 2015.

Table 2.7 Growth rates of gross fixed capital formation in select countries, 1976–2015

(Annual average)

Year	US	France	UK	Japan	Australia
1976–80	6.07	2.08	0.12	3.84	6.62
1981–85	5.18	−0.68	3.12	2.81	3.68
1986–90	2.02	6.00	6.08	8.77	2.01
1991–95	3.28	−0.91	1.45	−0.08	4.48
1996–2000	7.73	4.49	3.43	0.01	4.18
2001–05	2.60	1.93	2.11	−0.88	9.14
2006–10	−3.17	0.61	−1.58	−3.33	4.51
2011–15	4.20	0.42	3.50	2.62	1.10

Source: Calculated from OECD data (2017)

This vindicates that the finance-dominated regime of the past few decades has led to an adverse economic performance in the European nations (Stockhammer 2008: 15–17). It can also be said that the declining trend in accumulation of physical assets in the global financial systems has adversely affected global economic growth (Crotty 2000: 30).

Impacts of financialisation

It is difficult to define financialisation. The increased importance of the financial sector relative to the non-financial sectors may be generally viewed as financialisation of the economy (Van Treeck 2009: 467; Stockhammer 2004: 720). However, it is also a global phenomenon, parallel to the process of globalisation. The globalisation of financial markets, the shareholder value revolution, and the rise of incomes from financial investment are the features of this process (Stockhammer *Ibid.*). However, in whichever way we try to define what financialisation is, it would be incomplete.

Financialisation impacts in many ways on many spheres – at the national or global levels or at the levels of individual firms and consumers. For example, about fifty years ago, we used to save first for a period of time to build a fund to buy a house or a car, and then afterwards purchase those with our savings. Nowadays we purchase first and start consuming those by taking loans, and then repay the loans in the future. Is it not financialisation of household consumption – financing current consumption from the future earnings? When this is brought into account, we can neither say the current disposable income determines the consumption demand, nor say demands (especially for durable goods, items available on credit purchases, and services, like education and health) are determined by the current prices only. What matters more now are the expected future earnings. This is an issue that will have some significant implications for our study that we develop later in the final chapters. Here we mention briefly some of the major areas of the impacts of financialisation.

Financial market integration

We mention at the Introduction of this book that a global financial web has been born. One of its reflections is the increasing financial market integration that is taking place in the process of financialisation. In the global web the financial markets of most of the advanced and emerging economies are now interfaced. They behave in close association as may be seen in the movements of prices in these markets. This ensures smooth financial flows in and out. Unhindered capital flows would result in efficient allocation of capital by the market forces – a principal proposition of the neoclassical market economics. Therefore, it is expected that an effect of financial integration would be reflected on the economic growth. A large number of studies, mostly empirical ones, have been undertaken particularly in the context of the European financial markets (Guiso et al. 2004). As happens in most of the empirical investigations, different sets of data or a slight change in the model specification or estimation methods yield different results. So, the issue of financial integration resulting in economic growth has remained a controversial one, as both positive and negative results are found (Gourinchas and Jeanne 2006).

However, the focus has recently shifted to financial market 'fragmentation'. In the context of the European sovereign debt crisis, most of the countries, by imposing some restrictions, are now trying to insulate their financial markets from external shocks (Rose and Wieladek 2014). Now the issue has just been reversed – financial fragmentation and economic growth (Schnabel and Seckinger 2015).

Global corporate web and concentration

That there exists a global financial web is evidenced in a study of the network of TNCs. Starting with a list of 43,060 TNCs, taken from a sample of thirty million 'economic actors' contained in the Orbis 2007 database, Vitali et al. (2011) employed a recursive search algorithm to single out the 'network of all the ownership pathways originating from and pointing to the TNCs'. It suggests a nucleus of 787 firms with control of 80 percent of this network. Again, a 'super entity' comprised of 147 corporations have a controlling interest in 40 percent of the TNCs in the network. The 'super entity' firms 'exert control over other firms via a web of direct and indirect ownership relations which extends over many countries' (Vitali et al. 2011).

Looking at this phenomenon from another angle, we see the rise in the concentration ratios in ownerships of firms. In the United States the top-three commercial banks owned just 10.5 percent of the total industry assets in 1990. By 1997 the figure increased to 19 percent. By 2000, through several mega-mergers, the top-three commercial banks' ownership increased to 31 percent of the industry assets. In 2003 we saw the largest seven commercial banks in the United States own nearly 50 percent of total industry assets. This concentration process was not limited to the United States only. In a study of several countries (namely Australia, Belgium, Canada, France, Germany, Italy, Japan, the Netherlands, Spain, Sweden, Switzerland, the United Kingdom, and the United States), the ratio of the assets of the world's largest twenty banks to the combined GDP of the countries was 20 percent in 1980, 32 percent in 1990, and 40 percent in 1998 (Group of Ten 2001: 55). Further, it is also seen that in the United States the seven largest commercial banks held 98 percent of the industry's derivatives (Federal Reserve Board of Governors 2006, cited in Crotty 2007: 30).

Economic fragility

Derivatives are perfect vehicles for speculation. It is further claimed that they also help escape regulatory safeguards, circumvent accounting rules, and evade taxation (Eatwell and Taylor 2000: 99–100). Moreover, they have been found to play a destructive role in the 1997 East Asian crisis (Dodd 2003). Financial speculations naturally make the economies more susceptible to crisis and intensify the downturn once it starts. Increasing financial fragility is therefore the result of a finance-dominated economic regime. Stockhammer has used the term 'finance-dominated', claiming that financialisation can 'positively or negatively' affect economic growth. The finance-dominated economic structure is characterised by moderate growth in aggregate demand, a high degree of fragility, and crises arising domestically or internationally (Stockhammer 2008: 3–4). Moreover, the instability of the global financial markets has significantly increased the incidence of banking and currency crises, which have culminated in serious recessions in the present era (Crotty 2000: 30).

Corporate governance and shareholders' value revolution

Shareholder value revolution, defined as the increased dominance of shareholders over the management in corporate governance, leads to corporate restructuring and shift in management priorities (Stockhammer 2004; Van Treeck 2009). The high dividend payout ratio, as desired by shareholders, means a policy shift towards 'downsize and distribute', as opposed to a strategy to 'retain and invest' that has been traditionally favoured by management (Lazonick and O'Sullivan 2000: 18). The shareholders being the deciding factor for corporate control, and in hiring and firing of managers and performance-related pay-packages, the management becomes keener to adopt policies closer to the shareholder's objectives of increased dividend payout. This lowers the real sector investment activity through retained profits. It is therefore argued that the shareholder revolution has curbed the management's ability to accumulate physical capital through retained profits (Van Treeck *Ibid.*: 469–70).

Economic policies

Some significant changes in the national economic policies have been noticed in most countries since the 1990s. It is contended that the rise of a rentier class has been instrumental in shaping this policy change (Epstein and Power 2003: 3). The growing powerful clout of the rentier class has been, to a large extent, the controlling actor in the economic scenario. Countries focusing on growth and employment instead of low inflation have been often penalised by rentier capital flight (Crotty 2000: 30). This rentier class influences the global financial inflow and outflow to financial markets through foreign institutional investments and has often contributed to the market crisis. The rentier class also influences the crises-management policies of countries. For example, in Korea, unlike in the previous crises of 1970–72 and 1980, the 1997 crisis management policies focused more on the interests of the financial rentiers through Monetarist policies and full-scale financial liberalisations rather than on the industrial interests (Chang and Yoo 2002).

A bird's eye view

These developments since the 1970s, which appear to be paradoxical in mainstream economic theories, seem to be perennial. Therefore, a fundamental question is why in the current economic scenario repeated developments of paradoxical phenomena are seen – do they not speak of a deeper problem in the economic system? Could there be a major underlying characteristic of this epoch that has fostered these paradoxical developments but is overlooked in mainstream economic theories?

A radical development we see in this landscape is the evolution of the financial economy revolving around the growing financial capital. The root of many of the so-called paradoxical phenomena may lie in this fundamental evolution. Therefore, we should begin with probing the concept of financial capital vis-à-vis the standard concept of capital in mainstream economic theories and then examine how financial capital evolves and accumulates in economic systems.

3 The twin concepts of capital
Historical roots

Since the Age of Capital, beginning in the 1850s, capital has been the driving force in economic systems, and the key factor in the current evolution of a finance-dominated regime is accumulation of financial capital. How can this evolution be examined? The task is not simple. Until recently there was little consideration of the term 'financial capital' in mainstream economic methodology, and consequently, almost no attempt was made to probe the causes of accumulation of financial capital in economic systems. The second problem is deeper – it is the elusive concept of capital itself, as framed in mainstream economics.

In economics the concept of capital is indeed a very broad one, and a subject of varied interpretations. It has a key place in economics as one of the two main factors of production, the other being labour. Capital accumulation and investment have been widely held by both Keynesians and Marxians as essential for economic growth (Stockhammer 2004: 719).

The evolution of the concept of capital is one of the most fascinating chapters in the history of economic ideas. It evolved in phases. The beginning of the industrial production in the late 18th and the early 19th centuries opened new avenues for advancement in production methods and technology, and it promised improvements in economic life. It had an impact on economic ideas also. Through this impact some refinements of the earlier economic ideas took place, and modern economics was born as a discipline. The concept of capital too continued to evolve in this journey. The earlier ideas of capital were changed in its meaning and scope.

However, even in modern economics the very definition of capital has been widely debated – what are its contributions as a factor of production and the rewards to it, how it is to be measured. How elusive and broad the concept of capital is can be fathomed from the fact that economists have failed to reach a consensus on the theory of capital. Bliss puts it:

> When economists reach agreement on the theory of capital they will shortly reach agreement on everything else. Happily, for those who enjoy a diversity of views and beliefs, there is very little danger of this outcome. Indeed, there is at present not even agreement as to what the subject is about.
>
> (Bliss 1975: 7)

Economic literature has long been grappling with two concepts of capital – physical capital and financial capital. Mainstream economists have tended to view capital as the capital goods, which are assets, while in common parlance as well as in other disciplines, like accountancy, capital is viewed as a monetary fund (equity plus debt), which is a liability. These two diverging notions of capital have led to the confusing treatment of capital in economic theories. The concepts have been raised in economic theory but have been treated differently by different schools of thought. The treatment of capital sometimes as capital goods and at other times as a monetary fund generates ambiguity. Cohen and Harcourt (2005: xxviii) have pointed out that the dual notions or interpretations of capital are also the origin of controversies surrounding the capital theory, because one of the notions of capital is given undue importance to the neglect of the other.

The notion of financial fund in economic ideas

In the early economic ideas, capital was viewed as a fund. This fund view is seen in the pre-classical writings. Several authors have pointed out that the pre-classical writers viewed capital generally as 'funds' (Cantillon 1755), 'advances' (Quesnay 1759), or 'accumulated values' (Turgot 1774–76) needed to start and carry out the production process (Hennings 1987: 327–33; Blaug 1996: 26–7). Nitzan and Bichler pointed out that the writings of social theorists before the mid-18th century contained little discussions on capital, although an early, singular instance of an analysis was found in the writings of Barbon (1690). Barbon essentially saw capital as a 'stock'. He contended that interest was in fact a 'rent on capital' and paid for the 'stock'. Barbon, in this sense, set a precedent to the analysis of 'real capital', stressing that interest was paid for the use of the stock of goods that could be bought with the money and not for the money itself (Nitzan and Bichler 2000: 69).

An explicit idea of the role of capital in production process is found in the writings of the physiocrats. The term 'capital' was, however, not in usage. Cantillon (1755) called it 'funds', emphasising the need for an accumulated sum of money to buy stocks of goods with which to produce or trade. He wrote of the farmer who needed sufficient funds (*assed de fond*) to do business (Hennings 1987). This was the time when the society was predominantly agricultural. The money capital as a fund was needed in agricultural production cycles to finance the lag between expenditure on inputs and return on outputs.

Quesnay (1759) regarded capital as consisting of a series of 'advances' (*avances*). He used the term 'advances' to mean money capital (*capital d'argent*) conceiving it to be invested in building, implements, stores of grains, cattle etc. His idea was that larger advances were needed to use these items more in production. He considered advances in the form of livestock, building, and implements (which we would call later as fixed or physical capital) to be the 'original advances'. On these 'original advances' a charge at the rate of 10 percent was included as depreciation in his famous *Tableau Économique*. He also considered 'landlord's advances' including drainage, building, and other permanent land improvements but they did not feature in the *Tableau*. He further included 'annual advances' (what can be referred to as working capital) towards the wages of agricultural labourers, seeds, and other recurring annual costs. Farmers in the *Tableau* were seen to use two-fifths of their own output, while one-fifth was sold to 'sterile' artisans in exchange for goods to replace worn-out fixed capital (Blaug 1996: 26–7; Hennings 1987). Evidently, Quesnay conceived of capital as both 'money capital' advanced by the farmers and 'fixed capital', when the funds were invested in the production process. The seeds of the ambivalent treatment of the two concepts of capital were already sown in his ideas, which would continue in the analysis of his successors.

Reflections along the same lines permeated through the writings of Turgot (1774). He generalised Quesnay's theory and developed a specific theory of capital, as a requirement for production. Turgot defined capital as 'accumulated values' and pointed out that advances for running of the production process were paid out of capital. Undoubtedly, he was referring to money or finance capital as a key requirement in the production process that was roundabout. However, there was no clear indication of whether he was regarding the 'advances' themselves as productive or the capital goods representing them as productive. He further contended that the rates of return on all possible investments were equalised by competition between the owners of various 'capitals' (he used the plural, *capitaux*). Therefore, this rate of return acted as a kind of thermometer of the abundance or scarcity of capital in the society (Hennings 1987).

Later on, the classical writers saw capital both as fund or money capital and as physical capital. But quite often in their analysis there was a confusing juxtaposition of the two concepts. As a classical writer, Marx made explicit reference to the role of money capital or financial capital in the capitalist system. Marx was writing in the second half of the 19th century when the industrial revolution had come to its full fruition and this historical setting was influential in the development of his concepts. The fund concept was inherent in Marx's M–C–M' formulation. On the other hand, the physical capital concept (which, later on, the neoclassical school stressed) also found its representation in his idea of 'constant capital'.

Marx wrote extensively on capital in his book *Das Capital*. To Marx capital represented both the stock of goods and the sum of values. He insisted that capital goods were 'capital' only in the capitalist society, thereby using the term to describe particular organisation of production in the society (Hennings 1987). Marx recognised that capital must essentially begin with a 'fund' or pool of resources, which then took on definite forms in the capitalist production process. In this subsequent form capital was essentially the physical capital, which Marx denoted as 'non-reproductive capital' or 'constant capital'. This included the means of production, raw material, and auxiliary raw material, etc., which did not undergo any quantitative alteration of value in the production process. They were simply applied in the production process – their intrinsic values being transmitted to the product being manufactured, but they did not add any value on their own to the product (Munro 2008: 4–5).

However, in his analysis it was the concept of 'variable capital' – a revolving monetary fund used essentially for wage payments – that got more prominence as the sole source of creation of value in the production process. In doing so, Marx remained true to his classical political economy roots, giving the key role to human labour in production process following Smith's idea of labour theory of value. In Marxian views, variable capital was a part of capital, which reproduced the equivalent of its own value and also produced an excess or surplus value. Surplus value was created solely by labour power and appropriated by the capitalist, as in purchasing from the workers his labour power, the capitalist purchased all the fruits of his labour power (Munro 2008: 5).

Marx further analysed the accumulation of capital through a process of appropriation of surplus value, expressed in his formulation as M–C–M′. The reproduction and accumulation of capital as money reached its most fetishized state in this relation (Pineault 2001: 5–7). It could be seen in this formulation that a major determinant of the accumulation process in a capitalist economy was the access to money, the capacity to mobilise money as capital, and reproduction of money values. In pre-capitalist societies the M–M′ form manifested itself as usury, but in societies dominated by the capitalist mode of production the M–M′ form was embodied and reproduced by the credit system as a specific commodity, as 'commodified' money capital (Pineault 2001 *Ibid.*).

An implicit fund idea was also present in Fisher's (1906) writings. Taylor pointed out that Fisher defined capital as the stock of wealth at any point of time. The flows of services generated from wealth were then defined as income (which we now see as rental income from financial assets). Thus, the concept was very broad, as anything that generated a service or yield as benefit (whether paid for or not) was viewed as capital (Taylor 2000: 117–18).

Explicit mention of 'finance capital' is found in the early 20th century economic writings. Pineault pointed out that Hilferding (1910) considered 'finance capital' as the combination of industrial and financial capital. 'Finance capital', according to Hilferding, was a category, which was identified as a particular form of capital in a new form of capitalism. The spheres of industrial, commercial, and banking capital, separated earlier, were now brought together by the need of finance. The basis of this new association was elimination of free competition among individual capitalists by forming large monopolistic cartels. To grasp this economic and social transformation in its complexity, Hilferding developed a sophisticated analysis of the institutional mutations. The institutional forms examined by Hilferding were the emerging universal banks, the large manufacturing corporations, and the buoyant and dynamic stock exchanges. Finance capital was understood by him as the product of the interaction between these three institutional forms, an interaction structured by and for the circulation of fictitious liquid capital (Pineault 2001: 3).

Next, we find Keynes using a variety of concepts of capital in developing his arguments. In his *General Theory* (1936), he seemed to switch between capital as working capital and physical capital, depending upon whether the reference was to finance or to investment. In *Treatise* (1930), on the other hand, most of the time capital appeared in his writing to refer to the working capital. The working capital concept undoubtedly embodied the fund concept as it referred to capital as resources required in running the production process. Keynes discussed the 'finance motive', giving some valuable insights. He pointed out finance was essentially a revolving fund, which for the community as a whole, was only a 'book keeping transaction'. So, as soon as it is expended, the lack of liquidity is automatically made good and the readiness to become temporarily illiquid is available to be used over again (Taylor 2000: 117).

One of the few to point out the distinction between the fund concept and the physical goods concept of capital, but often ignored, was Joan Robinson. In the context of a suitable unit for measurement of capital Robinson (1953–54) pointed out that capital, in the form of yet 'un-invested' finance, was a sum of money and so were the net receipts of businesses. But it did not co-exist at the same time with its invested form. This meant that while capital was a sum of money, the profits were not yet earned, and when profits (quasi-rents) were earned, capital had ceased to be a sum of money and was a plant. So, any unit of capital should necessarily encompass the scope of both these ideas (Harcourt 1972: 19).

To sum up, there has been no unambiguous treatment of the concept of financial capital as a fund in early economic ideas. Financial capital, as a fund of surplus resources, was the earliest form of capital in human history which was needed to finance the undertaking of economic activities. Yet, there has been little analysis of capital as a fund of liquid resources and its essential role in initiating the economic production process.

Shifts in the focus

In the first half of the 19th century technological innovations began to fuel up rapid industrialisation in Western European nations. In this context, it was not surprising that later on the neoclassical economics laid more and more stress on incorporating the idea of physical capital or the capital goods as the means of production that embodied technology. Consequently, the focus shifted singularly on physical capital. As a corollary to this idea, debates concerning the macroeconomic aggregation and quantification of the stock of physical capital with different vintages became a marked feature of neo-neoclassical economics.

Economic ideas and development of its notions are naturally influenced by the milieu of the economic thinkers. In the second half of the 19th century, technological advancements and innovations (which were embodied in capital goods) in large-scale manufacturing by machines played a key role in economic development. Therefore, the notion of capital in the form of physical capital could hardly be ignored by the economists of the time. Attempts to analyse the role of capital goods in aiding labour in the production process surfaced even in the writings of the classical economists witnessing the first industrial revolution in the late 18th century.

In neo-neoclassical literature the controversies on the problems of measurement of physical capital, and the returns to it in the production process, took centre stage. Böhm-Bawerk used a concept of capital as aggregate of intermediate products used as the produced means of production. This concept was criticised by Menger, who wanted to stress the 'abstract concept of capital as the money value of the property devoted to acquisitive purposes' against Smith's concept of the 'produced means of production' (Krizner 1976: 4–18). Vaughn commented that Mises, following the similar tone, pointed out that the concept of capital had a meaning only in the context of a market in which monetary calculation was meaningful. To Mises, there was no meaning of the idea of an aggregate fund of capital. The market value of the existing group of capital goods was subject to continual change since entrepreneurial plans revealed unanticipated conflicts that annulled the expectations of some and exceeded the expectations of others. Therefore, the calculation of the value of the capital stock in aggregate of a country was meaningless (Vaughn 1976: 7.7, 7.8).

Misesian argument clearly contributed in erasing the line of demarcation between the financial capital as a fund and the physical capital created by this fund. In the neoclassical paradigm capital as a fund appeared on the liability side of the balance sheet of a firm as an accounting entry only. Far more important was the physical capital on the asset side, which was put into the action of production. As a result, the creation of financial capital, as a fund and financing of economic activities by it, dropped out of the neoclassical view.

In the milieu of paradoxical growth process since the late 1960s attempts have been made to develop various notions of capital, drawing analogies with the neoclassical concept. In many directions a plethora of notions associated with capital has emerged. The transition of the industrialised economies into knowledge-based ones along with the growth of the service sector has brought into focus the key role of human capital, replacing the erstwhile labour in economic theories. Economists are found to be engaged enthusiastically in developing notions and theories of human capital, and assigning a determining role to it in economic growth.

Subsequently, it is recognised that economic systems do have endogenous growth. But no satisfactory explanation of this endogenous economic growth could be obtained in the traditional neoclassical framework with labour and physical capital, which treats the sources of economic growth as exogenous and brought about primarily by technological advancement. Now incorporating the notion of human capital, attempts are made to build endogenous growth models. It is assumed that investments in skills and education build the human capital, and investments in research and development (R&D) leading to creation of intellectual property build the intellectual capital.

In another direction, natural capital is also finding a place in economic discussions, especially in the branch of economics of environment. Natural capital is taken as the stock of natural resources including soils, minerals and metals, air, water, forestry, and all living organisms. It is inherent in ecologies and, as an underpinning of the economy and the society, provides free goods and service that make human life possible. There is also a notion of social capital. It is viewed as the networks of relationships among people who live and work in a particular society, enabling the society to function effectively through reciprocity, trust, and cooperation. Yet another notion is public capital or infrastructure capital that refers to the government-owned assets such as roads, railways, bridges, tunnels, electrical grids, telecommunications, water supply and irrigation, city systems, sea and air ports, and so on. These provide the services necessary for the economy to function properly.

These are several important branches of the mainstream economics and the ongoing researches on these areas have contributed a large volume of literature. They draw on the analytical tools of the mainstream economic analyses, and widely use those in their investigations. However, the contribution these branches make as a feedback to enrich the mainstream by clarifying or strengthening its existing notions are not always very clear.

Since the 1990s the focus has been shifting towards the importance of financial capital and we see a revival of the earlier fund notion of capital. It is an undeniable fact that the last two decades has seen an increasing influence of the financial sector and explosive accumulation of financial capital. The notions of fund and financing can no longer be considered abstract notions and their existence cannot be denied either. With the development of financial markets and financial products, fund capital has started playing a role, having a life of its own. The arrival of the age of ICT has made the accumulation and transaction of financial capital unhindered. As a result, financial markets have developed at unprecedented levels. In this scenario, financial economics has emerged as an important branch of mainstream economic analysis. It questions many of the mainstream hypotheses and has contributed new insights, particularly in respect of decision-making under uncertainty of the future.

The primary focus of financial economics is on the interrelations of financial variables under uncertainty. Broadly speaking, its two main areas of study are pricing of financial assets and corporate finance. The first concerns the investors as the providers of fund capital, and the second concerns the companies as the user of fund capital. Most of the studies on financial economics frame the questions in the context of time, uncertainty, options, and information. Time brings an important dimension because 'money now' can be traded for 'money in the future'. This brings into the analysis the mechanics of discounting the future to its present value. But the future is uncertain. So the risk–return relationships are important in decision-making. Moreover, in a transaction involving the future there are options for either of the party to make some other decision at a later time, which will change the subsequent transfers of money. Information plays an important role since knowledge about the future may reduce the risk involved with the future monetary values. As an important branch of economic studies, financial economics finds a place in the curricula of many academic institutions, especially at the postgraduate level, with some of the recent texts being Kerry (2010), Frank, Edwin and Zhou (2011), Bianconi (2013), Leonard and Ziemba (2013), and Ivo (2014).

Financial economics, although it revolves around the concept of financial capital, does not focus on financial capital of an economy in aggregate, as it is built on the foundations of microeconomics and decision theory. A study of the sources of accumulation of financial capital (and thereby wealth or net worth) and its implications for the financial economy as a whole are not within the scope of the microeconomic framework of financial economics. However, one of the most important contributions of financial economics, particularly significant for our study here, is the notion treading upon the future – current transactions are now made on the future. The final chapter of this study will bring out its implication for the financial economy.

Historical roots of financing

Even in the primitive society some fund was needed for financing or initiating and performing economic activities. In the primitive subsistence agricultural societies, surplus food grains were required to take up the activities of tools making. This was required for fulfilling the consumption needs during the time spent on producing the tools and implements (or what we may say the capital goods). This fund of surplus food grains can be considered the first from capital or the fund of resources. Earlier, even for the primitive hunting and gathering tribal societies that preceded the primitive subsistence agricultural economy, a fund of food was necessary for the production of primitive hunting instruments – the primitive form of production capital.

With the emergence of property rights, agricultural production was organised on a larger scale for non-subsistence purposes. The word non-subsistence does not mean here that production was for the market. With property rights ensured, hoarding of food grains was a more feasible motive for the landowners in the society. In such an economy the 'wage fund', consisting of surplus consumption goods, was used as compensation for hiring assistance for non-agricultural production of implements and tools. The subsistence farmers also needed a fund of consumption goods to take up the maintenance and production of his implements. Thus, even in the non-monetary ancient societies a fund of resources was always needed in the production process. Therefore, we may say that capital existed in human societies since the earliest time in both the forms – as a fund of resources and as stock of goods.

With further developments in the society there arose a wealthy section of people who specialised in lending the fund of resources to others. This meant financing the activities of others, such as in trade and commerce. Along with it came a functioning credit system. A mercantile class emerged that specialised in lending the fund for both production and trading activities. This mercantile class, to facilitate both the lending activities and the trade that required movement over considerable distances, innovated to a disembodied financing mechanism using the system of credits.

The historical record suggests that credits and debits were older by about two thousand years than the oldest known coins, which appeared only in the 7th century B.C. The written records of credit, which acted as some kind of bills of exchange, were also prevalent before the emergence of coinage. Historical evidence also suggests that most of the commerce in the earliest societies were conducted by credits and debits, rather than by precious metals. Innes (1913) pointed out that the principal instrument of commerce in early Europe for many centuries was the 'tally' – a stick of squared hazel-wood that was marked to indicate the amount of the purchase or debt. It was created when the buyer became a debtor by accepting a good or service from a seller who automatically became the creditor. The name of the debtor and the date of transaction were written on two opposite sides of the stick. The stick, in turn, was divided in a way that the notches were cut in half, to ensure name and date appeared on both the pieces of the tally. The creditor retained the longer piece (stock) and the debtor retained the smaller piece (stub). When the debtor cleared his debts, the two pieces of tally were matched to verify the amount of the debt. Acting as transferable, negotiable instruments, these tallies were circulated mostly among the traders. The 'stock' was used by the creditors to purchase goods and services or to clear their own debts. Thus, by means of these tallies, purchases of goods were done, loans were made, and debts were cleared. The constant creation of credit and debits and their extinction by cancellation against one another formed the whole mechanism of commerce (Tymiogne and Wray 2006: 6–7).

As the mercantile class tried to find an intangible, disembodied form to represent the fund of resources, the written records of credit or bills of exchange emerged to facilitate both lending and trade. Bills representing the fund of resources are essentially a primitive form of financial capital. While a fund of consumption items or any other good is concrete and less liquid, financial capital even in the primitive form was disembodied and more liquid or transferable.

Emergence of money as a universally accepted means of payment, which acted as a store of value and a mode of financing production, trade, and commerce, was a much later phenomenon. The neoclassical contention of money arising to overcome the problems of barter is very much away from the historical evolution of money. As Tymiogne and Wray point out, coins appear to have originated as 'pay tokens', being mere tokens of the Crown's debt and imposed by the state on its subjects to ease payment of taxes (Tymiogne and Wray 2006: 7–8).

Financial capital, viewed as that which finances or helps in undertaking other economic activities, preceded money capital. Even when money came to be established as a universally accepted means of payments, credits, now valued in money units, continued as a part of financial capital and 'money capital' emerged as another part of the financial capital, which was held in money form.

With growing trade and commerce, the surplus of mercantile money capital used as loan capital emerged as the interest-bearing money capital. Then, in the industrial economy, the company system evolved as a form of business organisation in production and trade. Here, financial capital, as the sources of finance of the companies, acquired a new dimension with share capital (in the form of money capital) as one of its components. The application of finance, or the financial capital, found in the creation of assets – fixed in the form of capital goods, quasi-liquid in the form of stock of output and debtors, and liquid in the form of money – was required to initiate and perform production and trading activities.

The line of demarcation and the link

In current literature an explicit distinction between financial capital and production capital was made by Perez (2002), who stressed the interaction between these two types of capital that moulded the different phases of technological revolutions (Perez 2002: 73–7). Stressing the liquidity aspect of financial capital, Perez underlined the 'mobility' of financial capital while production capital was 'tied to concrete products' (Perez *Ibid*. 2002: 71). However, the formation of financial capital and its process of accumulation remained outside the purview of Perez's study. But the study established clearly that it was financial capital that financed the production capital and the mismatch between the two may occur.

In an earlier study, Taylor (2000) explored the concept of capital on a similar line of reasoning, demarking its fixed and fluid components. He considered an interesting definition of capital as a stock (or a surplus), which in turn was composed of two parts – a fixed (or sunk) component and a fluid (or liquid) component. The fixed component was represented by the un-depreciated portion of produced means of production. Taylor considered depreciation simply as an accounting device for transforming (over some relevant horizon) the sunk capital back into fluid capital. In other words, it was an instrument for effecting savings by the business organisation, and had no relation to the physical wear and tear referred to as economic depreciation. So, fluid capital was created by the depreciation reserves of the existing 'produced means of production', in supplement to the 'excess of past and current savings over past and current investment' (Taylor 2000: 18–19).

The fixed component in Taylor's demarcation was evidently what is referred to as physical capital, and the fluid component was the fund required for financing what is often referred to as circulating or working capital held in liquid form. The characteristic that makes capital fluid or liquid is that it is 'free to be embodied, through investment in anything, anywhere' (Taylor *Ibid*. 2000: 19). Thus, it is marked by 'fungibility', which fixed capital does not have. Evidently, Taylor is identifying both disembodiment and liquidity as the distinguishing feature of fluid capital. He stressed the fact that depreciation reserves created fluid capital to recover the amount invested in sunk capital.

Taylor's study made a significant contribution by bringing into the focus of economic studies the recovery of sunk capital and thereby creation of financial capital through depreciation of fixed assets. It appears that to him the fixed capital (or production capital on the asset side of balance sheet), and the fluid capital (or the financial capital on the liability side of balance sheet) were just not accounting entries. Depreciation creates a dynamic link between them. However, what would be its implications for an economy as a whole was not examined. This is an important aspect of our study which we will develop later.

We may conclude that keeping aside some recent attempts to loosely associate the term capital with several other aspects – social capital, human capital, infrastructure capital etc. – we have essentially a twin concept of capital: capital as a monetary fund (not only money but also monetary claims) and capital as the produced means of production financed by the funds, that is the physical or production capital. For this purpose we need to understand the dichotomy as well as the link between the two in the financial economy.

4 Financial breeding

Legitimisation of interest on money

Emergence of capital, a monetary fund, as a commodity naturally needed its price to be specified. As we show, this price is the interest on money. Historically, emergence of capital as a monetary fund and interest on money (transacted as a loan) were intertwined in the same evolutionary process. However, in mainstream economic literature, interest appears to be far more elusive than the concept of capital as capital goods, or more precisely, the productive machines embodying the aspect of technology. The stringent focus of the early neoclassical economics on physical capital thwarted not only the concept of capital as a monetary fund, but also made a conceptual muddle of interest and profit – interest was often considered a return on capital (that is, physical capital employed in the production process) rather than a cost of capital as a borrowed fund.

There was an historical context of this muddle. Even in the 19th century, a taboo on charging interest on money loans prevailed in the society, at least psychologically. A stigma was attached to usury – lending money at interest. If charging interest was not justified 'ethically', could it be justified by linking it to the economic activities that enabled interest? This was the background to the non-monetary theories of interest: a myopic view that neglected the fund aspect of capital.

Establishing the legitimacy of charging interest on money loans as an economic construct of human civilisation has a long history. Why must money, a barren commodity, yield a return? It does not have any natural growth on its own, like livestock or grains and plantations. This question came up frequently in the economic writings of the 17th and 18th century. Later on, when interest on money – an economic construct that artificially creates and assigns a new property of self-breeding to money – got accepted as a fact of economic life, the question of its implication for the economic system became far more important than justifying it by 'why and whence' theories of interest.

A close study of the historical roots of the phenomenon of interest and the attempts in economic literature in theorising the nature and causes of interest is essential to understand this implication – the process of breeding more money from money in the form of interest, and thereby multiplying itself to accumulate the financial capital (Roy 2009).

The historical roots of interest

The phenomenon of interest, although it manifests today most visibly as the interest on money loans, precedes the arrival of the money economy. The writings concerning the legitimacy or otherwise of interest on loans arrive very early in human history. For example, Kautilya (4th century B.C.) in 'Arthashastra' dealt quite elaborately on the rules and regulations regarding transactions related to loans and deposits, specifying the interest rates to be charged on various types of loans according to their riskiness (Sihag 2008: 7–9).

Evidence of contract interest on commodity loan is found much before the evolution of metal money. Credit, in fact, preceded the evolution of metal money by over two thousand years. Before the evolution of money economy, various commodities functioned as media of exchange. It is now widely believed that the difficulties (for the debtor) in making interest payment in varying, differentiated media of exchange served as a major contributing factor for standardisation of monetary units (Homer and Sylla 1963: 17–19). Along with the presence of contractual interest, there was also effort to prevent abuses of credit systems. In most of the ancient civilisations there were codes laying down the maximum interest to be charged for different loans.

In the ancient world, experimentation with several media of exchange led to the selection of one or two among them to serve as the commonly accepted medium of exchange. Law or custom sanctioned debt repayment in some commonly acceptable commodity of value – the legal tender emerged as the money of the economy. Before the town civilisation developed, food and animals were the most important forms of this denominator used by the original Sumerians, Indo-Germanic, and Semito-Hamitic peoples (Homer and Sylla *Ibid*. 1963: 19–21).

In the ancient Orient, development of town culture put a priority on credit and inanimate objects like silver, gold, lead, bronze, and copper were lent at interest. The early Hindu Laws provided for the right to negotiate such transactions. Detailed laws regarding default in payments of debts were laid down in Kautilya's 'Arthashastra', one of the earliest economic treatises of ancient India. The linkage of interest rates to the perceived riskiness of the borrower finds a place in 'Artha-shastra', where Kautilya recommended a higher risk premium for undertaking greater risk. He also proposed appropriate upper limits on the interest rates to be charged by lenders. The temple of the goddess Athena at Athens, for example, lent money to the state between 433 and 427 B.C. at 6 percent (Homer and Sylla 1963: 20–1; Sihag 2008: 7–10, Gkamas 2006: 122–23).

Religious, social, and legal prohibitions on contract interest

With the development of credit instruments, also appeared its abuses and most of the early legal codes tried to prevent the abuse of credit or altogether prohibit the use of it. For example, the Israelites did not permit lending at interest. The Iranians, as late as 450 B.C., considered that taking interest on a loan dishonoured a man. The ancient Indian literature set up maximum permissible rates of interest. The Babylonians and Romans permitted credit but limited the rate of interest, while the Greeks forbade personal bondage for debt, though not limiting the rate of interest. Nevertheless, loans based on real estate or pawns were mentioned in most of the ancient literatures, including the Bible, the Zend-Avesta, and the Vedas. The need for restriction on interest rates could be judged by the fact that the earliest historic interest rates ranged from 20 to 50 percent per annum for loans of grains and metal (Homer and Sylla 1963: 21).

The dissent against the practice of usury was voiced in the writings of philosophers like Plato (428/427–348/347 B.C.), Aristotle (384–322 B.C.), Plautus (254–184 B.C.), Cicero (106–43 B.C.), and Seneca (1 B.C.–A.D. 65). The dissent was well documented in the medieval period too. With the breakup of the Roman Empire, there was a general downturn of economic activities and this, coupled with the arrival of Christianity with its teachings, meant a new hostility towards interest taking. Certain passages in the New Testament were interpreted as expressing the divine prohibition towards usury, which strengthened the opposition to usury. Initially, interest taking was prohibited only by the Church and for the clergy, but soon this prohibition by the Church was extended to the masses (Böhm-Bawerk 1890: I.I.8–15).

From 'usury' to 'interest'

The Latin word 'usura' means use of anything – in the case of usury, the borrowed money – so that usury is the practice of using money. On the other hand, the word interest is derived from the Latin word 'intereo', which means to be lost. From its substantive form 'interesse', the modern term interest is developed. Thus, interest is the loss associated with lending of money (Homer and Sylla 1963: 71).

The difference between usury and interest dominates the scholastic analysis of usury in the medieval period. It was from the exceptions to the canon law against usury that the medieval notion of interest developed. Compensation for loans was held to be unjust if it was a gain to the lender but justified if the compensation was not net gain, but rather a reimbursement for the loss of the lender. Interest thus came to be considered the compensation due to the lender because of a loss, which he had incurred through lending. The concept was derived from Roman law, which considered interest as the difference between the lender's position after giving a loan and that in which he would have stood if he had not loaned. It was the damages, including broadly the profit that the lender might have made with the money loaned, and often a compensation for delayed repayment of loan. The term 'interesse' in this sense became standard around about 1220 A.D. (Homer and Sylla *Ibid.* 1963: 71–2).

The medieval traders and moneylenders devised their ways to escape the stringent prohibitions by establishing both direct and indirect exemptions. The direct exemptions included the exemption of the usury practices of Jews. Various means were devised to accommodate for interest taking within the prohibitions imposed. These included purchase of annuities, the taking of land as a mortgage for the money lent, the use of bills of exchange, partnership arrangements, and taking compensation from the borrower in the shape of 'interesse' on the deferred payment. In the case of a culpable neglect (technically called 'mora') on the part of the borrower to fulfil the contract obligations, the lender was entitled to compensation in the shape of 'interesse'. Two further devices virtually made interest taking possible without lifting the legislative prohibitions. Under one, the borrower agreed beforehand that the lender should be released from the obligation of authenticating the borrower's 'mora'; and under the other, a definite rate of 'interesse' was agreed on in advance. Thus, in effect, a loan was given nominally without interest, but the creditor actually received as 'interesse' a regular percentage for the whole period of the loan (Böhm-Bawerk 1890: I.II.6). In fact, the economic system had become too complicated to survive without a proper credit system, which naturally would be characterised by interest on money capital.

Providing economic justification for interest

Since the early 16th century, an important change started to take place in the discourses on interest in pre-modern Europe. The theological underpinnings that had dominated economic literature till then gave way to arguments of economic origins (Böhm-Bawerk *Ibid.* 1890: I.I.16–17). The traders and merchants with growing need of monetary finance for their activities began to feel keenly the restraints of the stringent prohibition of the canon laws. In the middle of the 16th century, literature supporting interest payments arrived from Calvinism, an offshoot of the Protestant movement in Europe. It gathered momentum during the 17th century, so that by the end of the 18th century there remained few theorists who supported in their writings the canon principles (Böhm-Bawerk *Ibid.* 1890: I.I.12). Arguments in support of the doctrine of interest, however, did not appear simultaneously in all the European nations. In countries with flourishing trade and commerce, the practical necessities and difficulties faced because of the prohibition soon manifested itself in voices supporting interest. In fact, in most of these nations, interest was a practical reality even before justifications arrived to support it (Böhm-Bawerk *Ibid.* 1890: I.II.51).

The 'why and whence' of 'interest' – the classical view

Interest was established as a fact of economic life, yet usury could not be justified. In this backdrop, the classical economic thinkers had to take a careful stance to conceptualise and theorise interest, bypassing the question of usury – the price charged by moneylenders for giving money loans. Discourses on interest before the 18th century focused on whether money, which in itself had no wealth-creating power, could (and should) yield an income in the form of interest as income from usury. From the 18th century the focus of economic theories shifted to 'why and whence of interest' (Böhm-Bawerk *Ibid.* 1890: I.I.2) in the production process, as distinct from usurers' monetary interest in the money-lending process.

In the pre-classical writings, however, there were some passing references to interest from a different stance. The early physiocrats gave little emphasis on the explanation of interest, which they left as a matter of short-term phenomena. Turgot, in his book *Reflections on the Formation and Distribution of Wealth* (1774), contended that since capital was necessary for all undertakings, the 'industrious' man would voluntarily share the profits of his enterprise with the owner of the capital who had lent him the funds. He saw lending of money as a trade, interest arising from the 'use' of money by the borrower. Interest, thus, arose from the use of the money, and not from the profit that the borrower hopes to make by using the funds borrowed. Moreover, Turgot saw interest as determined by purely monetary forces by the number of borrowers in the market demanding money loans and the number of lenders willing to lend money. The idea was clearly of interest as a monetary phenomenon and laid a foundation for a monetary theory of interest.

On the contrary, to avoid the pitfall of justifying in effect the usury interest on money, the classical writers had to take recourse to a tricky route of viewing interest as a return on physical capital employed, and thus contended that interest was a non-monetary phenomenon. The pre-classical writer Turgot recognised that interest was a voluntary share of profit but he did not confuse the sources from which it was paid with the reason for which it was paid. But the classical writers created this confusion. In their writings, interest became synonymous to profit.

Adam Smith (1776) did not thoroughly examine the emergence of interest, but in identifying the reasons for interest, he mentioned that there was necessarily a profit from capital when the capitalist was using his money capital in the employment of labourers in productive process. He contended that the source of interest was an increased value given to the product over the values, which labourers created – a deduction that the capitalist (presumably by the virtue of his ownership of capitalist means of production) made in his favour from the returns to labour, and so the workers did not receive the full value created by them, but were obliged to share it with the capitalist. Böhm-Bawerk pointed out that Smith's ideas, though far from perfect, had much influence on later interest theories, especially the 'productivity' and 'social' theories of interest (Böhm-Bawerk 1890: I.IV.4–15).

Ricardo's muddling of interest with profit was more categorical. He specified that interest as a phenomenon was a form of return linked solely with 'produced means of production' as capital. This contributed, in turn, to the 'tripartite' division of factors (land, labour, and capital) and their rewards (rent, wage, and profit/interest), which continued to dominate classical and neoclassical thinking for many years (Fetter 1977: 2.6.16). This often led to a neglect of monetary forces in the classical theories. Ricardo, for example, specifically contended that the rate of interest was not regulated by any rate fixed by the monetary authority but solely by the rate of profit obtained from the 'employment of capital' (Conard 1959: 15–19).

The 'productivity' approach was characterised by the assignment of the surplus value, the source of interest, to one of the factors of production, which was considered productive. The approaches that emerged during this period were all looking for the cause of the 'surplus value', which arose in the act of production. While the direct productivity theories assigned the 'surplus value' creating power to capital, the 'use' theories explained the origin of interest in a roundabout way, making the productive use of capital as an element of cost which, like every other element of cost, demanded compensation (Böhm-Bawerk 1890: II.I.31–3). The 'abstinence' theories held that surplus value was the equivalent to the abstinence – the sacrifice on part of the capitalist in not consuming the surplus. On the other hand, opposing the abstinence theories, the 'exploitation' theories held that labour was the sole source of surplus value and interest arose as the capitalist's appropriation of the surplus value.

Non-monetary neoclassical theories of interest

Since the work of Adam Smith in 1776, for more than a hundred years, economic discourses, having no concrete theory of interest, were in a confusing muddle of interest and profit in the so-called productivity idea of interest. This prevailed until the work of Böhm-Bawerk, *Capital and Interest: A Critical History of Economical Theory* (1890). Later on came the work of Irving Fisher, *The Theory of Interest* (1930). These two are the seminal works in the subsequent developments offering concrete theories of interest. Following them a plethora of interest theories came out. Unfortunately, muddling of interest and profit continued. In the works of both Böhm-Bawerk and Fisher, as well as in the subsequent developments following them, it became deep rooted in the formulations of the concrete theories. Further, more confusion brewed, particularly in the 'productivity' theories of interest that we will discuss next, as it became unclear whether these were the theories of interest or the theories of production capital. Neoclassical theories of interest and theories of capital often tended to overlap and, as a result, they falter in bringing out a separate theory of profit alongside a theory of interest.

With the coming of the industrial revolution, the economic production activities shifted to large-scale industrial production using machines and a class of entrepreneurs emerged who organised the production activities mostly with borrowed capital. They earned a handsome return by virtue of ownership of the means of production – the machines or the capital goods in production. Production activities, thus organised, not only allowed for the payment of interest on the monetary fund borrowed, but also allowed in excess of that a return to the entrepreneur. This was what Böhm-Bawerk (1890) famously referred to as 'natural interest'.

The idea of finding out an intrinsic natural value, as the reference point for a usually fluctuating economic phenomenon, was quite common in the classical paradigm. Classical writers were uninterested in short-term changes and looked for more basic forces or the long-term movements that determined the natural values, about which the daily rates might fluctuate. For example, they talked about natural prices (the exchange values of commodities), natural wage rate, etc. Following this classical tradition, Böhm-Bawerk intended to bring out a theory of 'natural' interest as a fundamental concept.

Productivity and time preference – the neoclassical debate

Böhm-Bawerk's work (1890) represented the key to the entry into the early 20th century interest theories, not only historically, but also because his theory contained the two dominant ideas that influenced interest theories in the early 20th century. These two key concepts of Böhm-Bawerk's theory of interest – the subjective concept of 'time valuation' and the objective technical concept of 'average period of production' – largely determined the divergence in the schools of thought that emerged in the early 20th century.

Böhm-Bawerk built his theories based on ideas similar to the time-preference ideas of Carl Menger (1840–1921), whose writings laid the basis of Austrian economics. To explain why interest rates were positive, Böhm-Bawerk argued that for three reasons difference existed in the time value between present goods and future goods of equal quality and quantity. Two of the reasons for this difference were subjective – in a growing economy people would expect larger incomes in the future and so would assign less time value to them, and for psychological reasons the usefulness of goods would tend to be less valued over time. Both the reasons, later called 'positive time preference', explained why people were willing to pay interest to get goods or resources in the present, or to insist on being paid interest if they were to give them as loan. The third reason given by Böhm-Bawerk, somewhat complicated and difficult to understand, was based on the concept of average period of production, or the time ratio between the input period and the output period. He argued that in roundabout production methods, or in the production process taking more time due to the introduction of capital goods, the same amount of input could yield a greater amount of output. This established the 'technical superiority' of the present over the future goods. The goods that would come in the future in normal course are less than the goods that could be produced using capital in a roundabout production method. Therefore, the net return to capital (or the interest) was the result of the greater value produced by the roundaboutness of production methods (Böhm-Bawerk 1890).

While a group of neo-neoclassical economists stressed the third aspect of Böhm-Bawerk's interest theory, the other economists, emphasising the 'psychological' aspects, criticised it. Instead, they gave importance to his idea of 'time valuation'. The psychological theorists, in fact, regarded Böhm-Bawerk's resorting to the 'average period of production' (and a consequent allowance to productivity factor) as his major shortcoming, especially in view of his own scathing criticism of productivity theories of interest (Fetter 1977: 2.1.29).

One of the most interesting debates this period witnessed was centred on the consideration of the 'time preference' and 'productivity' concepts in the theory of interest. One of the best known of these exchanges was between Böhm-Bawerk and John Bates Clark, concerning the concept of capital. Economists like Fetter, Patten, and Taussig accepted Böhm-Bawerk's theory in parts, emphasising Böhm-Bawerk's 'time preference' explanation of interest rates. Others, such as Seligman and Seager, tended to reject the theory of interest rates that emphasised the 'productivity' of capital along the lines of Clark (characterised by Fetter as 'technological' theories). Irving Fisher took an intermediate position regarding the role of time preference and productivity (Ryan 2002: ch.3).

Time preference – from Fisher to Mises

Fisher, with the publication of his book *The Theory of Interest* (1930), pioneered the birth of the 20th century non-monetary or 'real' theory of interest. He identified the rate of interest as the premium on the exchange between the present and the future goods, based partly on a subjective element of time preference, or 'human impatience', and partly on an objective element of 'investment opportunity'. The theory of interest, according to him, was similar to the theory of prices, of which it was considered a special case. Fisher saw 'human impatience' – the marginal preference for the present over the future goods – as a 'derivative of marginal desirability', the subjective element, which determined ordinary prices (Fisher 1930: II.IV3–4). Fisher started with a much broader concept of time preference and pointed out that it might indeed express any situation – either preference for the present over the future goods, or preference for the future over the present goods, or no preference in respect of time. However, in expressing this time preference, Fisher used a term – 'impatience' – which necessarily involved a supposition that the present goods are preferred. Fisher justified the use of the term 'impatience' as a fundamental attribute of human nature, and reverted to the exclusive consideration of positive time preference – the preference for the present goods over the future (Fisher 1930: II.IV.26–9). 'Productivity theorists' like Henry Seager (1913) felt that Fisher, in rejecting Böhm-Bawerk's third explanation of interest for the 'technical superiority of the present over the future goods', had denied a role to the productivity of capital in determining interest rate (Ryan 2002: 27).

Frank Knight, who had a clear theory of profit, unlike others muddling interest and profit (1921), came out with 'pure productivity' theory of interest in his contribution to capital theory in the 1930s as another non-monetary theory of interest. Conard argued that Knight based his theory on the ideas of Clark (1899), who propounded a concept of capital, which included not only land and natural agents, but also every other intangible right to income in which 'a fund of pure capital' might be invested (Conard 1959: 79). Many economists of the time were quite uncomfortable with Knight's proposition. The underlying reason could be that it gave almost a monetary fund view of capital – an idea not befitting the neoclassical idea of capital – and hence his interest theory tended to become, in effect, a theory of usury interests – an idea unacceptable at the time. Mises (1949) criticised Knight's 'permanent-fund-of-capital' view of physical capital, pointing out that like the 'productivity' theories of interest, it made a mistake in treating interest as the net income generated perpetually by the productivity of the abstract capital (fund) which was temporarily embodied in particular lumps of physical capital. He further contended that Knight's erroneous view of interest resulted from defining capital as an aggregate of capital goods or 'produced factors of production' (Conard 1959: 79; Krizner 1976: 4.26).

With the 'psychological' theories of Fetter, the exclusive focus came on the role of time in the emergence of the phenomenon of interest. Economists of the time had to be careful in their theories to avoid the pitfall of justifying usury interest. Fetter took this stance by offering a theory of 'economic interest' as against the 'contractual interest' on money loan, which was clearly interest in the form of 'usury'. He pointed out that while 'contract interest' was the payment for contract loans made in terms of money, 'economic interest' or 'implicit interest' represented the difference in the values of like goods available at different times.

Fetter was one of the forerunners in psychological analysis of 'economic interest', naming it 'a theory of capitalisation'. He opined that the theory of capitalisation must give a simple and unified explanation of time value wherever it was observable. It must also establish the theory of rent as the income from the use of goods in any given period, contrasting this clearly with the interest as the *agio* or discount on the goods taken over successive periods. Fetter contended that the 'productiveness' of a material agent was its quality of giving a scarce and desirable service to man and, to adequately explain this service of goods, a theory of rent was needed, as rent was related to the 'production' of scarce and desirable uses of things. Fetter's 'economic interest' theory then proposed the valuation of these different rents or incomes, distributed through different periods. Given the prospective series of future services given by a material good, interest should explain the valuation set contained in the goods for the future uses. Thus interest, as presented by this theory, expressed the exchange ratio of the present and the future services or uses (Fetter 1977: 2.4.17–19).

While Fetter led the way to a restatement of the stand of the purely 'psychological' interest theorists, Mises (1949) pioneered, following Mengerian ideas, another branch of interest theory subjugated to capital theory, in which time preference continued to play the key role. This branch is known as the Austrian theory of capital and interest. Mises specifically underlined their point of difference from Böhm-Bawerk's theory, stressing that it was Mengerian ideas that were more in keeping with the Austrian tradition. Like the purely psychological economists, Mises criticised the empirical and technical garb of the 'average period of production' used by Böhm-Bawerk to represent the concept of time preference. Mises pointed out that time preference manifested itself in the phenomenon of 'originary' interest which was the discount of the future goods against the present goods (Krizner 1976: 4.13–12).

Consideration of the time element in the process of production and, specifically, incorporation of an inter-temporal capital structure characterise Austrian macroeconomics. In considering the Austrian theory of interest and capital, a focus on the works of Mises were perhaps most justified by the thought that 'the theory of capital and interest occupies a central and characteristically Austrian position in the general Misesian system' (Fetter 1977: 2.1.33, 2.4.13–14). However, the Austrian position on capital and interest was far from a homogenous one. While Böhm-Bawerk's notions of time preference and average period of production were often loosely identified with the Austrian approach to capital and interest, Mises tried to reformulate Böhm-Bawerk's ideas in the 'strictly subjectivist' Austrian mode. His approach to the problem of interest was based on subjective time preference and he did not give any illustrative role to objective, or physical, conditions governing production in a capital-using world (Fetter *Ibid.* 1977: 2.4.14). He introduced the concept of 'originary interest': the 'ratio of the value assigned to the want-satisfaction in the immediate future and the value assigned to the want-satisfaction in remote periods of the future', expressed in a market economy as a discount of the 'future goods against the present goods' (Krizner 1976: 4.7–21).

Mises pointed out that the 'originary interest' was not a price determined in the market by the demand for and the supply of capital or capital goods. Rather, it was the rate of 'originary interest' that determined both the demand for and the supply of capital goods. How much of the available supply of goods was to be devoted to consumption in the immediate future and how much was to be kept for future consumption was determined by 'originary interest'. Thus, saving and capital accumulation were not done just because there was interest. Interest was neither the incentive for saving nor the reward for abstaining from immediate consumption – rather it was the ratio in the mutual valuation of the present goods over the future goods (Krizner 1976: 4.18–20).

The neoclassical debate that began in the early 20th century remained far from being concluded even after a century. What exactly is interest? Is it a return to the capitalists on the capital goods they use in production or it is to them a cost of capital (fund), as a payment to be made for the borrowed monetary fund they use in production (for buying the capital goods as well as working capital), or is it just a psychological discount factor people use to value the future in present terms? There is no straight answer to this question. It is a helpless situation – without clearly defining what we were examining, we jumped into examining its origin. As we mention at the beginning of this chapter, why it is paid and the sources from which it is paid are not the same thing. Turgot did not mix them up, but the classicists and the neoclassicists did.

The direct 'productivity' theories, following the Ricardian tradition, assigned the 'surplus value' or surplus goods creating power to capital, which was clearly inconceivable and hence abandoned. Nevertheless, the 'use' theories explained the origin of interest in a roundabout way, making the 'productive use' of capital an element of cost which, like every other element of cost, demanded compensation (Böhm-Bawerk

1890: II.I.31–3). When interest is viewed as an element of cost of the productive use of capital that demands compensation, confusion creeps in, since charging of depreciation (capital consumption allowance) has been an age-old practice. The productivity theorists simply overlooked this fact, and in effect proposed the same compensation to be paid twice – as depreciation and as interest. Introduction of machines or capital goods in production, a marvel created by the industrial revolution, moved the economists of the time so much so as to give capital goods the credit of all the three – interest, depreciation, and, above all, profit. Misesian time preference theory of interest, therefore, had to delink Fisherian time preference from the notion of productive use of capital, as interest, along with depreciation, would mean paying twice for the use of machines.

Whether in the time preference or in the productivity theory, we see the source from which interest is paid to be the future growth. What make it possible that there will be more goods (income) in the future than in the present? To Böhm-Bawerk it was the 'roundaboutness' of production methods with the use of capital goods, which ensured higher production, and to Fisher it was the investment opportunities, which made capital goods productive. Therefore, both Böhm-Bawerk's and Fisher's arguments for a positive interest were not stand-alone; but so was the Misesian conception of time preference. All presumed a growing economy with future growth – there would always be more in the future than in the present and not the other way around. Had there been stagnation, clearly no question of time preference, and hence positive interest would come. The positive interest originated, in these theories, either due to the outcome of the use of machine or capital goods in production, or due to the psychological preference of present over the future or discounting the future, but not as something to be paid for the use of monetary funds. Thus, the clutches of the age-old view on usury interest remained effective, and the canonical prohibition on it could be carefully kept satisfied by these theories. The cost we paid for these erroneous approaches in viewing money interest was simply muddling of interest with profit as well as interest theory with capital theory in earlier economic studies. These ideas still play a dominant role in abstract economic studies.

Monetary theories of interest

The dominance of the non-monetary theories of interest, viewing interest as a non-monetary phenomenon, continued in economic literature until the early 20th century, when the monetary theories of interest came, claiming that the money interest that was paid for using a monetary fund was simply a monetary phenomenon. With this, the reflections of the apparently invisible clutches of the age-old canonical prohibitions on usury interest were finally removed from the economic ideas about money interest.

The monetary theories of the 20th century had three roots: the first, following the Swedish approach, was pioneered by Knut Wicksell (1898) in his book *Interest and Prices*, and developed later by many economists including Bertil Ohlin, Eric Lindahl, Gunnar Myrdal, and Bent Hansen. The second, which followed the English neoclassical tradition, was best represented in the works of D. H. Robertson. The third, and the most famous, was found in the writings of John Maynard Keynes and his followers. The first two were, again, grouped together under the head of 'loanable funds theories', while the third was the 'liquidity preference theory' of Keynes (Conard 1959: 155).

The monetary theories particularly stressed the influence of possible changes in the supply of money or in its velocity on the rate of interest. More importantly, these theories, specially the Keynesian liquidity preference theory, held that the emergence of the phenomenon of interest was closely related to the unique features of money and psychological attributes of holding money (Conard *Ibid*. 1959: 108).

The loanable funds theory had two variants. One of these variants viewed the equilibrium rate of interest as that equal to the supply of and the demand for claims on interest-bearing securities. The other variant of this theory stated that the interest rate would be in equilibrium at a level which equated the supply and demand for loanable funds. However, it may be pointed out that the two variants of the theory imply the same thing because the supply of loanable funds can be thought of as being demand for claims while the demand for loanable funds may be regarded as offers of claims (Conard *Ibid*. 1959: 155–56).

Wicksell, often regarded as a monetary theorist, nevertheless synthesised monetary and non-monetary considerations considering both the 'natural' (non-monetary) and 'money' rate of interest. While Wicksell, like Ricardo, regarded the money rate of interest as an abnormality, unlike Ricardo he did not neglect the monetary conditions. In fact, in a way the monetary theories of interest reflected a synthesis of non-monetary and monetary considerations. Both the variants considered short-run market equilibrium to be achieved rapidly with the interest rate determined by the monetary forces, and a longer-run, more complete equilibrium to be arrived very slowly, through the adjustments in slow-moving variables like levels of income in a manner consistent with non-monetary theories. Wicksell's analysis was dynamic in the sense that in his frame of reference the system did not even 'rest' at equilibrium (Conard *Ibid.* 1959: 156).

Keynes, in his *General Theory of Interest, Employment and Money* (1936), vigorously criticised what he called the 'classical' theory of interest, presenting a new theory of interest. Keynes contended, 'The rate of interest is not the price which brings into equilibrium the demand for resources to invest with the readiness to abstain from present consumption', as postulated by these theories, but 'the price which equilibrates the desire to hold wealth in form of cash with the available quantity of cash' (cited by Conard 1959: 163).

In analysing the determinants of the demand for and the supply of cash balances, Keynes pointed out that the supply of cash, that is, the stock of money available at any one time, was fixed by the banking system. The demand for cash balances, again as a stock, on the other hand, was influenced by various motives for holding money balances. Two of these motives – the 'transaction' motive (reflecting the need for working balances) and the 'precautionary' motive (reflecting the need of preparedness for unforeseen circumstances) were assumed to be interest inelastic (Conard 1959: 163–64). The other motive, the 'speculative' motive or 'finance' motive for holding cash balances, was postulated as interest elastic. The speculative motive had a major role to play as a determinant of the rate of interest in Keynesian theory.

Historically, the Keynesian concept of using money for speculative motive was perhaps the first formal economic discussion on speculation as an economic activity. Economic speculation is simply making monetary gains by buying cheaper and selling dearer. In earlier economic literature, the prolonged absence of discussions on economic speculation as a fact of economic life was possibly due to the same canonical prohibitions that categorically spelt out that buying cheaper or selling dearer was a sin.

The medium of speculation, in Keynesian theory, was bonds or securities, whose price fluctuated with interest rate. Therefore, these securities gave an opportunity to make speculative gains through buying them cheaper and subsequently selling them dearer. For performing this act of speculation, obviously some money balances would be required that might be used in the course of buying securities.

Noticeably, Keynes did not justify general speculation as such on any commodity: it was just a special case of stock market activity. Further, his notion of speculative motive did not directly justify usury either as a price of money in buying or selling any monetary fund. When a small monetary fund of a common man is kept in banks, it earns interest. His motives are neither speculation nor production activity, but to get interest on the money deposits. The interest we see here is simply the usury interest, which was not the case in the pure Keynesian formulation. Keynes restricted his view on interest as a reward for parting with money for a period in speculative activity in the security market and it came in the form of speculative gains. Moreover, so far as these speculative activities were on the existing shares or bonds, the changes in the rate of interest or the bond prices they would generate could not be linked with the savings and investments in the production sector for so-called simultaneous macroeconomic determination of money income and interest. This is, however, overlooked in the Hicks-Hansen formulation of the Keynesian theory, combining it with the savings and investments in the production sector and establishing that interest in the Keynesian theory is partly monetary and partly real.

In Keynesian liquidity preference theory, the total demand for cash balances, or more specifically the residual speculative cash balances, determines the market rate of interest, given the total supply of cash balances as fixed by monetary authorities. Thus, interest in the Keynesian theory is a monetary phenomenon only. Keynes, in fact, stressed the fact that the rate of interest was determined in his theory without any reference to either saving or investment demand and this was specifically what Robertson criticised (Conard 1959: 164–65). However, later on, in the Hicks-Hansen formulation of the IS-LM model for simultaneous determination of interest and money income, although it was claimed to have been developed following the Keynesian theory, savings and investments were also brought into the analysis. But what is overlooked in this technical formulation is that whereas savings and investments are flow items, the Keynesian demand and supply of money are actually for cash balances in the form of stocks. In current literature on heterodox economics there has been growing discomfort with the IS-LM model. In fact, Hicks himself has commented on its limitations, although after forty years (Hicks 1980).

There are three major differences between the 'loanable funds theories' and the 'liquidity preference theory'. First, while 'loanable funds theories' are described with reference to flows over a period of time, the 'liquidity preference theory' is stated in terms of stocks at a point of time. Second, while the 'loanable funds theories' are usually stated as demand for and supply of securities, the 'liquidity preference theory' is stated in terms of demand for and supply of cash balances. Third, while 'loanable funds theory' proceeds by analysing the supply and demand for the securities in terms of the sources of supplies and demands, the 'liquidity preference theory' proceeds by setting the supply of money as a datum against the demand for money determined by various motives for holding money. Conard pointed out that each of these theories was appropriate in the perspective of a definite framework of analysis, each having a convenience that the other did not have. Essentially, both the theories stressed the much-neglected monetary variables, which were key variables in the short-run analysis of market rate of interest (Conard 1959: 232).

Financial breeding – money in the concept of time preference

From the confusing mess of the classical and neoclassical theories of interest muddling interest and profit, an important element has emerged in economic studies – the concept of time preference. In the neoclassical theory of interest due to Fisher, interest rate determines the relative price of the present and the future consumption. A person with positive or higher time preference would prefer consuming now to consuming in the future and so has to bear a price, the interest. Conceived in this way, interest rate clearly acts as a discounting factor – discounting the future values to their present. Fifty biscuits now or seventy biscuits after a month, which one is preferred? A person with positive time preference may prefer fifty biscuits now to seventy a month after as he can take into account the interest element. But a person with zero time preference would always prefer seventy biscuits after a month rather than fifty now, as seventy is, needless to say, greater than fifty – there is no time dimension in his perspective. Nevertheless, if this second person also had some time preference, relatively low, he might have preferred, say, sixty biscuits now rather than the future seventy biscuits. Fisher's concept of time preference, or discounting the future to its present, was developed in the context of theory of interest. Keynes used the idea of discounting the future earnings to the entrepreneur from an additional machine invested to its present value by a preferred discount rate, usually the market rate of interest, not in his theory of interest, but in his theory of marginal efficiency of capital.

Interest rate as a discounting factor of future earnings brings another notion – the risk or uncertainty involved in all expectations involving the future. Not only the positive time preference, but also the assessment of risk involved in the future outcome plays a role in determining the interest rate as the discounting factor. In our example, if the future outcome of seventy biscuits is less certain, or risky, then the person with positive time preference might prefer, say, even forty-five biscuits today than seventy after a month.

What is important to notice in the conception of time preference is the presumption that the future, by economic number or quantity, would always grow – it is always expected to be more than the present. If there is economic stagnation – the fifty today remains tomorrow or the day after just the same fifty only – the question of time preference or, let us say, interest would not have come. We know that natural biological entities breed and multiply. That is their natural law of growth. Does such natural law apply to economic entities also? Well, it may not be so, but we have constructed economic systems incorporating this element of future growth in economic entities, specifically the availability of goods or income in the future. From Böhm-Bawerk to Fisher to Mises, all have presumed this to explain positive interest.

When production of goods is presumed to multiply in the future for whatever reasons, why would money be left out from this presumption? Moreover, if money does not also multiply likewise in the future to keep pace with the goods, there would be a clear mismatch resulting in deflationary devastation in economic systems. Further, money is a store of value that represents a command or claim over the goods. Therefore, our example above of time preference in terms of number of biscuits should naturally exist in time preference of money also – say, fifty dollars now (as a store of value) might be more preferred to seventy dollars (as a store of value) after a month. Hence, it is a natural corollary of the notion of time preference theories that a barren economic entity like money should also grow in the future. Can we then disregard the usury money interest, a charge just on money loan, or on the store of value, which is supposed to grow in the future? Therefore, with the introduction of capital as monetary fund in production, we have constructed an economic system with an element of future growth in monetary fund also – the growth in monetary fund becomes a necessity intertwined in the process of the growth of goods production by the use of capital goods. This makes capital an item bearing a double charge on the production of output – on one hand interest is charged for the capital as monetary fund (borrowed), and on the other, depreciation or capital consumption is charged on the machines bought out of this fund. Over and above these two charges, there is of course the element of profit as return to the entrepreneur.

This is only one half of the story – more and more productive employment of capital goods would bring more and more production of goods and so more and more money would be required for not only providing the necessary monetary finance for introducing capital goods, but also to match the transaction requirement of the increased flow of goods. The other half of the story tells us about the implications of financial breeding – with the interest as a return, the monetary fund keeps on multiplying like self-breeding biological entities. The growing monetary fund would require, in turn, growing investments in capital goods. Otherwise, how could the growing monetary fund get absorbed? By constructing an economic system with an element of future growth, we have created a situation where growth necessitates further growth. This leads to another question – how could the growing flow of the goods and the growing flow of money mutually match each other in the operations of such an economic system?

5 Critique of neoclassical economics and revival of the idea of circuit analysis

The study of economics as a modern discipline purports to be the study of economic wealth, as it begins with Adam Smith's book *An Inquiry into the Nature and Causes of the Wealth of Nations* (1776). Yet, the creation of wealth, or the stock of financial capital as such, in the form of accumulating stocks in economic systems, does not appear explicitly in the mainstream economic analysis. The reason is simple. An understanding of the accumulation of stocks in the economic systems requires an understanding of the flows since stocks accumulate or de-accumulate through the flows coming in and going out of it. However, the stock-flow relation in economic systems has been generally ignored in mainstream economic analysis.

Unfortunately, the study of the stock-flow relations in economic systems cannot be done in the neoclassical methodological framework that forms the basis of mainstream economics. As we will see later, the circuit theory viewing economic systems in terms of economic flows and consequent creation of stocks could give us an alternative methodological framework for probing the causes behind the accumulation of financial capital in macroeconomic systems.

The discomfort with the neoclassical tools of analysis is not new in literature, even though it forms the core of the mainstream economic theorising. A wide discontent with the neoclassical school of thought appears in several economic schools of thought. This includes the Post-Keynesian, Austrian, Marxist, Circuitist, and Evolutionary schools, which are, often quite loosely, clubbed together as the heterodox schools of thought. The term 'heterodox' means unorthodox or dissenting, and the core dissent underlying these divergent schools is against the acceptance of neoclassical methodology as 'the methodology' of economic analysis.

Given the wide spectrum of economic analyses and the fact that the complexities of the real economic world must be reflected in the theoretical construct, exclusive dependence on a particular method of analysis is unwarranted. Different economic questions surely would warrant different ways of analysis that require different theoretical and empirical tools. Indeed, a single economic question may need different ways of looking at the answers to imbibe truly the complexities of the issues raised. The crucial point is that the methodology chosen for a particular analysis should assist in answering the questions the study has raised, not moulding the questions to fit the methodology. The methodology is, after all, never an end in itself but means to undertake the desired analysis. Dogmatic adherence to a particular methodology makes one believe that nothing exists that does not fit into one's specific model.

This being so, we begin by examining why the neoclassical methodology fails to deal with stock-flow dynamics of economic systems. What are the limitations of this methodology that inhibits analysis in this direction? Here, we must categorically distinguish the stock-flow dynamics of a system from the neoclassical conjecture of the Walrasian *tatonnement* or the direct or indirect causal adjustments postulated in the case of divergence from equilibrium positions. In search of an alternative methodology for the study of stock-flow relations, we first trace the historical origin of circuit school of thought and then turn to examine the revival of the circuit approach in current literature and its problems.

Neoclassical theory – how has it disappointed?

The term 'neoclassical', as Colander points out, was initially used by Thorstein Veblen (Preconceptions of Economic Science, 1900) as a negative description of Marshall's (1890) economics (Colander 2000: 131). The concept of marginalism, the reliance on mathematical models, and the mechanical concepts formed the distinct feature of neoclassical analysis and, as we will discuss, continues to form the backbone of neoclassical analysis. Colander pointed out that the term did not sufficiently describe the present body of mainstream research, which moved beyond the methodological tools for which the term was initially coined (Colander *Ibid*. 2000: 129–30). However, the essential ingredients of the neoclassical theory that developed in the 20th century have continued in the mainstream research. For several reasons, these tools are largely inadequate and misleading for a study of the present-day economic scenario with mounting accumulation of wealth or financial capital as well as debts.

Methodological individualism

The first basic tenet of the neoclassical body of work is the methodological individualism or the analysis of 'collective' behaviour in terms of rational, utility-maximising individuals, or what is called the '*Homos economicus*' postulate. The complexities of economic life are reduced to the profit-maximising behaviour of rational individuals abstracted from the socio-political dimensions (Hosseini 1990; Arnsperger and Varoufakis 2006). In the last thirty years there have been attempts to break away from this mould of rational individuals with perfect knowledge by introducing economic actors who are imperfectly informed and irrational. However, the basic methodological idea remains the same – to analyse the socio-economic phenomena under consideration by focusing on individuals whose actions are understood at the individual level and then the knowledge derived at the individual level is synthesised to understand the complex social phenomena under study (Arnsperger and Varoufakis *Ibid*. 2006: 2–4).

Closely connected with the idea of methodological individualism is the idea of methodological instrumentalism, which postulates that all behaviours are preference driven or means for maximising preference satisfaction. While in the newer developments of neoclassical theory (as psychological game theory), the preferences are not considered independent of the agent's socio-economic relationships, the economic man still remains rooted to fierce means-end instrumentalism, leading to the models where preferences (exogenous or endogenous) remain separate from the structure of the interactions in which they are involved (Arnsperger and Varoufakis 2006: 4).

A corollary to the above-mentioned lacunae of the neoclassical theory is the treatment of individuals as abstracted from their socio-political contexts. Individuals may demonstrate some irrationality but they still inhabit a model where their socio-political considerations do not impact their decisions. The evolution of economic or political institutions is not given any role in this construct. This proves a serious flaw in representation of the real-world problems where an economic man is very much a historical, political, and social man too.

In an analysis of accumulation of wealth, the neoclassical methodological individualism and abstraction from socio-political dimensions are major hurdles, since, here, the evolution of economic institutions and structures like corporate structures and the political influences of such structures have a significant role. Attempts to consider the motives at the individual level of the economic entity cannot succeed without considering in tandem the collective motives of social and political institutions or groups. The accumulation of wealth at individual level is necessarily determined in social context and seeing it abstracted from the political and ideological conditions is meaningless. In the macroeconomic framework, the continuous accumulation of financial capital and corporate wealth that has marked the last three decades need consideration of economic, social, and political institutions, as well as their interplay, rather than the decision-making of individual economic entities only.

All great thinkers of the discipline, beginning from Adam Smith to Marx and Keynes, have given human motives and behaviour in conjunction with the social setting a key place in their theories. The discipline began its query as a 'study of wealth', as Smith (1776) effectively put it. Yet, wealth, as we see it in real life today, and the query into the causes of its creation on a macroeconomic level, are nonexistent in the present economic literature. In neoclassical literature the concept of capital has become so mechanical and abstract that while physical capital goods and the problems of its measurement are discussed widely, wealth as capital gets little attention. Even the concept of financial capital or wealth held in form of paper assets has remained unanalysed in neoclassical macroeconomics, though its shadow remains ever omniscient.

Equilibrium analysis

The second distinct tenet of neoclassical body of thought is the axiomatic assumption of equilibrium. For its dependency on methodological individualism, prediction at the macro level was difficult in neoclassical methodology. Therefore, it was necessary to introduce something that ensured that the agent's instrumental behaviours were coordinated in a manner that aggregate behaviour becomes sufficiently regular to give rise to solid predictions (Arnsperger and Varoufakis 2006: 6). Equilibrium analysis allowed this even though it did not come up from the model's assumptions. Instead, equilibrium remained an axiomatic truth around which the analysis was centred.

The equilibrium analysis of the mainstream economics came from the induction of Newtonian mechanics to economic theory. The excessive dependence on mathematical formalism and attempts to make the neoclassical theories modelled on the mechanical models of physical sciences led to a divorce of these models from reality (Omay and Atasu 2004). In fact, the equilibrium concept in economics has remained one of its most criticised concepts throughout, one of the early and most intense one being found in the Cambridge capital controversy.

The famous Cambridge controversy reflected the discomfort with neoclassical methodology especially with equilibrium theory and the long-run capital theory. Joan Robinson was particularly critical of the 'neo-neoclassical' concepts of equilibrium. Her critique was expressed best in the article (1953–54) 'The production function and the theory of capital', as:

> The neo-neoclassical economist thinks of a position of equilibrium as a position towards which an economy is tending to move as time goes by. But it is impossible for a system to *get into* a position of equilibrium, for the very nature of equilibrium is that the system is already in it, and has been in it for a certain length of past time.
>
> (p. 85, italics in original)

Another definitive criticism of equilibrium theory came with Janos Kornai's development of the idea of 'anti-equilibrium'. Kornai, a leading socialist economist whose own models were based on the Walrasian world of the Arrow-Debreu model, grew increasingly disillusioned with the neoclassical approach by the 1960s that culminated in the publication of his famous book *Anti-equilibrium* in 1971 (Kornai 1971). Kornai pointed out that the Walrasian theory, which formed the basis of mainstream economic analysis, failed to give a deeper understanding of capitalism and socialism. Neoclassical theory ignored the political setting in construction of models, but the political setting (capitalist or socialist or any other) invariably influenced the economic behaviour (Kornai 2007: 147, 180–81).

Even the mainstream economists of the 20th century admitted that not only was the equilibrium theory of classroom economics inadequate for modelling the complex modern economy, but also the modern economies were in fact generally out of equilibrium. In the early 1960s there was a growing discontent with equilibrium theory, and by the 1990s several economists, especially in the United States, broke away from equilibrium theory. However, the later mainstream economists, instead of finding newer methodological tools for analysis, began to adopt unanimously the rational expectations models introduced in the early 1970s. The gamut of research in the later years showed an attempt not to break away from the equilibrium and rational expectations theories but to find ways to modulate rational expectations theory to represent the complexities of modern economies (Phelps 2007: xiv–xv).

The models, for example of the real business cycle, turned out more mathematically complex and tried to imbibe the unpredictability of real business cycles without sacrificing the mathematical neatness of rational expectation equilibrium. The mainstream models have turned more and more mechanical in their attempts to keep the formalism of equilibrium theories while introducing complexities of modern economies. The obsession with model building leads to a sustained attempt to mathematically express complexities and this makes the models mechanical. Most neoclassical theorists, as Colander reiterates, see the central element of modern economics as the 'modelling approach to problems' (Colander 2000: 137). Earlier, in this context, Solow pointed out:

> Today, if you ask a mainstream economist a question about almost any aspect of economic life, the response will be: suppose we model that situation and see what happens. . . . There are thousands of examples; the point is modern mainstream economics consists of little else but examples of this process.
>
> (Solow 1997: 43)

Abstract mathematical models remain a central element of the neoclassical analysis whereby other methodologies of analysis, without such mathematical formalism, are disregarded. Mathematics undoubtedly is a wonderful tool for economic analysis, and modelling of economic problems helps to clarify and analyse the relevant conditions better. However, this can hardly be relevant for all economic questions. Economic questions that are intertwined with important social, political, or evolutionary considerations cannot be modelled without almost always abstracting these crucial considerations. Again, while modelling may help analysis, they need not necessarily be based on the neoclassical methodology with complex mathematical formalism. The relevant question here is the clarification and presentations of economic questions and the presentation of a theoretical construct of the questions. Colander has pointed out that several leading economists – David Romer, William Baumol, Joe Stiglitz, Ken Arrow, Paul Krugman, Amartya Sen, to name a few – have operated outside the neoclassical framework in portions of their work. Colander accepts that though modern economics is open to ideas, it is but 'begrudgingly open', so that graduate schools and new researchers generally stick to the limited neoclassical framework (Colander 2000: 137).

The analysis of economics, in an out-of-equilibrium framework, is important for understanding accumulation. Accumulation, traced by actual stock-flow relations in economic systems, necessarily excludes the question of equilibrium of the desires of economic agents. More precisely, the concept of equilibrium or disequilibrium becomes not only redundant but also an obstruction for proper analysis of stock-flow dynamics. In fact, in the Walrasian concept of general equilibrium, all desired economic flows in an exchange economy (or the desires to supply of and demand for goods and money) are matched to each other and hence no accumulation should take place.

Neglect of money

The neglect of money remains a crucial feature of the neoclassical construct. The role of money here remains limited with an emphasis on the 'real' sector, which, in the neoclassical construct, can be analysed in isolation from the 'monetary sector'. In the neoclassical general equilibrium construct, there is no consideration of money as a store of value, or the medium of deferred payments. In this construct money is primarily a means of exchange and originates to reduce the 'transaction costs'. This understanding necessarily ignores the 'hierarchical relations or social symbolism' behind the rise of a commodity as the 'means of exchange'. Similarly, banks, financial institutions, and their instruments (along with money) are seen as to originate only to improve the market efficiency. Credit and banking in this theory follows coinage (Wray 2006: 2–4).

This view of the origin of money is widely contested by the heterodox writers, who stress that the written records of credit and debit transactions precede coinage by thousands of years, with the evidence of the development of financial accounting prior to coinage. The origins of credit and debt relations are traced by many economists to the elaborate system of tribal war fines, and later on taxes, designed to prevent disputes. Coinage is believed to have arrived later on to facilitate the payment of such fines and taxes. So, both coinage and markets did not originate spontaneously for greater 'efficiency' in economic transactions, but rather came about with a direct interference from the rulers and authorities (Wray 1998; Goodhart 2005: 759–61; Tymiogne and Wray 2006).

It must be noted that the consideration of money as primarily a means of exchange appeared with the classical writers. Smith (1776) emphasised that the adoption of money came from division of labour and to get over the problems of direct barter – an idea shared later on by Menger (1892) and Mill (1909). There were, however, several analytical problems with this approach, which were soon recognised. One of the most vexing problems was regarding the correct definition of utility of money which dominated the late 19th- and early 20th-century economic thought (Graziani 2003: 5–8).

By the end of the century, several economists had disagreed on this concept and asserted that money yields direct utility as well, specifically the one that an agent gets from holding liquid money balances. Graziani points out that the roots of this idea can be found in Marshall (1890) and Wicksell (1898), and was later developed by Fisher (1911) and Hicks (1933 [1980]). Fisher stressed the importance of liquid balances in an uncertain world, assigning a key role to the liquidity of money. Hicks held that money yields utility as a protection against uncertainty and, so, the demand for money is present in conditions of uncertainty. This underlined that money could be considered capable of yielding direct utility. Again, the Keynesian approach of money also defined it as cash balances having the function of protecting agents from uncertainty, which many heterodox economists have stressed as a key to the proper understanding of money (Graziani 2003: 9–13).

While some economists working within the neoclassical framework stressed the role of money as a store of liquidity, such considerations were neglected in the mainstream neoclassical analysis. The discussion of money supply was generally restricted to an analysis of the 'deposit multiplier'. In this approach, it was held that the growth of the money supply was 'exogenously controlled' by the central bank. This is the foundation of the Monetarist approach led by Milton Friedman. By the late 1970s, this view dominated the policymaking and led to the efforts by the central banks to control inflation by targeting monetary aggregates (Wray 1998).

In the 1970s came the amalgamation of the rational expectations hypothesis and classical monetarism to create what was called the 'new classical theory'. This school stressed the neutrality of money as long as the monetary policy was predictable. In effect, no credible policy could control inflation by reducing money growth rates (limited by the unemployment and growth trade-off), implying that money becomes irrelevant. The view that finance becomes 'neutral' if market impediments are removed hampers our ability to understand phenomena like credit rationing, sticky wages and prices, and complex input–output relations, all of which could leave money non-neutral in the short run (Wray *Ibid.* 1998). During the 1990s the New Monetary Consensus (NMC) approach to monetary theory and policy formulation was developed within the neoclassical framework, which stressed the link between inflation and interest rate changes through the central bank policies, but failed to contribute to the understanding of non-neutrality of money. The analysis of money as a key element of production process was ignored (Wray 1998).

In a nutshell, the neoclassical equilibrium framework is inherently contradictory to the coexistence of money. The Walrasian perfect world with rational individuals and no uncertainty cannot, in principle, co-exist with the monetary economy, as the simultaneous determination of all the present and the future prices rules out any possible demand for liquid balances (Graziani 2003: 11–13).

Exchange economy and the neglect to production and distribution

The methodological framework of neoclassical economics does not allow the study of economic flows and the resulting accumulation or de-accumulation of stocks in economic systems for the simple reason that its methodological construct presumes an exchange economy with the objective of identifying the point of exchange equilibrium. It has neither a theory of production nor a theory of distribution. In respect of production, the neoclassical theory assumes that goods are already existing like 'manna from heaven' so that the question of how they exist in the first place and its concerning problems are not explored (Walsh and Gram 1980). In respect of theory of distribution, Turner (1989) points out that Joan Robinson allied the neoclassical doctrine with the neglect of income distribution since, in marginal analysis, given equilibrium, distribution was already determined within the system of exchange itself, implying that by definition the question of distribution was excluded (Turner 1989: 107). At best, the neoclassical theory can say, using the formulation of a value added production function with labour and capital (as the two factor inputs) and constant return to scale, that the value added production would be fully distributed among the two factors, if they are paid according to their marginal products. This is known as the product exhaustion theorem of so-called marginal productivity theory of distribution, as mathematically derived from Euler's theorem.

There are two more fundamental problems with the neoclassical formulation of the value added production function and the marginal productivity theories of factor remuneration. Getting over the Ricardian tripartite division of factors of production, if we consider distinctly four types of factor remunerations (namely, wages, profits, interest, and rent), it becomes extremely difficult in neoclassical economics to define the corresponding four factors of production and identify and measure the factor services. Identifying the marginal products of these four factors becomes even more difficult. In fact, until recently in the context of financial economics, the conventional neoclassical economics did not distinguish between interest and profit, as they were muddled in the notion of 'returns to capital' employed in production, particularly in the neoclassical growth and trade models. The return to capital is a catch-all term in neoclassical economics that includes interest, depreciation, and profit. To be more categorical, one may say that the neoclassical theory has profit maximisation as its basic tenet, but it does not have a clear theory of profit to segregate it from interest. Is it not rather strange that the neoclassical theories, so rich in its mathematical formulations, do not have a theory of profit in its analytical framework? The idea of profit as 'normal profit' to be included in the cost of production as an element of costs is not clear – it is never spelt out what determines its quantum or rate and how. Moreover, if it is so, then the idea of profit maximisation as a rational behaviour does not go with it, since what is 'normal' should not be left for being maximised by individual choice.

The second problem we see is the formulation of value added production as a function of labour and physical capital. Here we see another muddle – that is, mingling of stock and flow variables. The value added production is clearly a flow variable whereas physical capital is measured as a stock. Value added production over time should be a function of not the stocks but the services rendered over time (flows) by the stocks engaged in production. Unfortunately, these flows of services are not observable, although the factor remunerations are, and so, one may argue, the stocks are taken in the production function as proxy of the flows, since the flows ultimately reflect on or determine the stocks. But, this argument may not hold in the context of the neoclassical trade theories.

Modern trade theories still today continue to build models with factor endowments of labour and capital, which are clearly stocks. On the other hand, they consider the factor remunerations, wages, and rate of return on capital for the services of the two factors (flow). Two amorphous notions are used, using the symbols 'L' and 'K', for model derivations. In the production function, they appear as the factor endowments or stocks, and for calculating the factor income shares, they appear as indicative of flow of services of the factors. Here, one may argue that the factor endowments or the stocks determine, in a way, the flow of services from them. Thus, we tend to argue both – in value added production function the flows determine the stocks (here stocks are proxy of the flows) and in the factor endowment production function with calculation of factor incomes, the factor endowments or the stocks determine the flows (here flows are approximated by the stocks). This is simply a hen and egg puzzle – the stock determines the flow or the flow determines the stock?

Nevertheless, in the neoclassical paradigm, these issues are not of much significance, so far as the general equilibrium exchange could be shown in an economy. With the production and distribution aspects dropping out from the picture, we are left with a situation where economic accumulation of stocks or wealth – whether in the form of profit, or surplus remuneration, or rentier incomes – also drops out from our analysis.

The methodological construct of the mainstream economics, namely the neoclassical economics, does not provide us any methodological framework for studying accumulation, or more precisely, the accumulation of financial capital. On the contrary, it takes us away from even conceptualising any such phenomenon. Therefore, in search of a suitable methodology for studying the economic flows, we have to look elsewhere. The importance of studying the economic flows had been noticed long ago by the French physiocrats in their circuit analysis. We first look at this historical root of the circuit theory.

The pre-classical appearance of the 'circuit theory'

The first attempt to analyse the economy in terms of flows of economic activities is evident in the concept of circular flow, as developed by the physiocrats. The pre-classical movement of physiocracy that preceded the first modern school (classical economics) was dominated by Anne-Robert-Jacques Turgot (1727–81) and François Quesnay (1694–1774). The physiocrats, a closely knit French community, were concerned not with an individual but with a common position. They called themselves Les Économistes, 'an admirably modern reference', although historians of economic thought 'settled long ago on the least apt of designations, the Physiocrats', for them (Galbraith 1987: 48).

The physiocrats asserted that the wealth of nations cannot be measured by its stock of precious metals but should be measured by the size of its net product. Further, any activity would generate a 'net product' or the surpluses if the value of the outputs of that activity exceeded the value of the inputs used for it. They stressed that only agriculture was productive, yielding a net product, while manufacturing and commerce were sterile, taking up as much value in inputs as they created in outputs. Quesnay's *Tableau Économique* followed this view closely. Quesnay developed many *tableaux* differing in their presentations.

The famous 'zigzags' that characterised the earlier ones were later abandoned (Brewer 2005: 1).

In Quesnay's analysis, three economic classes are considered – the 'proprietary' class consisting of landowners, the 'productive' class consisting of all farmers in agriculture, and the 'sterile' class made up of artisans and merchants. The circuit dynamics come from the flow of production in money values among the three classes and each sector spending money on produced stocks of output (grain and crafts) of the other sectors, leading to direct and indirect exchanges.

The circuit construction of the economy, however, did not begin with the physiocrats, although it came as an explicit model of analysis for the first time in their analysis. Before Quesnay, Cantillon in his *Essai* (1755) also conceived of the economy in terms of flow of goods among different sectors, although he did not develop an explicit tableau. Cantillon's formulation was almost identical in structure to Quesnay's arithmetic tableau, so much so that Schumpeter argued that Cantillon was the first to draw a Tableau Économique, which, barring the differences that hardly effect the essentials, was the same as Quesnay's (Brewer *Ibid.* 2005: 1–4).

Cantillon closely analysed the circulation of money between the city and the countryside and the amount of money required for this, or in other words, the determinants of the velocity of circulation of money. In his construct, the circulation of money happens with landlords spending in the city the rents which the farmers have paid them in lump sums, and thus the city traders get this money. This is used by the city traders to buy the farmers' agricultural produce. Effectively, large sums of money are at the beginning distributed in small amounts, which are then collected to make payments in substantial amounts to the farmers. The *Tableau Économique* of Quesnay was clearly based quite closely on Cantillon's account of intersectoral circulation (Brewer *Ibid.* 2005: 13–14).

However, Cantillon did not take into account the general (or sectoral) shortages of capital acting as a constraint on production, which found a place in Quesnay's disequilibrium analysis. There was no analysis of the role of advances in his account of circulation, as he implicitly assumed an economy in which the same pattern of production repeated over the years, and every year an individual was spending the entire money income that he or she had received. Quesnay's tableaux brought in the decline (or expansion) of advances depending on the division of spending, underlining the working of the economy in disequilibrium (Brewer *Ibid.* 2005: 13–14).

With the coming of the classical era of economic thought, the focus on the circuit construct of viewing the economy was lost completely. The rise of the industrial economy and the market for exchange of the commodities produced by the industries made the classicists more concerned with the intrinsic value of commodities that determined their market exchanges. With the impressive growth of the industrial economy the focus of economic analysis shifted entirely to the factor shares or factor prices like wage, rent, and profit in the industrial process of production. The classicists, in their contemporary milieu at the time of an emerging industrial economy, were sceptic about the analysis and conclusions of the physiocrats, particularly that manufacturing did not produce any surplus.

The advent of the neoclassical era led to a focus on the individualistic approach, convergence to general equilibrium, and treatment of money as merely a medium of exchange. The market that allowed for the exchange economy to function assumed a key importance. The neoclassicists did away with the classical value theory and developed the analytical framework for explaining the market exchanges in terms of equilibrium of demand and supply forces determining the prices. This framework of equilibrium analysis, further theorised by Walras (1874) to extend from partial to general equilibrium, drew apparent respectability because of the ease of using mathematics. The neoclassical framework of equilibrium analysis sent the circuit framework of conceptualising the economy to complete oblivion with the incorporation of Newtonian mechanics into economic theory (Omay and Atasu 2004).

Marxian analysis and circuit theory

In the writings of Karl Marx, we find another revival of the circuitist tradition. His theory accorded a key importance to the relevance of the physiocratic notion of the economic circuit for the theoretical determination of the economic logic of capitalism. Marx held that while Smith took over in his analysis the idea of circulation of capital from the physiocrats, his exposition and interpretation of the movement fell short of Quesnay's insights.

In Marxian analysis we find a full statement of the capitalistic process of circulation. Here, we get an analysis of the dynamics of the process of circulation of capital between the functional classes and between the economic productive sectors in a two-class, two-sector capitalistic economy in terms of the 'reproduction schemes'. Marx's formulation of the circulation process of extended reproduction under capitalist system is described as M–C–C′–M′. As the process repeats, money grows from the initial to M′, M″, M‴, and so on.

However, in our understanding of the circuit analysis that we intend to build here, Marx's formulation of the circuit was incomplete in the sense that it did not spell out wherefrom these additional flows of money would come into the circuit to make M grow to M′, M″, M‴, etc. Yet, it was not noticed that without ensuring this additional flow of money, Marx's formulation could not work. The Marxian economists often pointed out that in this formulation hoarding of money or under-consumption might lead to the crisis of profit realisation. Our point is that, even when these are not there, a problem of bringing more money flow into the circuit necessarily exists for monetary realisation of profits.

The analysis of the social circulation process of capital led Marx to several fundamental results, some of which could already be found in Quesnay's analysis. A key result among this was that the consumption and investment expenditure by the capitalist class was conditioned by the availability of money, and not by the money income of the previous period (as suggested by classical political economy) or by the money income of the present period (as suggested by neoclassical economists). The capitalist class had the command upon the general purchasing power. This, when spent, either in the form of consumption or in the form of investment or both, the money spent returned back to the capitalist class either as the profit of the industrial capitalists and the interest of the moneyed capitalists, or as the rent of the landlords. As in Quesnay's construct, the capitalist class being the proprietor class used to spend what it earned on production. This meant that it advanced the surplus value to itself under the form of its own effective demand. In turn, the working class used to spend what it earned.

However, in the circuit construction of the economy a key element is the understanding of monetary flow. This understanding has remained central to not only Marxian analysis but also to the analyses of Keynes and Kalecki. Kalecki made an explicit reference to his intellectual debt to Marx on this particular point in his essays on the 'Theory of the economic dynamics' (1954). In particular, he credited Marx for having developed the first analysis of the monetary circuit as well as the principle of effective demand of a capitalistic economy. Keynes, on the contrary, gave credit to Malthus as being the founder of such principle. All the heterodox authors – the mercantilists, the physiocrats, Marx, Kalecki, and Keynes, and the post-Keynes-Kalecki economists – who have discussed the process of circulation of capital, consider money as a medium of finance also.

The theory of monetary circuit

Though the physiocrat's method of conceptualising an economy as a circuit of flows lost its importance with the coming of the classical and the neoclassical schools of thought, it continued to appear and underline the analysis of a few great economic thinkers like Marx, Keynes, and Kalecki. Yet, a definite school of thought focusing on the circuit tradition did not develop. It was only after the 1950s that we see the arrival of a circuit school of thought with attempts to use the circuit tradition to analyse the monetary flows in an economic system.

The modern version that now represents the circuit school of thought is the theory of monetary circuit (TMC) that has been developing predominantly in Germany, Italy, and France since the 1950s. This version has its roots in the description of circuit theory found in Knut Wicksell's *Interest and Prices* (1898), which has influenced many German and French authors. The term circuit in fact, reproduces the German *Kreisalauf*, a term used by German writers to describe the circulation of money and goods.

Following the Keynesian heterodoxy, the revival of circuit theory came as a response to the dissatisfaction with the neoclassical doctrines. Keynes, in various sketches of the *General Theory* (1936) considered the 'entrepreneur economy' that came closest to the real monetary production economy. Again, in his book *A Treatise on Money* (1930), he assigned a key role to the consideration of an economy in the form of a circuit of monetary flows. However, such considerations were not followed up later in his book *The General Theory of Employment, Interest, and Money* (Lavoie 1992: 773; Graziani 2003: 3–4; Ertürk 2006).

In Germany and France, the revival of circuit theory was carried out by different groups of economists. In Germany, this revival was carried out by the school of Monetary Keynesianism, which stressed seeing the market mechanism in terms of monetary circuit, rejecting the neoclassical marginalism and treatment of money as a product of the market. Graziani pointed out that the development of circuit theory in France had been due to three groups centred on the works by three leading economists – Bernard Schmitt (1972), Alain Parguez (1975), and Francois Poulon (1982; Graziani 2003: 2–4).

The basic circuit construct

The monetary circuit, in its current version, stresses the links between money and the real economy in a world with time. The TMC, as this school of thought is usually referred, challenges three basic tenets of neoclassical theory – the individualistic approach, convergence to equilibrium, and the treatment of money as merely a means of exchange and just a stock. The modern circuitists are critical of the individualistic approach of the neoclassical theory, asserting that any theory based on an individualistic approach cannot build a truly macroeconomic analysis. In the circuit perspective, simple aggregation of individual behaviour functions cannot yield a truly macro theory (Bossone 2003: 142; Graziani 2003: 18).

The starting point for a macroeconomic model is the identification of the social groups present in a community followed by defining the conditions necessary for their reproduction and perpetuation over time. The classicists, for example, started with a subdivision of the society into a number of classes, each with different wealth endowments, as also Marx, who distinguished between proletarians and capitalists. Similarly, Keynes clearly distinguished between the consumers who evaluate consumption goods according to their immediate utility and the investors, who evaluate capital goods according to their subjective and uncertain profit expectations. In the theory of monetary circuit, we similarly find a distinction between the producers having access to bank credit and the wage earners not having access to bank credit with different initial endowments (Graziani 2003: 18–19).

Unlike the neoclassical theorists, the circuit approach, so far developed, does see money not only as a means of exchange but also as a means of payment. Money in the circuit construct enters the market as bank credit. When a firm uses a bank overdraft it is actually acquiring goods or labour without giving any real goods in exchange, and thus using money as a means of payment (Graziani *Ibid.* 2003: 17). While Keynesians stress the impact of money held as idle balance on the macro economy, circuitists assert that money exerts its influence on the macroeconomic construct when it is used to buy commodities and not when it is held idle. The focus is on the subsequent payments – from the initial creation of liquidity to the use of money in purchases and finally the destruction of liquidity. In fact, such analysis is named the theory of monetary circuit as it centres on examining the complete life cycle of money creation by the banking sector, circulation in market, and destruction (Graziani *Ibid.* 2003: 17–18).

Graziani outlines the three basic tenets of the theory of monetary circuit as the rigorous distinction between firms and banks, the endogenous determination of money stock, and the rejection of marginal theory of distribution (Graziani *Ibid.* 2003: 1). The circuit starts with banks extending credit to firms, termed in circuit literature 'initial finance', which allows the firms to undertake the process of production. The extent of credit demanded by the firms and extended by the banks must, in turn, equal the wage bill for the scheduled level of production. The firms use the borrowed money to pay the workers who are hired to produce commodities, both consumer and producer goods. These are then sold – consumer goods to the workers and the investment goods to the other firms. The sales proceeds on consumer goods (and the purchases of corporate bonds, if any, by the workers) return the money advanced to the workers. This money is then used by the firms to repay their debt to the banks and this repayment of debt in this model destroys the money created by the initial finance. This completes the circuit circulations in a cycle. It must be noted that all productive activities in a capitalist economy require finance, not only in a growing economy but also in stationary economy. In a stationary economy, where flows of income and production are assumed to remain unchanged over time, finance is needed because at the end of a circuit circulation the proceeds from the sales are used to extinguish the debt advanced initially by the banking sector (Seccareccia 2003: 173–76).

The paradox of profit in the theory of monetary circuit

It is evident that in the monetary circuit the wage earners must spend their income entirely on the purchase of consumer goods. It is only when the wage earners spend their entire income that the circuit can close with a return flow of the money to the firms. If the wage earners save a portion of their income in the form of liquid balances, money does not return in full, and hence the firms cannot pay back the banks an amount equal to this savings. Therefore, in the next cycle, if the same level of production is to be maintained, the money supply must increase to finance the same scale of production. The new quantity of money in this second circuit will equal the wage bill and the liquid balances saved by wage earners at the end of the previous cycle (Seccareccia *Ibid.* 2003: 176).

In this construct, it can be seen that the firms cannot make any profits even when the wage earners spend all their incomes, which is called the 'paradox of profits'. Without any external money flow, the only money existing is what the banks create in financing the production. Therefore, the amount of money that firms can recover by selling their products within the circuit is at the most equal to the amount which they have paid to the wage earners. In other words, there is no possibility that firms, as a whole, can realise their profits in money terms and pay interest owed to the banks (Zazzaro 2003: 233). Thus, even in the most favourable case of workers spending all their wages, the firms are anyhow unable to pay interest (Bellofiore et al. 2000: 410). Injection of new money and conversion of short-term debt obligations into long-term obligations are necessary to allow interest repayments and close the circuit cycle. It must be noted that this repayment problem comes from the liquidity constraint inbuilt in the circuit process, whereby a given stock of money is injected at the beginning of the circuit circulation, which obviously has not included the interest component. Interest payments, therefore, require new money from the banking system (Bossone 2003: 152).

The current research on circuit formulations continues to be concerned with these questions of the paradox of profit and interest payments that have been plaguing the theory of monetary circuit ever since its inception. The most unsettling problems for the TMC include: explaining aggregate profit, debt repayment and debt servicing, and the paradoxes of money saving by the households (Graziani 1989; Bellofiore et al. 2000; Nell 2002; Rochon 2005). This indicates that a sharp inconsistency in the TMC formulations characterises the monetary circuit school since in the real world firms do make profits, pay interest, and repay loans, and the households may save.

Solving the insoluble riddles in the theory of monetary circuit

The current literature on the theory of monetary circuit continues to centre on explaining these apparent paradoxes in the circuit framework. Several explanations have been attempted to deal with these paradoxes. Some explanations suggest that firms also borrow the profits and interest at the beginning of the circuit and spend them in order to retrieve them later. Some researchers have suggested that money creation covers both the wage bill and the investment expenditure. This solution also implies that investment is autonomous and does not depend on the saving behaviour or hoarding. In this case, investment is financed by bank credit rather than by selling equities to the households (Seccareccia 2003; Rochon 2005).

Allain presents an alternative solution which continues to assume that initial finance is restricted to the wage bill. This solution is based on the assumption that firms sell goods at prices exceeding their unit costs, but the realised monetary profits are not used to pay back the banks. This implies that money profits remain in the circuit, allowing additional transactions, so that profits come from their own expenditure. Thus, velocity of money is higher than unity and monetary profits are positive (Allain 2007).

Gnos offers another alternative solution to this paradox. His approach assumes that the firms simply sell goods at a price exceeding the factor cost so that they can earn profits (Gnos 2003: 334). This is consistent with Keynes's approach in *The General Theory* (1936) in formulating the principle of effective demand – the entrepreneurs attempt to determine the amount of employment at a level they expect will maximise the excess of the earnings over the factor cost. Gnos points out that this approach asserts that profits, nominal and real, are included in the circuit of money wages. Moreover, whatever the period of time under consideration, firms repeatedly pay wages and sell goods, and the production processes overlap one another, so that firms will have no difficulty gaining profits out of wages, provided that the buyers are prepared to purchase goods at prices exceeding factor costs (Gnos 2003).

Messori and Zazzaro propose that, in a growing economy, firms are not at the same stage of their life cycle. Therefore, those which go bankrupt do not pay back the banks; and the start-ups need large loans, but initially do not make profits. Therefore, money remains available in the circuit that enables the other firms to realise profits (Messori and Zazzaro 2005). In other words, as the economy develops, new firms keep entering the market and, while some are successful, others ultimately fail and thereby provide money for realisation of profits by the successful ones.

These attempts to explain the paradoxical results of the theory of monetary circuit overlook the need to re-examine the underlying tenets. One of the vital flaws is that most of the writers in this tradition have started with the monetary sector and then subsequently tried to build the goods sector in consonance. In other words, the primary concern remains restricted to the study of money flow, not the economy as a whole. However, such study of monetary flows in isolation may be misleading and lead to a neglect of the crucial link between the real and monetary sector. In fact, the theory of monetary circuit takes a diametrically opposite view from the neoclassical theory, which considers only the real sector.

The single injection of money or credit by banks as assumed is also an oversimplification. This assumption of abstract injection at the beginning of a circuit treats money as 'manna from heaven', which is in a way reminiscent of the Walrasian general equilibrium model's treatment of goods. Many circuit theorists suffer from overshadow of equilibrium analysis at various stages of their arguments. One vital place where this is indicated is the preconceived notion that the sum of all the flows in a circuit should equal to zero at the close of the circuit. They tend to analyse the circuit at the close, but in reality, the circuit never closes. This comes from the usual misconception that circuit means full endogenous circularity without any external input or output, which may happen only in the special case of a completely closed circuit. A completely closed circuit, which necessarily makes endogenous circularity of all the items of flow, creates another pitfall as it acts as an inert black box, which, with no open end, takes nothing from and gives back nothing to the rest of the world. Another misconception that 'repayment of loan destroys money' remains with most of the writers.

Creation of wealth, both real and monetary, in the circuit is completely absent. This is because the stock-flow dynamics is ignored since the theory of monetary circuit is concerned only with the monetary flows. Moreover, most of the circuitists consider in their circuit constructions, for the sake of simplicity, that the circuit flows are unidirectional. But in reality, in an economic circuit every transaction flow is two directional – for every inflow there is an outflow, and stock accumulates (de-accumulates) when the inflow is more (less) than the outflow. Unidirectional flow may arise only in special cases, say of extraction of natural resources.

In a nutshell, the insoluble riddles in the TMC in respect of the paradox of profit, or repayment of bank loans, household savings, and payment of money interests, stem out from the neglect of the circuit theorists to accept a simple fact which their own monetary circuit theory reveals – monetary profit or payment of bank interest and loans cannot exist within a closed monetary circuit, with a given amount of money in circulation. Circuit theorists continue to grapple with problems like the realisation of money profits, and repayment of debt and interest by the firms in the circuit. They neglect the present-day issues and complexities of economic activities – for example, the trading opportunity of an economic circuit with the rest of the world or even with its own future, which we will show in the subsequent chapters. Overshadow of the neoclassical legacy remains in many cases throttling the development of a proper circuit framework. However, the circuit framework has a huge scope for exploration. If these shortcomings of the TMC are addressed, this methodology may help in analysing the accumulation of wealth and indebtedness as creation of stocks through the flows in economic systems and provide an alternative macroeconomic framework of economic studies.

6 The circuit construct

Nascent corporate production economy

The evolution of money capital as a fund capital and the appearance of interest on money loan formed the pillars of the subsequent financial evolutions that took place under the corporate economy. How did the corporate economy evolve and operate leading to financial evolutions? We begin with this question. The birth of the corporate system in modern history can be traced to the late 16th and early 17th centuries when joint stock companies were first established with pooled investment from shareholders (Wilson 1995: 43–4). The inception of the joint stock companies was interlinked with mercantile trade and consequent colonial conquests of Western European powers during the late 16th and early 17th centuries. In fact, providing capital for the colonial and mercantile voyages was one of the reasons for the evolution of the earliest joint stock companies. One of the earliest joint stock companies was the East India Company, established in 1600, with the monopoly of trade in India granted by the Royal Charter.

The industrial revolution in Western Europe, traced from the second half of the 18th century to the first half of the 19th century, opened new avenues for earning returns through investments of money capital in large-scale industrial production for market. The earlier joint stock mercantile companies now shifted their activity towards this new avenue. A nascent corporate production system started to take shape in Western Europe in the 1840s. The decades of 1840–60 may be marked as the beginning of the age of corporate capital or simply the Age of Capital (1848–75), following the historian Eric Hobsbawm (1975).

The beginning of the nascent corporate production economy was supported by, and contributed to, several other evolutions. The most important ones were the evolution of states with political boundaries and the constitutional set-up for enacting their legal systems. The revolution of 1848 in Western Europe, known as the 'spring of nations', led to the formation of the nation-states. This new political system, called the state, provided the legal environment for corporate organisation. The earlier joint stock companies were dependent on the sanctions by the Royal Charter. Now there was a legal system by which a company might be established for production and trade. With the beginning of a nascent corporate production economy, a new construct of an open economic circuit came into existence in the Western European countries.

The background

While the joint stock companies were the forerunners of the modern companies that emerged in the West in the second half of the 19th century, we may trace out two other roots of this evolution. The joint stock companies mobilised money capital from many shareholders; but from where and in which form did this money capital come? Further, what guided the investment of money capital from simple mercantile trade to large-scale production activities by establishing factories? The answer to the first question lies in the mercantile conquests of the Western European countries since the late 15th century and the resultant specie flow that ultimately transformed into the Gold Standard money. To answer the second question we notice the technological possibilities opened up by the industrial revolution for carrying out large-scale production activities and, side by side, the organisation of the modern companies that aided mobilisation of huge money capital from the public by ensuring limited liability for the shareholders.

The mercantile conquests and specie flow

North West Europe experienced severe monetary scarcities and liquidity crises in the later part of the 14th and the 15th centuries, popularly called the bullion famines. The bullion famines led to a frantic search for money which was relieved somewhat by the discovery of copious quantities of silver and by debasements (Kindleberger 1984: 26–7; Munro 2009: 6). The money-hungriness of these early economies and the quest for gold had a key role to play in the early explorations. Kindleberger pointed out that search for gold was an important motivation behind Columbus's voyage of 1492. Columbus's diary of exploration for less than a hundred days mentioned 'gold' sixty-five times (Kindleberger 1984: 25).

Western European powers continued their efforts since the late 15th centuries to divert precious metals into their countries by various means. The Spanish Crown tried to monopolise the flow of silver into

Europe. The Spanish wars in the 16th and 17th centuries were encouraged by the treasure hunts uncovered in the New World. Another powerful nation-state, Portugal, discovered gold in Brazil in 1680, leading to new inflows of specie to Portugal. London gained from this flow of gold since Britain had formed an alliance (Treaty of Methuen) with Portugal in 1703 to channel the flow of specie through London. Spooner, as well as Kindleberger, opined that this infusion of capital was instrumental in paving the way for England to lead the industrial revolution (Spooner 1972; Kindleberger 1984).

Industrial revolution and evolution of the corporate structure

The second phase of the industrial revolution that emerged in Britain in the first half of the 19th century marked a beginning for a new wealth-generation process through large-scale industrial production. There was a parallel evolution of the corporate system to aid this process of wealth creation. The institutional structures evolved at this juncture proved befitting for the creation and accumulation of wealth that was needed also for furthering the industrial revolution in large-scale manufacturing. One such manifestation was seen in the invention of the steam engine and its subsequent improvisation in railways leading to the establishment of railway companies.

A crucial feature of the development of the corporate structure was the 'limited liability' of the shareholders. It allowed appropriation of profits through dividends without loss-sharing by the shareholders and thereby facilitated a huge mobilisation of capital that would be difficult in a proprietor holding or partnership firms with unlimited liability. An essential corollary of the limited liability concept was the development of the stock exchanges or share markets for share transfers, which evolved earlier in the time of joint stock mercantile companies. Along with the limited liability of the shareholders, transferability of shares had a key role in mobilising money capital for the expansion of the corporate economy.

The concept of limited liability got widespread support simultaneously in France and England in the late 17th century from the investors who wanted to exploit the expanding profiteering opportunities of the era given by the companies, without committing to any unlimited personal liability. Immediately following the industrial revolution, there was a marked rise in entrepreneurial activity – in England 236 patents were taken out in these years, compared to the 204 in the next forty years. After the revolution, there was an extraordinary increase in the floatation of joint stock companies (Dean 1972: 98–9; Wilson 1995: 43–4).

Development of stock markets was an essential corollary to the growth of the corporate mobilisation of equity capital. While the earliest stock markets were seen in the medieval stock markets of Italy, the modern stock market was traced to the 17th century in Amsterdam. In the early 17th century, the Dutch and the British East India Companies issued shares to the public to fund their imperial enterprises, granting the investors a share of profits in the form of dividends. These shares were also made freely transferable to attract those investors who might be unwilling to be attached irrevocably to the fate of the companies. Amsterdam's early stock market was loosely organised. The first formally organised exchange was established in Paris in 1724. With the French Revolution and the consequent disruption of commerce and trade there, the attention shifted to London, and the London stock exchange was opened in 1802. This marked the beginning of modern stock exchanges, with regular trading and a fixed, self-regulating membership (Henwood 1998: 12–13).

As the corporate system expanded, it required greater monetisation. The inflow of colonial trade surplus provided the much-needed liquidity infusion. The mercantile companies obtained a huge share of the inflow of capital and liquidity in the mercantile period. In 1689 the paid-up capital of three foreign trading companies was nearly half a million pounds out of the total paid-up capital of £630,000 of all British joint stock companies. In contrast, by 1695 the total paid-up capital of the joint stock companies in England was nearly £3.5 million, of which £2 million was attributable to the Bank of England and foreign trading companies. Thirty-eight percent of the estimated paid-up capital in 1695 was in foreign trade, about a quarter in banking, 12 percent in water supply undertakings, 4 percent in mining, and less than 15 percent in manufacturing (*Ibid.*).

In the 18th century, new forms of finance like trade credit or book debt also played an important role in financing the corporate system. For its circulating capital the nascent corporate system took the advantage of the existing elaborate mechanism of credit. Firms could devote most of their initial capital resources to fixed investment and, by using the circular flow of credit, could acquire working capital by a process of running creditors' balances of much larger amounts than that of debtors. It was possible to run the entire production process on credit – paying for raw materials, interest, dividends, and royalties could be done on credit. Again, although the companies some gave credit to the buyers of manufactured goods, they could either get their drafts on the customers discounted or get advances from commission agents to whom the goods were consigned. Thus, a web of credit, which was vital for infusion of liquidity in the corporate economy, existed at its onset. The merchant firms supplied the industry a large part of its circulating capital and played a dominant and decisive role in the development of the corporate economy. Financing of stocks by mercantile capital was more important than industry's self-finance, at least up to the beginning of the 19th century (Crouznet 1972: 44).

Accounting procedures and credit mechanisms also evolved during this period to allow liquidity infusions in the corporate production economy. Accounting procedures of double entry book keeping played a crucial role in this evolution. Under the double entry book keeping the value of the assets must equal the value of liabilities and the shareholder's equity. In other words, the asset a firm owns equals to what it owes in value terms. Following this principle, the system in practice was that whatever a firm had, including the inventories, was valued at market prices to bring about the symmetry with what the firm owed to others and the equity it possessed. This meant that market values were assigned also to the assets that had not yet been marketed and were illiquid resources. In this system any position of surplus of assets over liabilities less the equity capital raised the firm's ability to raise credit money from the market.

In the 19th century, the development of the corporate structure in Western capitalist countries got further impetus from enactment of some laws in their favour. One of the most important was the Limited Liability Act of 1855. The Joint Stock Company Act of 1844 did not provide limited liability shield to the general shareholders, since it regarded companies as partnership with members remaining liable for the debts of the company. It was the Act of 1855 that introduced limited liability for the shareholders, although there were some fears that it might encourage fraudulent practices by the promoters of companies. These two acts were revised and combined in the Joint Stock Company Act of 1856 (Brazier 1996: 10).

The Acts of 1855 and 1856 opened new horizons for the corporate system and the historical judgement on the case 'Salomon versus Salomon and Co.' in the House of Commons in 1897, which gave a disembodied, formless existence of the 'corporation' as a separate legal entity. This historical ruling provided that the ownership of the assets the corporation created with the pooled investment of the shareholders was vested on the corporation itself, but not on its shareholders.

This endorsed on the corporation an identity separate from its individual shareholders. The shareholders, it was ruled, were simply the 'investor owners' not the 'asset owners' (Ramsay 1998: 215–16).

This economic construct – that is, the separation of the corporation from its shareholders and the limited liability of the shareholders – had a profound impact on the later development of the corporate structure. The limited liability brought hopes of unlimited gains from investment in companies while absolving the liability if the companies became unsuccessful. It ensured that if the company went bankrupt the shareholders would bear a loss equivalent only to the value of the shares they invested, the remaining liability of the accumulated loss being vested on the formless entity of the corporation, or in effect, on the society at large. But as long as the company made profits the shareholders would continue to earn dividends. Naturally, the enactment of limited liability companies brought in incessantly many speculators willing to invest their money in companies.

The evolution of the nascent corporate system had a key role in the industrialisation of the West in the 19th century. It would not be an overstatement to say that the industrialisation of Western nations would not have been possible without the helping structure of the corporate system. The financial capital required for the growth of the industries could hardly be provided by the proprietorship or partnership organisations of firms. The adoption of new technology, which was still at a nascent and experimental stage, required investment of huge capital. This became possible only through the pooling of capital from numerous shareholders.

As a corollary to the separation of the corporation as an entity distinct from its shareholders came further development and growth of the stock exchanges that facilitated the sale and purchase of company shares. This was an added feature of the system whereby the shareholders, if desired, could sell the shares held to others willing to buy the same in the stock exchanges. It made sure that the money capital of the shareholders remained quasi-liquid in the corporate system. The added attraction in this system was the possibility of windfall speculative gains from the price appreciation of the shares, which gave further inducement to invest in company shares.

The golden era

From the beginning, monetisation of its stock of goods and infusion of liquidity was a crucial question for the nascent corporate economy.

There were two avenues to address this. The system of trade credit against the book debt meant that the production process could be carried on using the credit machinery even in the absence of sufficient liquid resources. Further, the specie flow from the colonial conquests and trade allowed the nascent corporate system of the West to monetise its stock of goods and acquire the required infusion of liquidity.

The period of the Gold Standard marked an era of unhindered prosperity for the corporate economy. There were several contributing factors. The 18th century marked the inception of the Gold Standard in Europe. It grew out of the earlier system of bimetallic coinage. In England the origins of the Gold Standard could be traced to 1717, when Sir Isaac Newton, as the master of United Kingdom Mint, reformed the coinage in a way that left gold overvalued relative to silver, even though the country was still legally bimetallic. This put Britain on a de facto Gold Standard and over the 18th century the convertibility of Bank of England notes into gold became the bedrock of the British monetary system. In 1797 there was a temporary suspension of the currency convertibility of Bank of England owing to the pressures of the French Revolutionary War, but the Gold Standard was restored in 1819 at the old parity. From the early 1870s most of the countries in Europe moved away from bimetallism to the Gold Standard. France, Germany, and the United States had introduced their Gold Standards by 1880. The period from 1880 to 1914 was characterised as the classical international Gold Standards and marked as one of the most remarkable periods of economic prosperity and stability (Snowdown and Vane 2002: 293).

The provision of liquidity under the Gold Standard meant an uninhibited process of monetisation and expansion for the corporate economy. According to Kindleberger (1973: p. 294) the prosperity under the Gold Standard and its liquidity and stability came from the effective monetary management by the Bank of England. The Bank of England acted as the international lender of the last resort ensuring the infusion of the required liquidity. In this period, marked by stable international cooperation among Western capitalist nations, minor international liquidity problems were solved by the tactic of cooperation among leading central banks and governments. When global credit conditions were overly restrictive, adjustment were undertaken simultaneously by central banks with the 'follow-the-leader' approach, Bank of England being the leader. In such situations central banks discounted the bills of the weak currency country, or lent gold to its central bank. So the resources a country could draw on, even when its gold parity was under doubt, far exceeded its own resources, as it included the resources of the other Gold Standard countries (Eichengreen 1992: 4–8).

However, it was not merely the international cooperation among the Western European countries for unhindered capital flows that made the Gold Standard a period of unlimited prosperity. This era for Western Europe, especially for Britain, France, Spain, Portugal, and Holland, was marked by still continuing flows of trade surpluses and the wealth amassed from the colonies that helped enhancing their gold reserves. The expansion of the corporate system required more and more monetisation. The colonial trade surpluses infused the required amount of liquidity to the nascent corporate economy, helping it flourish by monetising its stock of goods.

The period of the Gold Standard (1880–1914), saw the Sterling being established as the dominant currency in the workings of the international monetary system. This dominance was made possible by the fact that Britain ran current account surpluses all through this period. The surpluses came from the strong exports of shipping and financial services and the income from earnings on earlier foreign investments. During the heyday of the Gold Standard, Britain was the world's largest exporter (Maddison 2006: 115; Meissner 2010: 65). Undoubtedly, in such a position it could dictate its terms of trade with its colonies as well as with other countries. An idea about the transfer of resources from colonies can be obtained from Madison's estimates of the 'drain' of resources from India to Britain. He puts it around 0.9 percent to 1.3 percent of the Indian national income from 1868 to the 1930s, or a transfer amounting to roughly a fifth of India's net savings (Maddison *Ibid*: 113). It must be remembered that India was only one of the major colonies of the British crown. Britain had about fifty smaller colonies till the 1930s. Beside this, it had trade dominance over other countries, like China.

To run the production process, a company need not keep the entire working capital in liquid form. The newer forms of finance and accounting procedures like trade credit and book debt reduced the requirement of holding liquid resources. The development of these accounting techniques meant that large investments could now be made and productions could be planned on a grander scale even without money in hand, simply by taking recourse to various forms of credit. Under the accounting systems of the period, the stock of goods were assets on the firm's balance sheets and they helped acquiring credit through hypothecation for the next production cycle even if they were not sold.

The 'golden fetters'

The 19th century witnessed a flowering of the corporate system in Western capitalist nations. The industrial revolution and technological developments helped further accumulation of stock of goods and hence financial capital of the corporate economy in the form of credits against the stocks. At this initial stage the Gold Standard did not prove an obstacle to the increasing expansion of the corporate system. Its growing monetisation could squeeze money from the rest of the world through colonial conquests and trade on one hand, and take the advantage of technological advancement and a functioning credit system at home on the other. However, the expanding corporate system would sooner find that money to be backed by gold was an obstacle to its monetisation process. This led to the next phase of evolution of credit money to be discussed later.

The term 'golden fetters' was used by Keynes to describe the difficulties of the Gold Standard in the post-World War I period (Eichengreen 1992). Before that the dominant role of Sterling as a currency at the centre of the world financial system ensured the smooth working of the Gold Standard. In the years following World War I, the exchange rate was allowed to move in line with market forces and, from 1920 to 1924, the Sterling–dollar exchange rate fluctuated with little official intervention to stabilise the Sterling. By the early 1920s the Sterling had dropped from the pre-war parity of $4.86 to $3.18 and by early 1925 it improved again to $4.78, leading Britain to return to gold parity in April 1925 (Argy 1981: 14–16). However, the inter-war Gold Standards proved to be less resilient than its predecessor. It was limited as well as fragile and involved much monetary management by the central banks.

As the corporate economy continued to expand, it needed continuous monetisation of its stock of goods. We will see later in the rudimentary formulation of the circuit that, as the corporate economy expands, on one hand continuous accumulation of stock of goods takes place and, on the other, nominal reserves as a source of financial capital grow continuously. Consequently, the corporate system will always be money-hungry and try to monetise its stock of goods.

There are many reasons for the Gold Standard becoming ultimately unworkable. First, under the Gold Standard, the obligation of convertibility to gold meant governments could not deflate to ease liquidity crunches. The liquidity needs of the corporate economy obviously required monetary and credit expansion. However, countries obligated to the Gold Standard could not undertake unilateral monetary expansion or increase public expenditure as it would threaten the Gold Standard (Eichengreen 1992: 12–18). Second, the colonial surpluses or mercantile exploits ensuring gold inflow ultimately reached their limits and could not be adequate to meet the growing needs of liquidity. Third, the international disputes over war debts and reparations marred the international financial cooperation among the Western nations, and stopped the earlier unhindered capital flows that had allowed the countries to tide over liquidity problems under the Gold Standard. The Bank of International Settlements (BIS) was founded in 1930 to address these issues but the ongoing political disputes related to war debts and reparations prevented the BIS from achieving any significant international monetary cooperation. World War I had greatly improved the US balance of payments position and weakened that of the others, so that the external accounts of many countries remained tenuously balanced on long-term capital flows from the United States. But, while the United Kingdom no longer remained in a position to act as the 'international lender of the last resort', the United States was not prepared to take up the role (Eichengreen *Ibid*. 1992: 4, 11).

Many scholars like Eichengreen (1992) viewed the obligation to the Gold Standard to be, to a large extent, responsible for the Great Depression of the 1930s. In the 1920s the external accounts of most of the Western countries remained dependent on the capital outflows from the United States. The precariousness on this situation was soon revealed. In the summer of 1928, the United States curtailed lending to these countries due to stringent Federal Reserve monetary policies, and the weakness in the external positions of the other countries was revealed. This led to a loss of gold reserves or foreign exchange reserves of these countries, threatening the convertibility of their currencies to gold. Moreover, along with the curtailment of US lending, there was also a massive flow of gold to France, leading to a further tightening of fiscal policies in parts of Europe and much of South America. A minor shift in US domestic policies had a dramatic impact due to the foreign reaction it provoked, given the Gold Standard constraints. Further, the bank failures in 1929 and the following financial chaos led to the liquidation of bank deposits and disrupted the provision of financial services, intensifying the instability of the situation (Eichengreen 1992: 12–18).

The depressionary forces in Western economies were amplified by the stock market crash of 29 October 1929 in the United States. The depression soon spread to almost every developed country in the world by 1930 and culminated in one of the longest and severest periods of economic depression – the Great Depression that continued all through the decade before World War II. By the 1930s, major European nations, including Britain, were off the Gold Standard. Keynes famously compared the abandoning of the Gold Standard as the breaking of the 'golden fetters', writing, 'There are few Englishmen who do not rejoice at the breaking of our gold fetters' (Keynes 1932: 288).

Monetarists, led by Friedman, opined that the rigid money supply and failure of the Federal Reserve to infuse the required amount of liquidity aggravated the downturn of 1929 to the mammoth Great Depression. In their book *Monetary History of the United States*, Friedman and Schwartz (1963) suggested that the exogenous changes in money supply were an important factor behind the Great Depression. They pointed out that the series of banking crises, beginning in October 1930 and ending in March 1933, reduced both the money multiplier and the money stock. This decline was not offset by the Federal Reserve with open market operations and therefore led to a sharp contraction in economic activity (Calomiris 1993: 62).

Though this monetary explanation of the Great Depression was not accepted by all economists, there had been some evidence of a contraction in the money supply in the United States in 1929. Field (1984) showed that the securities market trading increased the demand for money in the late 1920s, pointing that speculative activities of the economy further aggravated the liquidity needs. There was, however, no increase in the money supplies in this period. Money supply was contracted in the United States in 1929 as the Federal Reserve raised interest rates to reduce the general price levels. Wheelock (1990) found a subsequent downward shift in the banks' demand for borrowed reserves that caused a reduction in the money multiplier which the Federal Reserve could not offset with money market operations. Wheelock (1992) showed that the money stock fell by a third from 1929 to 1933, with a rise in the value of the dollar by 25 percent in the same period. Further, the real interest rate – that is, the interest rate adjusted for the changes in price level – rose sharply during this period. All these indicated a tight monetary situation.

Friedman and Schwartz (1963) attributed these policies of the Federal Reserve to a change in its leadership at the helm of the Reserve (Calomiris 1993: 62). But, the obligations to the Gold Standard, in fact, left fewer policies open to the Federal Reserve. Moreover, the speculative needs of the economy exerted further pressure on the liquid balances. In this situation, the contraction in money supply proved disastrous, aggravating the downturn to a massive Depression. The Gold Standard proved to be a detriment in the way of monetary expansion by the countries. The time had come to move into a monetary system suited to the needs of the expanding corporate economy.

Circuit construct – the nascent corporate production economy

At this point it would be useful to consider the organisation of the corporate production economy in terms of circuit flows and stocks. In the political plane, the Revolutions of 1848 gave birth to the nation-states in Western Europe. Simultaneously in the economic plane, the Age of Capital gave birth to two new kinds of economic entity – the large-scale corporate production units for market and the national economies built around it. How did these national economies that emerged in the West operate? For this we take the circuit view of the economy – the economic circuits that prevailed as the national economies of the West.

The economic circuit in Figure 6.1 traces the directions of economic flows, formation of economic stocks and their accumulation through the flows, and the economic agents undertaking the activities in the economic circuit that emerged with the nascent corporate production economy. There are four economic agents at the aggregate level – the corporate sector engaged in production and trade, the household sector (consisting of workers and high net worth individuals), the commercial banks engaged in monetary deposit taking and lending, and the government issuing the Gold Standard money. In Figure 6.1 these economic agents are put in the rectangular boxes.

The economic flows among these agents are marked by lines with arrow heads indicating the direction of the flow of the items and the economic stocks resulting from the flows are encircled in the chart. There are four types of economic stocks – stock of goods, retained profits by the companies (nominal financial capital), monetary reserves of the banks, and the gold reserve of the country or the government. Natural resources of the country as the gift of nature are of course a stock, but it is not created by economic flows. Economic flows rather draw from this stock the material resources for production. For the sake of simplicity, we have not shown separately the stock of net financial assets of the HNIs, who are included in the household sector, or the money loan given by the banks to the household sector and the loan interest they get in return. The household savings (primarily by the HNIs), flowing into the financial market as investments on bonds and equity shares, and as bank deposits in the commercial banks,

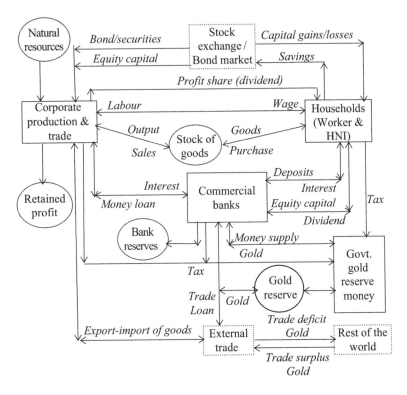

Figure 6.1 Nascent corporate production circuit, 1850–1930

Note: Construction explained in the text

HNI = high net worth individuals

Source: Prepared by the authors

constitute the stock of net financial assets (less of loans, if any) of the household sector.

At the centre of the circuit we find the corporate production circuit and the rest of the circuit flows revolve around it. This is shown in Figure 6.2. The figure shows on the upper part the money income flows as wages from the corporate production sector to the household sector and in exchange the household sector supplies labour to the corporate production sector. On the lower part, the circuit shows the output flow.

The corporate production sector, through its output, builds its stock of goods produced, from which sales are made to the household sector. Through the purchase of goods by the household sector, money

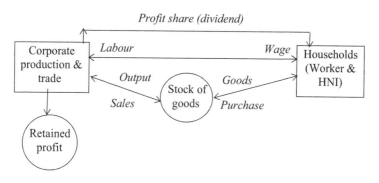

Figure 6.2 Central part of the corporate production circuit
Note: Construction explained in the text
Source: Prepared by the authors

then flows back as sales revenue to the corporate production sector, financing the production activity (payment of wages) in the next cycle. The simple circuit depicts here the economic flows in the rudimentary production cycle.

The circuit diagram shows only the direction of the flows, not the quantities. Creation of the stocks that may result from the flows can be examined only when we bring into consideration the volume of the flows, for economic volume of the flows is measured by money (values). When we bring the flow of money into the picture we see that the money that can flow back to the corporate production sector can be at most the money it has paid earlier as wages, which is the money income of the households or the cost of production of the corporate production sector. Thus, provided that the households spend their entire money income, the corporate production sector gets back its money outlays as cost of production and the production cycle continues as before. Then where is the profit of the corporate sector? This is another way of bringing out the paradox of profit of the TMC. When the household sector saves a part the money flow it has received as money income, the corporate production sector, from within the circuit flow, would get less than its money outlay as cost of production or wage payments. So, there would be liquidity problem in financing production in the next production cycle and the corporate sector would be forced to cut down production. This would be the typical case of Keynesian paradox of thrift.

The corporate production economies, as the circuit shows, is always at the edge of a crisis – it can never realise profits over and above the cost production – the money it puts into the flow as cost of production is at most the money it can get back from within the circuit (that is, from within the national economies of the nascent corporate production system), unless there comes some additional money flow into the circuit. But is it not a fact that the corporate production sector does make financial profits? It also accumulates financial profit and invests it to expand its activities. How can this be possible? In what ways it earns profits when it could not realise profits from the money flow within the circuit?

To answer this puzzle we need to notice that in this production circuit profit accrues to the corporate production sector first as surplus production. Since the corporate sector charges a mark-up profit in the money value of the output over the cost of production, this surplus is necessarily generated as unsold stock of goods. The household sector, even by spending the entire money flow it has received by supplying labour, can never buy the entire output flow of production at the mark-up price. Thus, the corporate sector will get back the money it has put into production and will be left with some amount of stock of goods that accumulate as surplus production at the end of each production cycle. With the given money flow in the circuit, the corporate sector can at best keep on running the production cycle, provided that the household sector does not hold back any part of the money flow it gets as income as idle money savings. The corporate sector can also keep on accumulating the surplus production, but with the current money flow in the circuit, it cannot monetise it to realise profits in money form.

In the upper part of the central circuit, as shown in Figure 6.2, we have marked dividend flow as profit share from the corporate sector to the household sector (particularly to the HNIs). This central circuit flow shows that unless the corporate sector can monetise its surplus production, it cannot pay this dividend on the equity capital it has mobilised from the household sector. The unsold surplus production, held as assets (at market value including the mark-up profit), is now reflected by a matching liability of nominal reserve of undistributed profit in the balance sheet of the corporate sector following the double entry accounting system. Moreover, when a part of the money capital of the corporate sector comes from the banking sector as money loan, which usually is, the corporate sector will not be able to repay it for the same reason – it does not have the liquidity. The operations of the corporate production circuit and its implications are discussed in greater detail in terms of sectoral stocks and flows in the Chapter 7 on rudimentary formulation of the circuit.

How does the corporate sector monetise the surplus production to get money profit that is essential for its business? One way this can be achieved is by squeezing the money that may have remained within the national economy, but yet outside the nascent corporate production circuit. Out of the earlier specie flow of the mercantilist period, some money remains with the household sector of the national economies. The nascent corporate production sector evolves by mobilising a part of this money as its equity capital. Then it grows with increased money capital by squeezing the remaining money through selling the surplus goods within the national economy. But eventually this opportunity dries up and the corporate production circuit has to explore other ways for monetising the surplus production.

The other avenue of injecting money into the circuit is exporting its surplus production to the rest of the world. For, even if a national economy could increase its gold extraction and thereby raise the gold reserve, it would only be able to issue more money to the banking sector. It could neither induce the household sector to buy more from the corporate sector taking bank credits, nor induce the corporate sector to produce more by engaging more money capital taken as bank loans, as there was already loads of surplus production that could not be sold. Therefore, the question is not just how to raise the money supply by the national government, but how to inject that money into the circuit – that is, to the household sector – so that selling the surplus production becomes possible within the circuit. Here, our circuit analysis reveals the well-known debate between the Monetarist and Keynesian schools – raising the money supply by the government or raising the government expenditure to raise the demand for the goods produced within the economic circuit. We find each of the two schools gives only a half story. Both are simultaneously needed.

The lower part of the circuit diagram in Figure 6.1 shows the open end of the circuit through which goods and money flow in and out of the circuit of a national economy to and from the rest of the world as export and import of goods in exchange for gold or Gold Standard money. Export brings money to the circuit and, by import, money flows out of the circuit. So economies having net exports (money value of export more than money value of import) would be able to build more gold reserves through the sale of surplus production to the rest of the world and ensure more Gold Standard money flows into its production circuit. This money flow, transformed into domestic money via banks, comes to the corporate production sector as the sale proceeds of the surplus products and as the gold equivalent of the foreign money, which has come, goes to the gold reserve of the economy. Whether or not the entire surplus production could be sold, and thereby how much profit could be realised in money, would depend on the money value of net exports, of which the export price obtained is an important element. In any case, whenever there is net export, the corporate production sector of a national economy would get an additional money flow as realised money profit. On the other side, whenever there is negative net export (that is, import value is more than export value), money flows out from the economy. Export by one economy means import by another economy, and so a positive net export of an economy is necessarily matched by a negative net export by some other economy or economies. So, by net export, a production circuit gets additional money flow simply by squeezing the money from outside, that is, from the importing economies in the rest of the world. This was indeed the story of 19th- and early 20th-century Western capitalism.

It appears that a corporate production circuit can overcome its monetisation crisis by exporting the surplus production to the rest of the world. But the crisis is not over. The circuit stays on the edge of a crisis. First, we notice that for its staying out of crisis there must always exist some economies in the rest of world that could be induced to import goods, implying that they must have the necessary Gold Standard money backed by gold reserve (or simply gold) to finance their imports. This is an essential condition for the nascent corporate production circuit of Western capitalism to stay out of its monetisation crisis. But this shifts the crisis from the exporting economy to the importing economy, since in this process, as Gold Standard money (or gold) flows out, depleting the gold reserve of the importing economies of the rest of the world, they start facing the same liquidity crisis. In the nascent corporate production circuits of these economies, there will be depression with piling up unsold stocks of goods, leading to contraction of goods production. The only way the nascent corporate production could survive in these economies is to operate in a different direction – to circulate its money capital, not primarily in its domestic circuit of industrial production and sale of goods and labour wage payment for it, but mostly in producing or extracting and exporting natural resource intensive primary products to the West. We may note that it is a historical economic construct of value addition that the value of goods produced by manufacturing is necessarily higher than the primary material used in production. So these economies would continue to remain with negative net export with unfavourable terms of trade.

The trade pattern we find from the circuit analysis gives an explanation of the Leontief paradox that contradicts the neoclassical theory of trade based on the Hekscher-Ohlin theorem. Historically, in the evolutionary path of the corporate system, the Western European economies were much ahead of the rest of the world. They were the earliest to reap the benefits of the industrial revolution. Moreover, the triangular trade pattern that prevailed in the colonised world beginning in the 16th century favoured the European powers in exporting the goods produced by their corporate production circuit. The counterpart that imported these goods was the colonies and the economies in the rest of the world. Our circuit analysis shows that the corporate production circuit of the West specialises in exporting the goods of the production circuit with the higher labour–capital ratio, and the importing economies in the rest of the world are forced to specialise in exporting material-intensive primary goods of the production circuits that employ less labour per unit of capital.

The other sources of crises come from a different route. We see that the corporate production circuit monetises its surplus production by the money profit through net exports, and thus gets an additional money flow over and above the initial money capital it put into circulation as wage payment. What would be the implication of this additional money flow received by the corporate sector for the circuit? Using it, the corporate sector can now repay in whole or part its money loan to the bank along with interest, and/or pay dividends to its shareholders in the household sector, and/or retain it for augmenting the money capital to expand its scale of production. If it repays the bank loan plus interest, the banks would face the problem of surplus money fund. This will push the interest rate down, unless the corporate sector requires higher amounts of further loans to expand its production. If the corporate sector uses the entire additional money to pay dividends, the increased money income of the household sector would create additional domestic demand for goods, which cannot be matched by additional supply, as the corporate sector would not be able to expand production without additional money capital. It would be the situation of classical quantity theory, where additional money flow would be reflected only in proportionate rise in prices. So in either case, the corporate sector would get signals to expand its production. Hence, besides repaying the bank loans and paying dividends, retaining a part of this money flow as undistributed profits by the corporate sector could bring a balance between these two possibilities.

With the increased money flow, the corporate production sector would tend to expand its production by keeping a part of its monetised profit as retained profit (not distributed to the shareholders) for enhancing its money capital invested in production. If it does not do so, there will be crisis in the domestic economy, either in the form of excess loanable funds with the banks, or in the form of inflationary rises in the price. But if the corporate sector does so, there will be another crisis – the crisis of accumulating more surplus production and the problem of monetising it by increasing the net exports to the rest of the world further. Thus, monetising the surplus production by the corporate production circuit by net exports does not free it from the crisis but brings the crisis back on a larger scale. It has to keep on increasing its exports and squeeze the rest of the world of the Gold Standard money (or gold). Unfortunately the gold reserve of the world is not infinite.

The nascent corporate production circuits that evolved in the West since the 1850s grew by squeezing the Gold Standard money (or gold) that was remaining outside the circuit in the domestic economy as well as abroad. It was its golden era of growth. But this could not continue for long. The limit was set by the available gold reserves in the economies. By the late 1920s the export-led growth regime in most of the Western countries was coming to an end, with a downward trend in export that was setting in. The Gold Standard, after its golden era, as reflected in growing corporate production circuits, became the golden fetters. The crisis of the 1930s made another organisational evolution necessary for Western capitalism. On one hand, the golden fetters of money supply were to be removed to increase supply of money (Monetarists school), and on the other, the additional money supply was to be brought into circulation in the form of enhanced demand for consumption, which was to be generated by the fiscal measures of increasing government expenditure (Keynesian school). In Chapter 8 we discuss this evolution in the creditisation phase of capitalism.

7 Rudimentary formulation of the circuit

The evolutions of the corporate economy can be distinctly marked by three phases – the first phase is the nascent corporate production economy in the early stage of evolution of Western capitalism in the second half of the 19th century. It was monetised with exogenous money, which continued until the 1930s. Next came the phase of creditisation with endogenous money in the post-war periods of monetary expansion and growth that lasted up to the 1960s. Finally, the third phase marks the arrival of financialisation with financial commodities that started in the late 1970s. Here, we will construct the rudimentary monetised economic circuit of the nascent stage of the corporate production economy that also lies at the foundation of our present economic structure. We will discuss the next two evolutions in the following chapters.

Understanding the operation of the rudimentary circuit is important. Only with a properly formulated rudimentary foundation can we analyse the evolutions in the subsequent phases. We must mention that in circuit construction we are considering the actual flows of economic entities, not the neoclassical abstract concepts of demand and supply. Therefore, the typical neoclassical questions, like what determines consumption or investment demands or the economic desires as such, do not arise in the circuit framework. To formulate the rudimentary economic circuit of the nascent corporate production economy in terms of an economic circuit, we would start with specifying its structural aspects.

Structural aspects

The early stage of corporate production evolved when there was only exogenous money. Though credit evolved much before money, endogenous credit money came much later, after the breakdown of the Gold

Standard because of the crisis of the 1930s. One of the sources of exogenous money under the Gold Standard was the external trade surplus implying inflow of gold. This inflow of gold to the circuit was essential.

We will see that this economic circuit was not a closed one. It kept an open end for transaction flows with the rest of the world in the form of trade exports and imports, which was essential for the realisation of monetary profit and thereby its expansion. The open-circuit framework helps analyse and explain the accumulation of wealth from the early stage of the corporate production economy to its current stage of financial capital accumulation. For otherwise, in a closed circuit, every gain also means an equal amount of loss, or every asset created means an equal amount of liability creation within the circuit.

In our circuit construction, first we segregate the structure of the economy into four sectors – the corporate production sector, the banking sector, the household sector, and the national government or the state. The state-issued Gold Standard money was exogenous to the circuit. The rest of the world existed outside the circuit for its external trade.

In this structure, the corporate production sector employed for production the labour supplied by the household sector. In exchange, the money wages were paid to the households. The household sector, in turn, using its money income, purchased the goods produced by the corporate sector. Thus, money circulated between the corporate sector and the household sector in the basic production circuit and the production cycles continued. In the nascent stage of corporate production economies (1850–1930), we do not find much role of the banking and the government sectors, which we see in the subsequent evolutionary stages. With the Gold Standard money, the banks could not create credit money, and the role of the government was restricted mostly to the collection of taxes to finance its administrative costs and maintaining the gold reserve of the country. Economic interventions by governments through fiscal management, which we see in the next phase of evolution, were not significant here.

Second, we should note how the state-issued exogenous money came into circulation in the circuit of production. Money was already in existence in different specie forms even before the advent of the corporate production system. It was in the possession of the various economic agents, like landlords, moneylenders or usurers, merchants, ordinary citizens, artisans, household producers, and the early bankers. With the evolution of corporate industrial production, the production activities were reorganised through transfer of a part of the existing stock of money held by these agents to the formation of the companies for corporate production and trade. In other words, the corporate sector and the banks channelized a part of the stock of the state money, held as wealth by the households in the earlier production economy, as initial stock transfers in the form of equity capital. Another part went to the banking sector in form of household deposits. Some money of course still remained with the households at the nascent stage.

This is in contrast to the single injection of money or credit by banks, as assumed in the TMC. Here, it is neither assumed that there is an abstract injection of money at the beginning of the circuit, nor is money the 'manna from heaven', as the Walrasian general equilibrium models assume about the goods. Further, there were no reasons to assume that the 'corporate production economy' evolved at one go and absorbed 'all the money' that was available in the entire economy. Such sweeping assumptions erase the evolutionary process of the corporate production economy and its intricacies – the process through which the corporate production economy could expand by squeezing the residual part of the state money remaining outside the circuit but with the households, besides squeezing money from the rest of the world.

In the nascent organisational structure of the corporate production economy, banks could not create endogenous money or credit money. The situation typifies the era of state-issued Gold Standard money. All transactions in the circuit flows were to be settled ultimately through physical transfer of Gold Standard money of the state. With the political reorganisation of the states as national economies and consolidation of the Gold Standard money, the government became the money-issuing authority. However, to issue the Gold Standard money the government had to back it up by the necessary gold reserve. For the sake of simplicity of the rudimentary circuit formulation, we may assume here that there was no *seigniorage* charged by the state.

To simplify the circuit formulation further, we may use some assumptions about its operations. First, temporary idle money of the corporate sector, as might be kept in bank deposits, is non-interest bearing. Second, we also suppress the time element necessary to specify the rates of various flows in the circuit. One way of doing this could be to assume all flow transactions take place instantaneously, making the time duration of a flow-cycle equal to zero. This would be a too-strict assumption. Instead, we assume that, with a given stock of money in the circuit, all the flows take place at mutually consistent rates over time without any delay. If they were not consistent then bottlenecks would arise and, when these rates change, the money stock required for the circuit would change. These aspects, which we keep outside the scope of this book, may be studied as technical dynamics within the circuit (Andresen 1996).

Third, we assume the banking sector distributes all of its profits to its shareholders, without retaining any undistributed profit. As the banking sector is not involved in production activities, it would be unprofitable for it to hold idle money, leading to loss of interest, unless it can issue its retained profits as further loans to the business, earning more interest income. We will keep aside this possibility of retained profits by banks, assuming all banking profits are distributed.

Fourth, we do not segregate the output into production of capital goods and consumption goods. The capital goods produced remains within the corporate production sector as a whole, either as the fixed assets of the firms producing consumption goods or in the stock of unsold capital goods of the capital goods-producing firms. Thus, as a whole, the stock of capital goods produced remains within the corporate sector. There is, of course, a possibility of some incidences of mismatch between the capital goods available and the capital goods required for production of consumption goods, when we segregate two types of firms – firms producing capital goods and firms producing consumption goods. In such cases, some interesting adjustments in the circuit flows would take place, in respect of wage income and purchases of the households, sales of consumption and capital goods, and monetary profits of the capital goods- and consumption goods-producing firms. We do not explore this possibility here. Our implicit assumption is that no such significant mismatch occurs which the corporate sector cannot accommodate through adjustments in the production of capital and consumption goods quickly over the subsequent production cycles.

In the circuit production cycles, we notice that the closing stock of the goods produced that may remain after sales is a current asset of the corporate production sector. This means a simultaneous creation of an equivalent amount of nominal reserves as liabilities in its balance sheet, when the market value of the stocks, including the profit, is taken into account. Further, the corporate production sector also charges depreciation as the cost of production and, through it, creates a further nominal reserve as a capital asset replacement reserve, or alternatively accounts the fixed assets at their written-down values. The repayment of loan instalments is made out of the money profits retained by the corporate sector as undistributed profits. In fact, creation of these nominal reserves out of retained earnings is a phenomenon that evolved in the corporate production economy, which we do not find in earlier production systems. We shall mark the endogenous generation of these reserves as the origin of financial capital in the circuit.

Formulation of the nascent corporate economic circuit

To indicate the circuit flows and stocks we use some notations. The three sectors in the circuit are represented by 'p' for the production sector, 'b' for the banking sector, and 'h' for the household sector. We distinguish seven types of economic flows as 'e' for equity capital, 'd' for bank deposit, 'f' for bank loan finance, 'w' for wages, 'π' for profits, 'r' for interest, and 'c' for consumption. Using these notations, we can indicate the items of initial stocks and transfers, the items of circular flows, and the items of economic outcomes as shown in Tables 7.1a, 7.1b, and 7.1c.

Table 7.1a Items of initial money stocks and transfers

Wh	Wealth (net worth) of the earlier household production economy
Mhep	Money capital provided by households to corporate production sector
Mheb	Money capital provided by households to banking sector
Mhdb	Money deposits of households in banks
Mh	Money remaining as an item of wealth with the households
M	Total exogenous money stock in the economy
Mb	Money reserves maintained by the banks
Mbfp	Money finance or loan given by the banking sector to the corporate production sector

Note: All tables in the chapter are prepared by the authors

Table 7.1b Items of circuit flows

L	Quantity of labour flow from households to the corporate sector
Mpwh	Wage money flow from the corporate sector to the households
Mhcp	Money flow through households' consumption to corporate sector
O	Quantity of output flow of the corporate sector
Opch	Quantity of goods (sold) flow from corporate sector to households
Oa	Net accumulation of stock of goods with corporate sector
Mpπh	Dividend money flow paid by corporate sector on household equity
Mprb	Interest money flow on loans, paid by corporate sector to banks
Mbrh	Interest money flow on deposits, paid by the banks to households
Mbπh	Dividend money flow, paid by banks on household equity
Пap	Accumulation of nominal reserve in corporate balance sheet

Table 7.1c Items of economic outcomes

ρ	Value added price of goods transacted
Пp	Profit of production sector
Пb	Profit of the banking sector
dp	Depreciation charged to the cost of goods produced

We notice that by definition of the items, the following relations hold:

$$M = Mhep + Mheb + Mhdb + Mh = Wh \tag{1}$$

$$Mbfp = Mheb + Mhdb - Mb \tag{2}$$

$$Oa = O - Opch \tag{3}$$

$$\rho = Mhcp / Opch \tag{4}$$

$$\Pi p = Mpnh + \Pi ap \tag{5}$$

$$\Pi b = Mprb - Mbrh \tag{6}$$

Operation of the nascent corporate economic circuit

The nascent corporate economic circuit is essentially an open circuit interacting with the rest of the world with the stock of goods produced, which constituted a part of its wealth as the net result of the circuit. This is similar to the concept of 'wealth' in Adam Smith's *Wealth of Nations*, as a stock, which has been lost in the mainstream economics for its concern over national income or GDP as an item of flow. The essence of the corporate production economy would be lost from our analysis if we do not consider its possession of the accumulated stock of goods, simultaneously creating the nominal reserves of retained profits, as an item of wealth in money units or the financial capital of the corporate sector.

The terms we use as wealth, financial capital, and net worth need some clarifications. In common usage, wealth means the movable and immovable assets one possesses. However, some or all of these may be created out of debts, which are to be borne as liabilities. Therefore, to arrive at a proper measure of wealth, we deduct all debt liabilities from the total value of the movable and immovable assets owned. This difference is called the net worth, which we define here as the financial capital. Thus, all the three – wealth, net worth, and financial capital – bear the same meaning. In the case of corporate financial capital (or wealth or net worth), one of its important elements is the nominal reserves of retained profits – an internal generation or, rather, the self-generation – besides the equity capital contributed by the households.

How many units of output (Op) the corporate production sector gives in exchange for the money the households spend (Mhcp) is a crucial question. The corporate production sector follows the principle of pricing its output at 'cost plus profit'. That is, the benchmark price charged per unit of output that covers the wage, interest, provision for capital consumption or depreciation, and an element of profit. We assume, for the sake of simplicity, this price is the 'value added price' of the corporate production sector, ignoring the cost of intermediate material used and other expenses like rent and taxes. The loan repayment instalments are paid out of the undistributed monetary profit. Hence, the profit mark-up also covers the dividends to be paid as well as the amount required for loan repayment, besides keeping some retained profits for the company. This is, in fact, the accounting price. As per our notation, it is:

$$\rho = [Mpwh + Mprb + \Pi p + dp] / O \qquad (7)$$

These specifications complete the circuit formulation of the early stage of the corporate production economy. We may note that, at the accounting price, sales in money value, as realised by the corporate sector, will be:

$$Mhcp = \rho. Opch \qquad (8)$$

To keep aside at the moment the economic dynamics of savings, we assume the household sector spends all of its money income on the purchase of goods marketed by the corporate sector. The amount of money that flows from the household sector to the corporate sector through purchase or sale of goods is then:

$$Mhcp = Mpwh + Mp\pi h + Mb\pi h + Mbrh \qquad (9)$$

The right-hand side of (9) is the money flowing into the household sector in various forms of income, which it can spend on purchasing goods. We must notice here that the dividend income of the household (Mpπh), which we have included here, is the dividends paid by the corporate sector from the profit realised at the end of the previous cycle, since dividends are paid only after realising the monetary profit at the end of a cycle. We have assumed that the banking sector distributes all of its profits as dividends to the household sector. Therefore, the banking sector's profit (Πb) that goes to the household sector as money flow (Mbпh) is simply the difference between the loan interest it earns from the corporate sector and deposit interest it pays to the household sector, that is:

$$Mbпh = Mprb - Mbrh \quad or, \quad Mbпh + Mbrh = Mprb$$

Hence, we can replace (MbПh + Mbrh) in (9) by Mprb and get an alternative expression for (9) as:

$$Mhcp = Mpwh + Mpпh + Mprb \tag{9a}$$

We may now see how much money flows back to the corporate production sector and what happens to the stock of goods it produces in each production cycle. Would the corporate sector be able to sell the entire output and realise profit within the circuit? The money value of the value added output produced in a cycle, at cost plus mark-up profit charged by the corporate sector is obtained from (7) as:

$$\rho.O = Mpwh + Mprb + \Pi p + dp \tag{7a}$$

We compare it with the money value of the output purchased by the household sector. From (8) and (9) we get the amount of output (Opch) that may flow as sales to the household sector at the accounting price set by the corporate at ρ as:

$$\rho.Opch = Mpwh + Mprb + Mpпh \tag{9b}$$

Comparing (7a) with (9b) we observe that, theoretically, the quantity of sales flow (Opch) could be at the most equal to the total output flow (O) only if,

$$\Pi p + dp = Mpпh$$

Evidently, this condition cannot be fulfilled in corporate production systems. A part of profit has to be retained (Πap) by the corporate sector at least to repay the bank loan, besides retaining the depreciation element dp. Hence, sales quantity (Opch) at this accounting price ρ would be necessarily less than the output quantity (O), leading to accumulation of a stock of goods (Oa), unless repayment of loans and depreciation charges are put to zero and the entire profit is distributed to the household sector as dividends. We will examine this aspect in the following section on circuit results.

Sectoral balance sheets and the flow accounts

We now present the circuit formulation in terms of sectoral balance sheets and flow accounts to check the stock-flow consistency, following the current practice in the theory of monetary circuit (Gnos 2003; Zezza 2004; Dos Santos 2004; Allain 2007). There are non-monetary items in the circuit flow, like quantity of labour, quantity of goods purchased and sold, and quantity of the stock of goods. To draw the balance sheets and see that they do balance, we require totalling the assets and liabilities as well as the flows to and from the sectors. This we do by converting these items into money values.

The accounting price of the items, charged by the corporate sector, is used as the unit for conversion of the non-monetary items to their money values. In respect of stocks, whether the price used for valuation should be the current price or historical price is an important issue. There are likely to be items of different vintages in the stock. The accounting practices usually take the historical prices, but we require here the current market price to focus on the economic dynamics.

The next question is at which point of time we construct the balance sheet, and over which period we observe the flows. For the sake of simplicity of observing the net effects of the flows in the circuit, we may assume that each flow-cycle starts at the end of the previous cycle without overlapping, and money, output, and labour flows take place accordingly. Clearly, the observed balance sheet items would be different depending on at which point of time we are constructing the balance sheets – beginning of a cycle, end of a cycle, or at any point in between.

Let us assume that we make this observation at the end of a flow-cycle. That means the initial stock transfers of equity capital from the households to the corporate sector and banks, deposits from households to banks, and money loans from banks to the corporate sector have been completed in the organisational evolution of the corporate production economy. Thereafter the corporate production sector has completed the production, disbursement of wages, marketing and selling the output, payment of interest to banks and dividends to households, and is about to start the next cycle. Simultaneously, the household sector has received wages, dividend income from the corporate sector and banks, deposit interest from banks, as well as fully spent their money income on the purchase of the goods produced by the corporate sector. Banks have also received the interest money from the corporate sector and disbursed the dividend and deposit interests to the households.

The household sector's balance sheet and flow account

The household sector's balance sheet is shown in Tables 7.1a–7.1c. The households' wealth in the liability side is, in fact, the notional net wealth as the net worth, which is the difference between the assets held and the liabilities (debt) incurred. These assets may be the bank deposits, investments in equity of the banking and corporate sectors (in the forms of Mhdb, Mheb, and Mhep), and the balance of the state money (Mh) held. We have assumed here that there is no household debt at the nascent stage of the corporate productions. In any case, with Wh as the net worth (notional wealth) of the household sector the balance sheet would always balance. We can see from Table 7.2 that here, with no debts, Mhep + Mheb + Mhdb + Mh = Wh.

Table 7.3 shows the household sector's flow account. The left-hand side represents the debit side, showing the outflows from the household sector in money values, while the right-hand side represents the credit side, showing the inflows to the household sector in money values. Labour flow from the households to the production sector is represented in value terms on the debit side by L.(Mpwh/L). The wage income (Mpwh), the dividend income from the corporate (MpΠh) and from the banks (MbΠh), and the bank deposit's interest income (Mbrh)

Table 7.2 Household sector's stock balance sheet

Liability		Asset	
Wealth (net worth)	Wh	Business equity investment	Mhep
		Bank equity investment	Mheb
		Bank deposit	Mhdb
		Balance of State money held	Mh

Note: For explanation, see text

Table 7.3 Household sector's flow account

Debit (outflows)		Credit (inflows)	
Labour	L.(Mpwh/L)	Wage income	Mpwh
Expenditure on company products	Mpwh + MpΠh + MbΠh + Mbrh	Business dividend income	MpΠh
		Bank dividend income	MbΠh
		Bank deposit interest	Mbrh
Money value of goods consumed	Opch.ρ	Money value of goods purchased	Opch.ρ

Note: For explanation, see text

represent inflows to the household sector on the credit side. Next, we see that it spends its money income, we have assumed entirely, on the purchase of the goods marketed by the corporate sector, and so it comes again in the debit side as expenditure. The money value of the goods consumed (Opch.ρ) is an outflow, while the same goods that come into the household sector through purchase is an inflow, making the term Opch.ρ appearing on both sides, following the double entry system. The flow account is thus balanced.

We note that if the household sector did not fully consume the goods it purchased (say durables) during the current period, it would be shown as surplus goods saved and included as assets in the form of stock of goods in the balance sheet, raising also the wealth (net worth) in the liability side at the market value of them. Similarly, if they did not spend the entire money income, there would be money savings. It would be reflected in the balance sheet similarly, increasing the wealth (net worth) on one hand on the liability side, and the money savings held as asset on the asset side. Thus, the household sector account would remain balanced, but it will generate economic dynamics within the circuit, which we examine later.

The corporate sector's balance sheet and flow account

Tables 7.3 and 7.4 show the corporate production sector's stock balance sheet and flow account respectively. In Table 7.4, equity capital (Mhep) bank loans (Mbfp) are liabilities of the corporate production sector. Similarly, notional reserves kept for depreciation (dp) and profits retained by the corporate production sector are treated as liability. On the other hand, the value of the accumulated stock of goods produced by the corporate production sector is its asset (Oa.ρ), as is the money balance of this sector (Mhep+ Mbfp).

The corporate production sector's flow account in Table 7.5 shows on the debit side the outflows from the corporate production sector and on the credit side the inflows to the corporate production sector.

Table 7.4 Corporate production sector's stock balance sheet

Liability		Asset	
Equity capital	Mhep	Value of stock of goods	Oa.ρ
Bank loan	Mbfp	Money balance	Mhep + Mbfp
Reserve (retained profit)	Пap		
Depreciation reserve	dp		

Note: For explanation, see text

Table 7.5 Corporate production sector's flow account

Debit (outflows)		Credit (inflows)	
Wages paid	Mpwh	Sale of goods	Opch.ρ
Interest paid on bank loan	Mprb	Closing stock of goods	Oa.ρ
Depreciation charged	dp		
Dividend paid	Mpпh		
Retained profit transfer to reserve	Пap		

Note: For explanation, see text

Wages paid (Mpwh), interest on bank loans (Mprb), depreciation charged (dp), dividend paid (Mpпh), and retained profit transferred to nominal reserves represent outflows. The value of the stock of goods sold, Opch.ρ, is an inflow on the credit side. The money value of the closing stock of goods (Oa.ρ), though yet unrealised, is treated as an inflow. We may note that the value of closing stock here, for our purpose of analysing the economic dynamics as mentioned earlier, includes the profit mark-up element of the selling price. In current accounting practice now, the value of the closing stock is measured at cost to exclude the unrealised profits.

We can show that the flow account balances. By construction of the accounting price, as shown in (7a), we have:

$$(Opch+Oa).\rho = Mpwh + Mprb + \Pi p + dp$$

Further, we have from (9b):

$$Opch. \rho = Mpwh + Mp\pi h + Mprb$$

in addition, we have the distribution of profit relation (5) that gives:

$$\Pi p = Mp\pi h + \Pi ap$$

So we can write:

$$(Opch+Oa).\rho = Mpwh + Mprb + Mp\pi h + \Pi ap + dp \tag{7c}$$

Comparing (9b) and (7c), we see the following relation must hold:

$$\Pi ap + dp = Oa.\rho \tag{10}$$

Therefore, the flow account of the corporate production sector, as well as the balance sheet, will balance with Пap + dp = Oa.ρ. Second, we see the corporate sector has sufficient money balance to continue its activities, that is, to start the next cycle, because through sales it gets back:

Opch. ρ = Mpwh + Mpпh + Mprb.

Therefore, if a business unit decides to quit, then at the end of the cycle, it would have exactly the same amount of money balance (Mhep+ Mbfp), if there were no accumulated loss in course of its operations, which is required for paying off the equity and the loan. After that, by selling the accumulated stock of goods (Oa) at whatever price, it would be able to realise on quitting the accumulated wealth in money value. We must notice here that the items of reserves, retained profit Пap and depreciation reserve dp, shown as liabilities in the balance sheet, are only notional liabilities.

The banking sector's balance sheet and flow account

Tables 7.6 and 7.7 show the banking sector's stock balance sheet and flow account respectively. In Table 7.6, equity capital (Mheb) and deposits (Mhdb) by the household sector, through which money comes into the banking sector, are liabilities of the banking sector. On the other hand, assuming that the banking sector gives as advances (credit) the entire money mobilised to the corporate production sector, we put (Mheb + Mhdb) as asset of the banking sector. The money balance (Mb), if any, shown here as may be held by this sector is an asset, with a corresponding notional entry as reserve on the liability side. For

Table 7.6 Banking sector's stock balance sheet

Liability		Asset	
Equity capital	Mheb	Loan to corporate production sector	Mheb + Mhdb
Deposits	Mhdb	Money balance	Mb
Reserve money	Mb		

Note: For explanation, see text

Table 7.7 Banking sector's flow account

Debit (outflows)		Credit (inflows)	
Interest paid on deposits	Mbrh	Interest received	Mprb
Dividend paid	Mbпh		

Note: For explanation, see text

simplicity of our circuit formulation, we have put this as equal to zero, assuming that the banking sector lends the entire money it mobilises through equity and deposits.

The banking sector's flow account is in Table 7.7, with the debit side showing the outflows of money and the credit side showing the inflows of money. Interest paid on deposits (Mbrh) and dividends paid (Mbпh) represent the outflows from the banking sector. Interest received on corporate advances or loan (Mprb) is an inflow to this sector, represented on the credit side. Here also the balance sheet and the flow account are clearly balanced. This comes from the assumption that the banking sector does not retain its money profit, so that Mbrh + MbПh = Mprb.

The circuit results

The results of the economic circuit may now be considered. We keep aside at the moment the economic dynamics that may arise when agents or sectors in the circuit try to change their stock-flow positions. First, we assume that the households do not save their money income, which are fully spent on purchasing the output marketed by the corporate production sector. Second, we assume that at the nascent stage of corporate evolution, there exists within the national economy some households outside the circuit, who are the producers in the non-corporate production economy or in the agriculture sector, and that they spend fully the money they receive in exchange for their products on buying industrial output of the corporate sector. In this context, we must remember that historically the agriculture–industry terms of trade have been found to be always tilted in favour of industry. We will see that the existence of such non-corporate production economy within the national economy, or the rest of the world outside the circuit, acts as the womb essential for the nourishment and growth of the monetised corporate production economy at this embryonic stage.

Accumulation of financial capital

The circuit shows that an essential characteristic of the corporate production economy is the accumulation of financial capital. Even with a given stock of money, there can be continuous accumulation of stock of goods on one hand and nominal reserve as a source of financial capital on the other. This will accumulate necessarily in the corporate sector only. This will be unhindered as long as no sector in the circuit tries to change their stock and flow; that is, neither the production sector repays the money loan, nor the households save or withdraw their deposits.

We have noted earlier that financial capital originates at the early stage of the corporate production economy through the accumulation of nominal reserves within the system. We can calculate the rate of accumulation of nominal reserves per unit of revolving money capital in the circuit. In relation (10) the nominal reserve is:

$$\Pi ap + dp = \rho.Oa.$$

Let us denote the revolving money capital, Mk as:

$$Mk = [Mpwh + Mprb + Mp\pi h]$$
$$= \rho.\ Opch \quad \text{by relation (9b)} \tag{11}$$

The rate of accumulation of nominal reserve on revolving money capital, denoted by θ, can then be expressed as:

$$\theta = [\Pi ap + dp] / Mk$$
$$= Oa.\rho/Mk \quad \text{by relation (10)} \tag{12}$$

Then using relation (11) we get:

$$\theta = Oa/Opch \tag{13}$$

This means the ratio of the units kept in stock to the units sold determines this rate. If this ratio is, say, 0.20, then after five production cycles, the corporate production sector will generate and possess an accumulated stock of goods with market value (and corresponding nominal reserves) equal to the money capital it has put into the production. The higher this ratio the faster will be the generation. This clearly indicates the motive of the corporate production sector to generate higher surplus output to be retained as stock, by charging its profit to as little sales units as possible. This simultaneous motive of inventory building is generally not recognised in the flat assumption of profit maximisation. We can show that the rate of accumulation can be manipulated by the choice of the rate of profit charged on output, the rate of dividend paid out of profit, and the rate of depreciation charged.

Let the rate of profit on the value of output be β, which is:

$$\beta = \Pi p / \rho.O \tag{14}$$

and the rate of dividend paid is δ, expressed as:

$$\delta = M p \pi h / \Pi p \tag{15}$$

From relation (10) we get the retained profit as:

$$\Pi a p = Oa.\rho - dp$$

or, $(1 - \delta)\, \Pi p = Oa.\rho - dp$

Now, using relation (14) we get:

$$(1 - \delta)\, \beta.\rho.O = Oa.\rho - dp$$

or, $\beta\,(1 - \delta) = [Oa/O] - [dp/\rho.O]$

or, $\beta\,(1 - \delta) = [Oa/O] - [dp/\rho.O] \tag{16}$

Since δ lies between 0 to 1, we see that, when $\delta = 0$, there is no dividend paid and the stock per unit of output (Oa/O) accumulates by the rate of profit β plus the rate of depreciation charged to the output. In case $\delta = 1$, that is, all profits are distributed as dividend, the stock per unit of output accumulates only by the rate of depreciation charged to the output (dp/ρ.O).

Further, the rate of return of the corporate production sector on its revolving money capital, Mk, can be expressed as:

$$\Pi p / Mk = \beta.\rho.O / \rho.Opch = \beta.\,[1 + \theta] \quad \text{(using 13)}$$

or, $\Pi p = \beta.\,[1 + \theta].Mk \tag{17}$

This relation shows that the quantum of profit Πp of the corporate production sector is the product of three factors – the rate of profit on output (β), the rate of accumulation of the nominal reserve (θ), and its revolving money capital (Mk).

Given the amount of revolving money capital (Mk) as fixed within the circuit, if the corporate production sector tries to increase its profit by charging a higher mark-up price on output, it will result only in higher accumulation of surplus production per unit of output (Oa/O) with a matching increase in accumulation of nominal reserve. In the Gold Standard, money revolving in the circuit (Mk) is fixed, and so the corporate production sector will not get additional money flow from within the circuit to monetise the surplus production that is accumulating. For this constraint, the corporate production sector will not be able to make further investment of the financial capital that is growing in the form of nominal reserves. This creates a crisis within the corporate production circuit. The corporate sector would neither be able to repay the money loan to the banks, nor be able to expand its production activities, although it is making unrealised profit reflected in piling up surplus production accumulating as its stock of goods.

The circuit must expand

We usually overlook the implication of charging depreciation to the cost of production and thereby creations of capital replacement reserve in the system design of the corporate production economy. Because of this reserve, when the corporate production sector monetises its surplus stock of goods it becomes able not only to repay its bank loan, but also to finance the replacement of its existing capital asset, without taking any further bank loan. Through depreciation charges, the corporate sector creates its own financial fund to replace its worn-out capital goods. Evidently, the banking sector would then face a crisis. It cannot put the money, which it has received as repayment of earlier loans with interest, again on lending unless the corporate production sector seeks new loans for expanding its stock of capital assets to increase production. Charging depreciation as a cost of production, therefore, is a source of creating a macroeconomic instability in the system – a mismatch between the funds required by the firms and funds available with the banks, unless there is expansion of corporate production.

The corporate production sector in the circuit also stays at the edge of a fundamental crisis. It is the paradox of profit. From within the circuit it cannot get additional money flow to realise its profit, which remains only in the form of accumulating surplus production and nominal reserve, but not in money capital. The corporate sector must sell the surplus production outside the circuit to get the additional money flow to realise its profits. However, here again comes another crisis. When the profits are realised as additional money flow from outside the circuit and when the corporate sector repays its bank loans, the banking sector faces the crisis of excess liquidity unless the corporate sector takes new loans.

Further, the corporate sector, on realisation of more money profits than needed to repay the bank loans, would face the problem of unemployed financial capital in the form of idle money balance with them, unless it expands. The corporate production circuit, therefore, must be able to sell not only its surplus production, either to the domestic households still outside the circuit, if any, or to the rest of the world, but also keep on expanding its production and sales.

Money-hungriness of the corporate production circuit

The economic circuit of the corporate production economy always remains money-hungry. With the current stock of money and continuously accumulating stock of goods, the circuit is highly fragile, since the entire money in the circuit, being fully in circulation, cannot be allowed to stay anywhere for long. We will elaborate this point further in the final chapter in the context of digitalisation of money. Further, it stays at the edge of a liquidity crisis since the accumulated stock of goods can never be monetised within the circuit. Nevertheless, when the stock of goods is monetised through sales outside the circuit, excess liquidity generates within the circuit. To absorb it the circuit flows must expand. Again, when it expands, this additional money gets absorbed in the circuit and brings the same problem back. Therefore, when additional money is brought into the circuit for realisation of profits, it necessarily requires further expansion.

The circuit of the early stage of the corporate production economy, therefore, lives on squeezing money from and expanding over the rest of the world. However, with expansion of the circuit, as the rest of the world starts getting absorbed within the circuit, opportunities for further expansion become constrained and crisis develops for the economic circuit. Money injections through monetary accommodation policy (providing liquidity only) would not be able to solve this crisis in the longer run, when the possibility of expansion to the outer world ends for the circuit. This we will discuss in the following section.

Sources of growth and economic dynamics

Using the economic circuit, we can distinguish three possibilities – growth of the circuit that may be endogenous or exogenous, and the economic dynamics that may generate within the circuit when the agents or sectors in the circuit try to change their stock positions.

Endogenous or malignant growth

In respect of endogenous growth, we see that the economic circuit of the corporate production economy has a source within itself in the form of continuous accumulation of stock of goods and nominal reserves or financial capital even with the given money and at the same rate of output. However, constrained by the supply of money within the circuit, this continuous accumulation of financial capital in the form of nominal reserves keeps inflating only the stock of surplus goods with the corporate sector. As such, this does not automatically lead to any endogenous growth of the circuit by which the rate of output and other stocks and flows in the circuit may grow. This is, therefore, a situation of malignant growth, not matched by simultaneous growth in other stocks and flows in the circuit. This happens when the corporate sector is not able to monetise its accumulated stock of goods and expand production activities of the circuit. Therefore, the circuit achieves either its overall endogenous growth with additional money flows from outside the circuit, or it faces the problem of malignant growth in accumulation of stock (and nominal reserves). Thus, a simple conclusion follows – endogenous growth cannot be achieved by the circuit without simultaneous exogenous growth of increased supply of money or gold under the Gold Standard. Moreover, to keep on increasing production, the circuit requires also an increasing supply of labour.

Sources of exogenous growth

The exogenous growth enables the economic circuit to raise its rate of output, and correspondingly the other flows per unit of time. The sources of such growth are – first, the technological and organisational innovations that raise the flow capacity of the circuit channels (we will see this in the final chapter on the digitalised global financial economy); second, increased mobilisation of labour and money from the rest of the world; and third, technological innovation that directly raises the productivity of labour. In reality, none of these sources can materialise without the others. The historical growth of the early stage of the corporate production economy, from the 19th century to the 1930s, vindicates the interplay of these three sources, contributing to the endogenous growth of the corporate production circuit in the West.

The importance of organisational innovation as a source of growth (though not usually considered in economic analysis) was realised even in the late 19th and early 20th century in various organisation and method (O&M) studies. For example, Taylor's scientific management (1911), and the introduction of a moving assembly line in Ford's automobile production in 1913, were part of the O&M studies which now fall under the discipline of management cybernetics and operations research (Banta 1993; Hughes 2004). The interplay of endogenous and exogenous growth brought about by these three sources, and the dynamics that they may generate within the economic circuit, could be an interesting area of study. We will note here only the conditions required for the exogenous growth.

In respect of continuously acquiring gold (money) and labour from the rest of the world, three conditions prevailed historically that made growth of the economic circuit of the West possible at the early stage. These are the supply of labour, or especially the slaves from the colonies in the rest of the world, the domestic wage-gap between the industrial and non-industrial sectors, and the possibility of exploiting the rest of the world through the terms of trade, especially in colonial trade favouring the corporate industrial production. So long as these conditions prevailed, the economic circuit of the early stage of the corporate production economy could continue to grow even with the Gold Standard money. Again, this was possible as long as some amount of gold or Gold Standard money remained in the rest of the world.

In the historical growth process the nascent corporate production economy monetised its stock of accumulated goods through trade with the rest of the world and transformed the nominal reserves of financial capital into monetary capital, repaid the bank loans, and widened its production activities by taking fresh loans as required. The banking sector also built up gold reserves, enabling them to issue more money loans. Side by side, the household sector in the circuit could also get some increased rate of flow of consumption goods with increased real wages.

The third source of exogenous growth is technological innovations that improve the labour productivity. However, this may have an impact on creating some adjustments as internal dynamics in the circuit. The increased rate of output flow, brought about by higher productivity, may lower the accounting price to some extent, and thereby enable the household sector to get more goods in exchange for their money income. This happens except when the corporate sector appropriates the entire benefit of growth by raising proportionately the rate of profit (β) or lowering the rate of dividend (δ). However, this is not likely at the early stage of growth. The corporate production sector would rather raise money wages to attract more labour and pay higher dividends to attract more equity capital investments from the households, which are required for its expansion. So, with the increase in the rate of flow of consumption goods in exchange for their money income, the household sector may tend to save a portion of their money income. This generates a circuit dynamic.

Internal dynamics of household savings

In the economic circuit constructed here, household savings would lead to a peculiar dynamic, depending upon whether or not for the corporate production economy there exists the opportunity to sell its accumulating stock through net exports to the rest of the world. Let us first examine the economic dynamics that household money savings may generate. If, in the growth process, the household money income becomes higher than what they require for their current consumption, there will be household money savings put into the banks to earn interest income. The initial impact of it will be on the corporate sector. The corporate sector will not get back its revolving money capital through sales within the circuit. The return money flow through sales within the circuit has now reduced by the amount of money savings of the households. The corporate production economy, facing liquidity crisis, will react initially by lowering wage payments through wage cuts, cutting down production, or both. Side by side, increased household savings in bank deposits will tend to lower the deposit interest. Therefore, the banks may lower the loan interest to induce the corporate production economy to take new loans from these new deposits. Eventually, taking new loans from banks and cutting down only the money wages by the amount of interest on this new loan, the corporate production economy would be able to meet its liquidity crisis, maintaining the same level of money capital and production and prices. This will wipe out the excess wage income while increasing the interest income of the household sector. An income redistribution effect will take place favouring the rentier income of interest.

We now consider two possible cases – whether or not the corporate circuit has the opportunity to sell its output to the rest of the world. If the corporate production sector had no opportunity to sell its output outside the circuit (that was the typical case of the national economies in the rest of the world), the net outcome of household savings would be self-defeating. It would result in only redistribution of income in the household sector favouring rentier income (interest on savings) against money wage income. The increase in interest income, in turn, is likely to induce the interest-earning households to save more, and result in further wage and interest rate deflations that would ultimately wipe out such savings. The circuit balance sheet and flow accounts would once again balance with higher deposits by interest-earning households, higher bank loans to business, and lower wage income compensated by higher interest income of the households. Thus, we see here a peculiar paradox of income redistribution that lowers total wage income and increases total interest income – the more the wealthy households save, the poorer the poor wage-earner households become. The income inequality this redistribution may breed within the circuit is an important finding of circuit analysis.

On the other hand, if there were opportunities for the corporate sector to increase the sale of its output outside the circuit (the typical case of the national economies of the West), similar redistribution would occur, with household savings increasing the interest income in the circuit, but without wage and interest deflation. Here household savings would not be self-defeating, but rather required by the corporate sector for expanding its output with the necessary money capital raised through either further bank loans or new equity finance. Thus, the corporate production sector and the rentier income earners in the household sector would become wealthier, without affecting the wage rate, rate of profit, rate of dividend, and rate of accumulation. Therefore, when opportunities exist for the corporate production circuit to expand net exports to the rest of the world, a redistribution of income would take place due to household savings, but without causing a slowdown in accumulation and growth. Therefore, the resulting income inequality in the household sector would not be so much as we saw in the previous case.

This was the story of prosperity of the early corporate production economies of the West until the beginning of the 1930s. There were opportunities for them to increase exports to the rest of the world, that is, outside the circuit. Later on, when trade opportunities with the rest of the world started contracting, the Gold Standard money made monetisation difficult for the circuit. The resulting effect was liquidity crisis. In the wealthy West, the household money savings aggravated the liquidity crisis. This liquidity crisis resulted in the Great Depression with wage, price, and interest deflation; unemployment; production cuts; and bank failures. At the edge of this crisis, the economic circuit needed an evolution – an evolution of a financial system that would ensure unhindered monetary flow into the system. This evolution came through abandoning the Gold Standard of exogenous money and creating endogenous credit money within the circuit. With this began the post-war creditisation phase that led to the maturity of the nascent corporate production circuit of the West.

8 Matured corporate accumulation

The creditisation phase

The post-war period, following the Great Depression, saw a flowering of the corporate economy and marked a period of unparalleled economic growth and prosperity of Western capitalist nations. This is the phase of creditisation with the endogenous money creation by commercial banks in the form of credit, which came after the breakdown of the Gold Standard. In this phase of post-war monetary expansion, the corporate production economy registered high growth and productivity in industrial production.

We call this the stage of matured corporate production circuits that evolved in Western economies after World War II. Here, the circuits continue to appropriate the surplus production and monetise it to realise money profits. The retained profit and nominal depreciation charge that accumulate as nominal reserves become the sources of internal generation of additional financial capital. Besides the foreign exchange earnings from net exports creating additional money flow, the credit money created by banks removes the monetary constraint of the Gold Standard for expansion. Therefore, the accumulation of financial capital and its investment in production could bring unabated expansion. However, as we will see later, as more and more liquidity is brought into the system through creditisation to cater to the never-ending need for expansion, the system becomes more vulnerable to liquidity crisis and ultimately moves towards another crisis – falling productivity and stagnating industrial production due to the stagnation in consumption demand for industrial products.

Maturity of the corporate economy – institutional evolutions

From 1945 to the 1960s, several factors helped monetisation and the consequent expansion of the system. We have seen earlier in our discussion in Chapter 6 that to overcome the problem of mon-etising the stock of surplus production in the circuit, two things are required simultaneously – monetary expansion (Monetarist school) and income generation through fiscal policy (Keynesian school). The matured corporate production circuits in the West evolved through the institutional evolution of both. We see the coming of credit money with centralisation of the banking system and abandoning the Gold Standard on one hand, and the move to Keynesianism by the states on the other. In view of the removal of the Gold Standard another institutional evolution, presumed as required, was the Bretton Woods system of international monetary management, which was, however, abandoned later. We begin with a brief account of evolution of these institutional frameworks during this period.

Centralisation of the banking system and credit money

While the obligations to the Gold Standard put obstacles on monetary expansion, the possibility of unhindered monetary expansion came with the breakdown of the Gold Standard and the move to fiat money. The breakdown of the Gold Standard is seen by scholars like Eichen-green as the key to the European recovery from the Great Depres-sion. The move to fiat money stimulated the economic recovery with output, prices, employment, and investment rising more quickly in nations that went off the Gold Standard (Eichengreen 1992: 21).

After the Great Depression the US economy became stronger. The political developments in Europe beginning in the 1930s caused huge gold inflows to the United States, leading to a dramatic rise in its money supply (M1) by nearly 10 percent per year between 1933 and 1937 and even higher in the early 1940s. Romer contended that the growth in US real gross national product (GNP), at an average rate of over 8 percent between 1933 and 1937 and over 10 percent between 1938 and 1941, was not due to any self-correcting response of the US economy, but because of this unprecedented monetary expansion that followed after 1933 (Romer 1992: 757–59).

We find the coming of the modern central banks when the Gold Standard began to collapse after World War I. Since 1920, Bank of England, under the governorship of Montagu Norman, had been making deliberate efforts to move away from commercial banking to become a central bank, and was finally nationalised in 1946. In the United States, the Federal Reserve was created by the US Congress in 1913. The formalisation of the banking system under central banks was a key development – it allowed endogenous generation of money by the banking system. The central banks, acting as the 'lender of the last resort', meant that the commercial banks could create credit money and use it to accommodate the demand for credit coming from the business sector. Rothbard pointed out that the essential purpose of central banking was to use the government privileges to remove the limitations on banking for monetary and bank credit inflation. However, the removal of the Gold Standard was also necessary because the operation of the Gold Standard would severely limit the inflationary potential of the banking system even under central banking (Rothbard 2008: 125–33).

In this system of banking, deposits generate loans or credit money, which, due to the 'money multiplier' of the fractional reserve system of banking, become multiple times the deposits. The post-Keynesian accommodationists (Moore 1988; Rogers 1989; Lavoie 1992; Smithin 1994; Rochon 1999) point out that the changes in money stock are driven in the first place by the private sector's loan demands, which the commercial banks are obliged to accommodate (Cottrell 1994: 593–96). As they create additional credit money in response to such demands, banks have to provide for extra reserves to meet the reserve requirements set by the monetary authority for maintaining the mandatory convertibility of bank deposits into fiat currency on demand. The central banks, to maintain the confidence of the banking system in itself as 'the lender of the last resort', cannot refuse to supply the needed reserves in the banking system. The best the authorities can do to restrain the process of creation of bank money is to adjust the terms on which they supply the base money (Cottrell 1994: *Ibid.*).

With every creation of a loan, there is a creation of a new deposit, and thereby, increase in broad money and the money supply – a two-way relation between loans and deposits. For the commercial banks to remain viable, deposits must be converted into loans, as they are liabilities of the banking sector on which interest has to be paid. On account of the fractional reserve system, loans created will be multiple times the deposits with the banking sector, as every loan is again a deposit, with credit generated being accommodated fully by the central bank, leading to an increase in money supply (Rothbard 2008: 161–70). The amount of bank money which banks could safely create was virtually unlimited provided that the banks made sure that the clearing losses were compensated by gains. A capitalist economy cannot function without credit and credit money – full-bodied commodity money is incompatible with capitalism (Wray 1990: 58).

The credit creation ability of the banks serves as a boon for the corporate economy, as it can overcome its liquidity problems as well as expand its level of production with credit money. With expansion of the corporate production, there is again further creation of nominal reserves in the balance sheet of the firms and, to monetise it, they will require more credit. With endogenous money, banks accommodate the increased demand for credit by the corporate sector and the accumulation of financial capital by the corporate sector becomes unhindered. A capitalist system cannot be constrained by commodity money or savings (Wray 1990: *Ibid.*).

Banks now can create credits and thereby increase the supply of broad money, but how will it come into circulation in the circuit unless it reaches people in the form of increased money income that would generate consumption demand for industrial products? Along with the centralisation of the banking structure, now we find a simultaneous move to Keynesian policies during this period that stressed income generation to boost up demand. It propelled the evolution of political governance supportive of fiscal management in the form of deficit financing and tax cuts. Deficit financing by the states played a crucial role in this period of expansion of the corporate economy.

Keynesianism and income generation

Keynesian economics was a dominant force in the aftermath of the Great Depression. The Keynesian fiscal policy emphasised government intervention to apply stimulus when the economy was going down and to curb liquidity in times of an excessive boom. During the post-war period this idea influenced policymaking in both the developed and the developing countries. Following the Keynesian principles, the policies of the New Deal came in the United States, and a massive public works program was instituted by President Roosevelt in response to the Great Depression. Mobilisation for World War II and a significant rise in government purchases of goods and services in the United States, from $14 billion in 1940 to $88.6 billion in 1943, had contributed to liquidity injection following the Great Depression (Case and Fair 2007: 474; Dowd and Hutchinson 2010: 8).

With the massive war-oriented expenditures of the 1940s and rising government expenditures, income increased sharply and unemployment fell. The Keynesian principles dominated US policymaking in the 1950s through the 1960s. In the United States the expansion of the corporate system has continued since the 1950s with increased credit creation by the banking system, government's deficit financing, and capital account deficits that maintained the international monetary order. The Keynesian economists – like Samuelson, Heller, and

Galbraith – became advisors to President Kennedy and influenced the Kennedy–Johnson tax cut of 1964 – a Keynesian program designed to stimulate economic growth through deliberate deficit financing (Skousen 2008: 517).

The US corporations in this period were able to expand their markets, productivity, and profits at unprecedented rates. Their after-tax profits from overseas investments grew from 10 percent at the beginning of the 1950s to over 20 percent by the early 1970s, fuelling their productive capacity further in the 1960s. This was helped by the international position of the American firms to dominate through the Marshall Plan in other developed markets in Europe and also by the US military occupation of post-war Japan. This period marked the rise of the United States as the dominant geo-political power (Barlow 2003: 32–3).

Bretton Woods and international liquidity in corporate systems

With the removal of the Gold Standard, an international monetary order was needed to ensure expansion of the corporate economy through international trade. The 1930s were marked by major trade imbalances of Western countries leading to the adoption of widespread protectionism and deflationary policies, competitive devaluations, and the eventual abandonment of the Gold Standard. The breakdown of the Gold Standard was followed by a restructuring of the international monetary system at the Bretton Woods conference in 1944. Delegates from forty-four countries assembled at Mt. Washington Hotel in Bretton Woods, New Hampshire to bring about a new international system of governing the exchange rates and foreign lending. Among the most important features of the system were the fixed but adjustable exchange rates and setting up two new international organisations, the International Monetary Fund (IMF) and the International Bank for Reconstruction and Development (IBRD) or the World Bank (Bordo 1993: Preface; Pilbeam 2006: 262). The proponents of the Bretton Woods system wanted a set of monetary arrangements that would combine the advantage of exchange rate stability with the independence to pursue the national full employment policies (Bordo *Ibid.* 1993: 5–27).

One of the immediate sources of liquidity injection in the international monetary system was the United States Marshall Aid Plan for the reconstruction of the war-torn European economies. The Marshall

Plan channelled approximately $13 billion as aid (grants and loans) to Western Europe between 1948 and 1952 (Bordo *Ibid.* 1993: 41). The Marshall Plan proved successful in propelling the US dollar as the main source of international liquidity. This helped the United States gaining huge financial power and influence as the supplier of the world's key currency. It also enabled the United States to avoid the discipline that the international monetary system imposed on the other states, and New York emerged in this period as the financial hub of the world economy.

The growing private and official demand for dollars was supplied by persistent balance of payments deficits of the United States throughout this period. From the early 1950s onwards, the United States moved from its post-war surplus to deficits of approximately $1.5 billion per year. As the demand for international liquidity was met with increasing dollar liabilities, the economic system witnessed stability and growth in the initial years of the Bretton Woods system. However, foreign dollar holdings exceeded the US gold reserves for the first time in 1960, leading to the reluctance on the part of its trading partners to accumulate more dollars as reserve currency. With the US involvement in the Vietnam War, its balance of payments position deteriorated further, although little was done to reduce the size of the deficits during this period. By 1971 it was apparent to speculators that the dollar was overvalued, and the US balance of payments surfaced a huge capital outflow in anticipation of dollar devaluations. In view of the massive speculation against the dollar, President Nixon on 15 August 1971 announced that the dollar was no longer convertible to gold, bringing an end to the Bretton Woods system. As was argued and predicted famously by Triffin (1960), the Bretton Woods system collapsed from the inherent contradiction in the dollar–Gold Standard. Triffin pointed out that as international trade grew, the demand for international reserves or the US dollar would also grow. To meet the demand for international reserves, the Bretton Woods system depended on the United States running deficits, while the countries running surpluses were purchasing dollars to prevent their currencies from appreciating. Hence, over time. the stock of the US dollar liabilities to the rest of the world increased and became higher than the annual addition to the US gold reserves from gold-mining activities. In other words, US liabilities in gold deteriorated and eventually the convertibility of the dollars into gold at $35 per ounce became practically impossible (Pilbeam 2006: 266–69; Cohn 2008).

Stagnation in the real sector

For the corporate production economy, the opportunities for continuous expansion of its production activities remained crucial. The needs of the corporate production sector and the banking sector were intertwined. If the opportunities for expansion of the corporate production economy dried up, the banks would face the problems of utilisation of the credit to be generated, as its deposit liabilities must be converted into interest-earning loans. It was a perennial problem since every loan created new deposits in the banking sector. On the other hand, the corporate system also depended on the banking sector for monetary expansion to monetise its accumulating stock of goods and thereby convert it into financial capital in liquid money assets. The financial capital thus generated would again seek further opportunities of investment. This in turn would reflect back on rising bank deposits through an increase in income.

Historically, the post-war growth of the corporate production system in the West was so much so that it was popularly called the 'Golden Age of Western Capitalism'. It was marked by a sustained increase in growth and labour productivity as the post-war reconstruction period allowed ample opportunities to expand. There were also financial markets that provided some avenues for investment in financial assets, but these were mostly the first-generation financial commodities like bonds, bills, and securities, which were linked with the production and trade activities.

However, the 'maturity' phase lasted for about two decades only (1945–65). The corporate production economy, that was the real sector of the economy, started facing a crisis again. The crisis in this phase came, first, with the drying up of opportunities to expand industrial production, as the consumption demand for industrial goods was reaching its saturation, while the investible financial capital kept on accumulating. Second, the productivity growth experienced by industrialised nations in the post-war period ended sometime around 1973 with a dismal productivity record. That there was a fall in both labour and total factor productivity during this period, compared to the preceding 'Fordist' era, was confirmed by several studies (Nordhaus 1982, 2004; Cullison 1989; Gordon 1995; Wolff 1997; Kozicki 1997). The combined effect of the two was stagnation in the real sector. This we discuss in Chapter 2 at some length.

The post-Fordist stagnation was followed by an explosion of investments in the service sector beginning in the 1970s, as corporate financial capital and the banking sector scouted for new avenues of investments. This growth of the service sector created what was known as 'the service sector paradox', as it grew in spite of the fact that service sector productivity was seen to lag behind the productivity of the manufacturing sector in Western capitalist countries (Kozicki 1997; Wolff 1997; Maclean 1997; Baumol 2001).

The service sector initially provided some outlet, but soon the opportunities for investment in the service sector also reached their limits. The maturity phase of capitalist economies was thus marked by decreasing demand and, consequently, falling investment opportunities in the real sector. A few downturns in economic activity surfaced, as the entrepreneurs' overestimate of demand for their output fell short of actual demand. This in turn made a number of bank loans, given to the corporate sector, non-performing and the banks had to become cautious in giving credit.

A growing mismatch was developing between the increasing need of the banks for extending credit and the firms' investment opportunities, which were decreasing. Consequently, the 1980s were marked by a flood of lending to the developing countries as the banking system looked for greater and greater avenues for credit creation (Eatwell and Taylor 2000: 36). This had an impact on the international financial systems and the balance of payments, particularly of the less developed countries (LDCs).

The international monetary system returned to floating exchange rates following the breakdown of the Bretton Woods system in 1971. In 1973 the first oil shock came. With the Arab–Israeli conflict, OPEC (Organisation of the Petroleum Exporting Countries) quadrupled the price of oil that led to a significant deterioration of the terms of trade of the oil-importing countries with the OPEC countries. The non-oil exporting LDCs were the worst sufferers of the rise in oil prices and recession in industrialised nations, as their import bills were going up against declining exports to the West. The LDCs, as a group, experienced massive current account deficits, which rose from \$8.7 billion in 1973 to \$51.3 billion in 1975.

The floating exchange rate system was legitimised at the Jamaica Conference in 1976. In addition to abolishing the official price of gold, the member nations of the IMF underlined the importance of special drawing rights (SDRs) for overcoming their international liquidity problems. The second oil shock came in 1978 with further rises in the OPEC price of oil, contributing to a global rise in interest rates. Major recessions set in in the United States and the United Kingdom in the early 1980s (Pilbeam 2006: 273–79). The 1970s and 1980s continued to be the periods of stagnant growth, productivity, and employment in the real sector of the developed and developing countries of the world.

The economic circuit with credit money

We may now present the economic circuit of the matured corporate production economy supported by credit money and try to bring out its implications. Compared to the earlier economic circuit of the nascent corporate production economy, the fiat money of the states now evolved, replacing the earlier Gold Standard money, and enabled credit creation by commercial banks. The central banks evolved as the monetary authority. The central bank now can issue money against the government security, control the money supply within the state and act as the custodian of the foreign exchange reserves of the state, and try to prescribe (fixed exchange system) or monitor (floating exchange system) the value of the domestic currency vis-à-vis other foreign currencies. The lower portion of the circuit diagram in Figure 8.1 depicts this evolution.

The circuit diagram traces out the circuit flows and the creations of stocks. A remarkable change is that the stock of gold reserve in the previous circuit is now replaced by foreign exchange (FX) reserve. Further, with net foreign exchange earnings, which build the foreign exchange reserve, the domestic money supply increases since the central bank issues domestic money against the foreign exchange. So, with trade surplus (or net exports), foreign exchange flows into the economy creating additional money flow. Trade deficit, on the other hand, leads to outflow of foreign exchange (or domestic money), meaning outflow of money from the circuit.

The inflow and outflow of foreign exchanges and variations in the exchange rates now determine the exogenous money of the circuit. There is another source of money supply – the endogenous money within the monetary circuit. The institutional evolution of the fractional reserve system brings a magnification effect on the creation of credit money by the banks. The credit money that the banks can now create multiplies in the process of money circulation as deposit–credit–deposit that generates from every additional money deposit.

Thus, the possibility of credit creation by commercial banks removes the 'golden fetters' of the earlier Gold Standard. Restriction on the supply of money is no more a problem in the corporate production circuit. Nevertheless, the banking sector now stays on the edge of another type of crisis – on mobilisation of deposits it must immediately lend it out

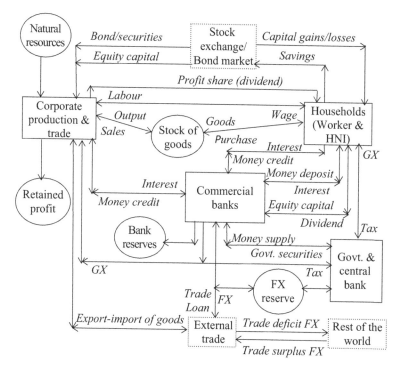

Figure 8.1 Matured corporate economic circuit: creditisation phase since the 1940s

Notes: Construction explained in the text

HNI = high net worth individuals; FX = foreign currencies;

GX = government subsidies and expenditure; GX–Tax = fiscal deficit

Source: Prepared by the authors

as credit. Where will this demand for bank credit come from unless the corporate production circuit expands its production activity?

The central part of the circuit, that is, the production flow, has remained the same as the nascent corporate production circuit we discuss in Chapters 6 and 7. The corporate production sector, by selling its goods produced at cost plus profit mark-up price, accumulates the surplus production in its stock. The problem of monetising the surplus production and thereby realising monetary profit within the circuit still remains. When the corporate sector monetises this surplus production through sales outside the circuit, either to the households still remaining outside the circuit but within the domestic economy, or through net exports to the rest of the world, it faces the problem of accumulating money capital more than it requires as revolving money capital for the current level of production. It must, therefore, seek to invest this accumulating financial capital by expanding its level of production. And as it expands production, the problem of monetising the surplus production accentuates and continues.

We also see that within the production circuit the 'paradox of thrift' remains – a rise in household saving creates accumulation of more surplus production and the corporate production sector fails to get the revolving money capital, which it has spent on production, flowing back to it. In the nascent corporate production circuit with the Gold Standard money, the household savings from wage income necessarily led to liquidity crisis for the corporate production sector, if it did not have net exports to the rest of the world. This in turn used to lead to the contraction of production, unless the corporate sector could recapitalise the money capital by taking money loans from banks or by bond and equity financing from within the circuit. But this was not possible as the money supply within the circuit was fixed by its Gold Standard money. Now with the endogenous credit money created by the banks, the matured corporate production circuit can quickly overcome this liquidity problem with bank credits.

When the corporate sector realises money profits, it is likely to pay dividends on equity shares that go to the household sector, and may even raise the money wage rate to get more workers from the households for increasing its levels of production. In both cases, the income of the household sector increases, creating the possibility of household savings. The internal dynamics that the household savings generates within the circuit of the nascent corporate production is discussed at length in Chapter 7. Now we examine its implications at the matured stage.

Household savings, as shown in the circuit diagram, flow either to the commercial banks as savings deposits or to the security market as investments in corporate bonds and equities. So far as it flows to the banks as deposits, there will be credit money creation by banks and the corporate production sector will get money credits to recapitalise its money capital. But if the household money savings are channelized to the capital market for speculative trading on the existing shares and bonds in the form of speculative holding of money, the corporate sector will not be able to recover the money capital through new credits by banks and it will face liquidity crisis in financing its current level of production. It is unlikely that, in such situations, with already unsold goods, the corporate sector would go for raising more money capital by new issue of shares in the security market. Thus, the flow balance of the corporate production circuit is quite fragile – a slight change in the direction and quantum of money flow, out of the household savings, may lead to a liquidity crisis.

An important distinction should be made here between the nature of wage income and that of dividend income. Wage income of the households flows over time during the production activities of a production cycle, whereas dividend incomes may come only at the end of a production cycle after the surplus production is monetised as realised profits through sales (whether outside or inside the circuit) and distributed by the firms as dividends. Therefore, while savings by the wage earners traps the circuit in liquidity crisis due to failure of the firms to get back their revolving money capital through sales to the households, no such trap can arise in the case of savings out of dividend income, since the question of dividend income arises only after realising money profits over and above the revolving money capital. Nevertheless, in the case of dividend income, problems may crop up in the circuit balance from another direction, depending on how the dividend money income is spent. A part of the dividend income is likely to be spent on the purchase of consumption goods, and another part saved in bank deposits or invested in purchase of equities or bonds. For the part spent on the purchase of consumption goods, there will be a possibility of inflationary rise in the prices of consumption goods, particularly when full monetary profit is already realised by the corporate sector by selling the entire surplus production. In that case the corporate sector will not have unsold surplus consumption goods left in its stock of goods – it has already monetised the surplus production through sales for generating the money profit from which the dividend has been paid. In this case, with the rise in prices, the firms will realise more than mark-up profits leading to accumulation of more money capital and thus get signals to increase their level of output in the subsequent production cycles.

On the other hand, when the dividend money income flow is saved, a part of it might go to the banking sector as money deposits. Now the banking sector will face the problem of lending it out, and so this will depress the rate of interest, inducing the corporate sector to go for increasing its production in the following production cycle by taking additional bank credits (money loan). The remaining part of the savings out of dividend income will go to the capital market for purchasing equity or bonds. This will enable the corporate sector to raise more money capital from the capital market through the issue of new equities and bonds. However, if this part of savings from dividend incomes is used mostly for speculative trading on the existing equities and bonds (for speculative capital gains rather than earning more dividend incomes), then the corporate sector will not have sufficient scope for raising fresh capital from the capital market. Thus, here also the flow balance of the corporate production circuit is quite fragile – changes in the direction and quantum of money flow, out of the dividend income, may destabilise the balance.

Even when the corporate production circuit recapitalises its money capital by bank loan or additional equity or bond financing, it stays on the edge of the crisis of continuously monetising the stock of surplus production. Like the nascent corporate production circuit, the matured production circuit also depends on export to the rest of the world to monetise its surplus production. With endogenous credit creation by banks, the corporate production sector can now overcome its liquidity problems only in the short run by taking bank loans, but not monetise the surplus production. In the long run it has to increase its sales to monetise the surplus production. It is only through monetisation of surplus production that it can repay its bank loan, pay dividends, and also retain some undistributed profit to internally generate money capital for expanding the scale of production. Thus, fundamentally the matured corporate production circuit faces the same crisis as the nascent corporate production circuit.

The stock of gold reserve in the nascent corporate circuit with the Gold Standard money is now replaced in the matured corporate production circuit by the FX reserve. What would be its implications for the developing countries in the rest of the world? As the corporate circuit of the West monetises its surplus production by net exports (export minus import) to the rest of the world, the additional money flow that comes into it has to be absorbed by increasing the money capital investment in production, so that all other flows in the circuit increase simultaneously to keep the overall circuit flow in balance. Therefore, a rise in net exports, leading to an increase in money capital and thereby production, will subsequently require even more rise in net exports. Since net export to the rest of the world means matching negative net exports by the economies there, the liquidity crisis of the West gets shifted and replicated in these economies in the form of deteriorating FX reserves due to a growing balance of payment deficits, which ultimately leads to devaluation of their currencies.

The new avenues of monetisation

Compared to the nascent corporate production circuit, however, two new avenues have now opened up in the matured production circuit for monetising the surplus production to an extent within the domestic circuit. The first one has come from the Keynesian mechanism of boosting up demand and thereby sales within the circuit through government fiscal deficits. For the economies in the rest of the world with negative net exports (imports more than exports) and consequent outflow of money from the circuit, this becomes essential for maintaining the sales of their corporate production sector within the circuit. These economies, therefore, tend to suffer from growing fiscal deficits, beside their balance payment deficits.

The second avenue for boosting up sales within the circuit is to induce the wage income earners in the circuit to spend more than they earn by taking bank credits. This will obviously help the corporate sector to monetise its surplus production and realise profit from within the circuit. But, when the wage-earning households pursue this consumerism and a part of the dividend income also goes for purchasing consumption goods within the circuit, there will be the possibility of inflationary rise in prices with zero or even negative savings, implying growing indebtedness of the household sector. There will be no capital formation in the circuit, other than in the corporate sector's retained profits and depreciation reserves. Moreover, the corporate sector will get back the dividends it has paid, through sales at higher prices, and realise in the following production cycles profits more than the mark-up.

To consume more or save more

Our circuit analysis here brings out a simple, yet important, puzzle of the mainstream economic theory. Should an economy save more or consume more for achieving economic growth? The classical and neoclassical conclusion was to save more, whereas the Keynesian prescription was to consume more. Saving more is necessary to create capital formation that may be invested as increased money capital for expanding production. But this will depress the flowing back of revolving money capital to the corporate sector through purchase (or sale) of the output produced, as the household sector in the circuit now consumes less. On the other hand, increasing consumption will boost up flowing back of the revolving money capital to the corporate sector through purchase (or sale) of the output produced within the circuit, but depress capital formation as the household sector now saves less. Considering the aggregate flow of money as given within the circuit we get no clear answer to this puzzle. For achieving growth of output, savings is necessary to create money capital and consumption is necessary to ensure that the additional output would be sold. But, the fact is, both cannot occur simultaneously.

This riddle could be solved if we disaggregate, as shown in Figure 8.1, the household sector into workers and HNIs, and the corresponding money income flows into wage income and dividend income or rentier income, including capital gains and losses. These three types of income flows are marked separately in the circuit diagram in Figure 8.1. We have already mentioned an important difference between the natures of wage income flow and dividend income flow over time. Wage income flows out of the corporate sector in the course of a production cycle as outlay of cost of production and flows back as sales when the wage earners buy the output. But dividend income flows only after the surplus production is monetised as realised profit through the sale of output, that is, at the end of a production cycle. So, we get a simple answer to the question – whether an economy should consume more or save more? The wage income earners should consume (not save) more to ensure that the revolving money capital flows back by the sale of output to the firms and the dividend income earners should save more to ensure capital formation required by the firms to increase output levels. We may mention here that historically the wage rate of the workers has remained more or less around the subsistence level, and nowadays are governed by the so-called minimum wages acts, which implies that the workers may not be able to save. The classical economic ideas conformed this in Ricardo's subsistence theory of wage, which had a reflection even on Marx's theory of surplus value. In modern times, besides the workers, we also have the salary income-earning employees in a slightly higher bracket. But again, being flooded with various types of bank loans, they are induced to spend more than they earn. From this observation surfaces a simple fact about the operation and growth of a production circuit, which has some far-reaching implications, but yet remains outside the scope of economic analysis.

Self-contained endogenous growth

Can the corporate production circuit be self-contained and have endogenous growth? Within its own circuit (without export or import outside) the matured corporate production circuit can operate and grow successfully when three conditions are simultaneously fulfilled – one, more workers, or workers with higher productivity, are engaged, even with paying higher wages, but they, at the same time, are induced to spend more than their income on purchasing the output produced, either out of past monetary savings or by taking bank loans. Two, the dividend income earners, by and large, should save their income and put it in new bank deposits or invest in new issues of shares and bonds creating additional money capital for the corporate sector from equity or bond financing. A third condition is necessary since inducing the wage income earners to spend more than their income cannot be stretched far. Therefore, there must be some other sector or source in the circuit, where outflow of money (spending) is more than its inflow of money (income), so that the sales in the circuit can increase through purchases by this sector when the circuit output increases. This source, within the circuit, is clearly the deficit fiscal expenditure by the government – the famous Keynesian prescription. So we have the third condition – the government must run fiscal deficit (increasing its public debts or debts to its central bank). Only when these three conditions are fulfilled, money flow, as may be returned to the corporate sector through sales, would generate money profit over and above the recovery of revolving money capital outlay in production.

The root of growing indebtedness

The matured corporate production circuit, when it grows within itself, necessarily pushes the household sector (not including the HNIs) and the government to growing indebtedness. This was not possible for the nascent corporate production circuit operating with Gold Standard money. These avenues for growth of the corporate production circuit now, or more precisely the growth of the corporate sector and the HNIs, are founded in the creditisation phase of the matured corporate production circuit with creation of endogenous money and Keynesianism in the state fiscal system. From this we get a clue to explain why economic growth in recent times is necessarily accompanied by growing public debt and household debt across the world. This will be an inevitable outcome of the circuit growth at its final stage of evolution into one global financial circuit, which we discuss next in the chapter on the financial circuit.

When growth of a corporate production circuit is not restricted within itself, that is to say, when a corporate production circuit can realise net exports through trading with the rest of the world, the need for indebtedness of the household and the government within the circuit would be eased to the extent of the money value of the net exports. But this will mean growing indebtedness of the importing countries with the matching negative export surplus (imports more than exports). The negative net export in these countries would necessitate more public and household debt in these countries. Thus, the matured corporate production circuit can operate successfully, realising its monetary profit only when it grows, which in turn means growing indebtedness of public and household debt, whether inside the circuit or in the rest of the world. The economic circuit reveals a simple fact: economic growth brought about by accumulation of corporate monetary profits necessarily means that there must be growing indebtedness – some others must become more and more indebted in the process.

Corroborating the circuit results

To corroborate the results of our circuit analysis, we may now look into the historical track of the maturity of the corporate production circuit during the period 1945–65. With the post-war reconstruction founded upon the institutional evolution of the endogenous system of credit money creation by commercial banks, the Keynesianism of the state fiscal system, and the Bretton Woods arrangements of international monetary transactions for a period of time, the corporate production circuits in Western economies came into the phase of maturity beginning in 1945. The golden era of industrial growth began. At the beginning, with innovations in industrial technology, the average productivity of labour was rising and so was employment, output, and even the real wage rate, raising the average standard of living in the West. The circuit growth became possible with growing net exports of these economies to the developing nations in the rest of the world. However, at its counterpart, the developing economies in the rest of the world, with widening negative net export, started facing growing indebtedness in the process – their balance of payments was dwindling, foreign exchange reserve was depleting, which pushed their currency to the verge of devaluation, and fiscal deficits were growing, leading to inflationary rise in domestic prices.

This golden period of Western industrial growth, however, did not last long. By the end of the 1960s the rise in the average productivity of labour was slowing down, as the initial benefits of new industrial technology was tapering off, and net exports of the West to the developing economies was stagnating and the developing economies reached limits of indebtedness. Above all, the consumption demand for industrial goods and services by the households was reaching its saturation point even in the West, as physical consumption of goods could not be stretched infinitely even with induced consumerism. Moreover, the operation of the economic circuit had already bred growing income inequality. This had its consequence on consumption demands. Consumption demands for the industrial final products and services came mostly from the urban households in the high income brackets, but they tended to save more with a higher propensity.

The result was stagnation in the production circuit, that is, in the real sector of the economies – surplus production was accumulating which could not be monetised, and so the money capital in the production circuit was stagnating. Consequently, the production flow of the circuit stopped growing. But endogenous credit creation by the banks, with its interest income flow and the government fiscal deficits, could not be restrained to tune to this stagnation in the production circuit. As a result, stagnation in the real sector was found to be accompanied by inflationary rise in prices – a paradoxical situation, which was named stagflation in textbook economic theories.

By the beginning of the 1970s the global economic scenario was a confusing mess. The economic circuit was once again found to be at the edge of a crisis – stagnation, inflation, growing fiscal deficits of the governments, and balance of payment crisis, accentuated by the oil price hikes forcing devaluation of currencies in many countries. With the consumption demand for industrial products reaching its saturation point, the corporate economic circuit sought another way of boosting up consumption expenditure by the households, that is, by service consumption. By the late 1960s service consumption started growing with the launching of newer service products, and the corporate production circuit found a new avenue for its expansion in service production. This growth of the service sector seemed unexplainable since its productivity lagged behind that of the industrial manufacturing sector.

However, the expansion opportunity for the corporate circuit brought about by the service production also proved to be insufficient for two reasons. First, like consumption of industrial products, service consumption cannot be stretched infinitely. Second, the service products of the 1970s – namely bank and insurance services, hotels, tours and travels, transportation, communication, as well as sports and entertainment – were, by and large, the high-end products meant for high-income groups or the HNIs. The larger section of the household sector in the lower income group remained outside the service sector net during this period.

The confusing mess in the global economic scenario continued in the 1970s and 1980s. There were apprehensions that another global economic crisis was brewing, and the economic circuit was awaiting another much-needed evolution at this edge of crisis. In the later part of the 1980s and in the early 1990s the ICT revolution opened a new horizon for investments in financial commodities. The evolution of a financial economy was in the making and a new economic circuit was born – the financial circuit. It is possibly the Final Circuit in the evolutionary path of the corporate economic circuit that originated in the 1850s, which we examine next.

9 The financial circuit
Leveraging the growth

The crisis that was brewing in the 1970s due to stagnation in industrial growth ended in the 1990s with the evolution of the financial sector, which opened up new avenues of investments for the accumulating financial capital. The ICT revolution that started in the late 1980s made financial transactions of money values possible almost instantaneously across the world. Since the 1990s a global financial web has been growing. It opened up a new horizon for financial transactions, creating as well as squeezing surplus flow of money values anywhere at any time. As its corollary, the nature and function of money was transformed. Other than for petty purchase and small savings that we see mostly in the developing and LDCs, transactions in physical currency notes became almost extinct in the developed world.

In the financial circuit, money values now flow through transactions in the digitalised financial web in the form of inflow (receipts) or outflow (payments) of financial accounts. Any transaction of money values can now be made just through account transfers. Thus, money has become digitalised and so virtual, acting only as a unit of account in a digitalised financial web. The monetary constraint that was imposed earlier on the growth of the economic circuits by the limits of physical money flow (Gold Standard or fiat) or the credit money that could be created upon it is finally removed completely.

The second impact of the ICT-led global financial web is seen in the emergence of a new generation of financial commodities – the derivatives and structured securities and their packaged combinations in diversified financials, which can convert any future flow of money value into a current financial asset that generates rental income. These financial commodities are bought and sold in the financial markets for making financial gains through price speculations or for hedging the risk of the uncertainty in future prices, as well as for earning the future cash flow from the asset as the rental income. The emergence of these new financial commodities and its implications are discussed at length by Crotty (2008). Conventionally, mainstream economic theories consider only two types of incomes from financial assets, namely the capital gains and the dividend income, and overlook the rental income in the form of future flow of money values from securities, whether asset backed or mortgage backed. This rental income is a distinguishing feature of the financial economy. Here, any mortgage loan or any other agreement creating a claim on a future cash flow can be converted through securitisation into a current financial asset. The holder of these financial assets gets the cash flow, as it comes as rental income, along with a possibility of capital gains on selling the asset.

Alongside these developments, the erstwhile national barriers to global financial flows were removed through institutional reforms that had started with structural adjustments in the developing countries, followed by the economic reforms of liberalisation and privatisation. To create a single global trade system by removing the trade barriers of countries, a new institution evolved, known as the World Trade Organisation (WTO), with which the current phase of globalisation began. In the era of globalisation, the erstwhile country-centric corporate production circuits, now also including services and diversified financial commodities, were merged through a process of financial integration into one global system – the global corporate system. Thus, another economic evolution took place. A global financial economy as a single economic circuit was born.

The financial economy has now become so complex with its intricate real-time linkages in the global financial web that no government or governments and their regulatory agencies together can make any effective regulation to monitor its operation. Most of the global financial transactions now flow through the TNCs and a number of corporate havens beyond anybody's control. In Chapter 2 we mention the global network of the TNCs and the 'super entities' as found in a study (Vitali, Glattfelder, and Battiston 2011). So, the circuit now works almost autonomously. The experience of the global financial crisis of 2008 has vindicated this.

We do not mean that this circuit already prevails all over the world. But it is extending and integrating the economies, having almost no economic boundary. The recent rise of the so-called emerging economies or the BRICs (Brazil, Russia, India, and China), with growing linkages with the global circuit, is a typical feature of this extension. It may be argued that the growth centres of industrial development are now shifting from the West to the East or South East, or that by the business process outsourcing of the foreign firms for cheap labour, a dependent production structure is evolving in the domestic economy. But such issues come only when we try to view these developments in terms of our prevailing notion of geo-political boundaries of national economies. However, these boundaries are becoming almost non-existent economically in the global financial circuit. In fact, the global financial economy, with its giant TNCs, neither really has a specified country centre, nor has any preference to be guided by the national interests of a particular country.

There are several other complex developments in the evolutionary process of the global financial circuit, like corporate restructuring, emergence of new-generation financial commodities and securitisation, and the changing role of banks. There were also concerns over leveraging and creating economic bubbles, and the onset of the global financial crises. We include a brief note on these aspects in the Appendix for the interested reader.

We now explore how the financial circuit operates – how it tends to grow to absorb the accumulation of financial capital within the single economic circuit and falls into financial crises that become systemic for it. A major concern, especially after the global financial crisis of 2008, is the economic crises to which the global financial circuit might lead us, in spite of its economic growth. We are now having a paradoxical situation of growth and crises, mentioned at the beginning of this book. Are not these developments, which appear paradoxical in our mainstream economic theories, in fact systemic for the global financial economy? We need to explain how the following phenomena arise:

- growing concentration of wealth and income in a few giant corporations and HNIs;
- rising capital intensity in spite of growing unemployment;
- rise in operational and financial leveraging to the advantage of larger companies;
- increasing financialisation leading to a growing share of rentier incomes;
- stagnating growth of production in the real sector and shifting production towards high-end products and shrinking production of wage goods or basic items of consumption;
- recurrent occurrence of financial crises at different segments of financial markets; and above all
- growing indebtedness of the state and the household sector.

The Final Circuit – global financial economy

We may now look into the operation of the global financial economy that leads to these paradoxical developments. Our analysis with economic circuit methodology would provide some answer to these paradoxes. We take up the analysis first by probing the corporate objective of leveraging and its implications.

Leveraging – growing capital intensity and rentier income share

In the functioning of our present economic systems a 'growth of dangerously high system-wide leverage' is seen from cross-country and firm-level evidence, which raises the systemic risk (Crotty 2008: 50–4). We also see that two more characteristic features of recent economic growth are increasing capital intensity of production and redistribution of income. Though both are found in the same growth process, in the current research directions they are treated as separate phenomena. Some studies focus on the former, often referring it as 'jobless growth', and some others examine the latter, considering it as a process of financialisation with rising rentier income in comparison to wage income. The root of this separation lies in the framework of mainstream economics where labour intensity (or capital intensity) of production is considered purely as a matter of choice of production technique depending upon the relative factor prices, independent of corporate financial decisions. Here we try to find a link between the three – leveraging, rising capital intensity, and redistribution of income shares.

In respect of rising capital intensity of production, some studies allege that the labour market rigidities, imperfections, or distortions are the cause of capital–labour substitution, leading to 'jobless growth' in recent years (Dutt 2003: 16, 25). Rowthorn (1995, 1999) and Bhaduri and Marglin (1990) consider the role of capital formation and capital–labour substitutions in creating jobless growth. There are also some studies that put forward categorically that the sharp increase of real wage rates is the cause of the rise in the capital–labour ratio (Ahluwalia 1992; Ghosh 1994).

In another direction of research, several studies focus on financialisation, defining it as the increase in the income share of rentiers at the expense of wage income. In this group, one may refer to the studies by Argitis and Pitelis (2001, 2006), Epstein and Power (2003), Dumenil and Levy (2004), Epstein and Jayadev (2005), Power, Epstein and

Abrena (2003), and Stockhammer (2004, 2005–06). The effects of financialisation on different forms of income redistribution are also considered. Some consider that shareholder demands for higher distributed profits lead to a declining share of wages in national income (Boyer 2000). Another implication of the shareholders value orientation is the increasing gap between wages and white-collar managerial salaries. In post-Keynesian models of growth and distribution, Palley (2006) and Lavoie (2009) have analysed this phenomenon of 'cadrisme'. Van Treeck (2007) has studied the effects of changes in interest and dividend payments on the firm's mark-up. There are also some efforts to create an integrated framework, introducing interest rates and debt in Kaleckian models of distribution and growth, to study the effects of changes in interest rate on income distribution, capacity utilisation, capital accumulation, and profit rate (Hein 2006).

We propose an alternative direction of research, to explain simultaneously both of these two phenomena in a single framework. Since both the phenomena, that is, rising capital intensity and income redistribution, are outcomes of the same process, we need to study the underlying common process, instead of separating them by different approaches. This common process of the recent economic growth, which is so far overlooked, is leveraging in corporate financial structure and production structure. In fact, increased leveraging is the other phenomenon that is observed in recent growth process. But current studies are yet to bring this into the directions of research and derive its economic implications.

Let us note how the corporate leveraging works. First, two components of leveraging are distinguished – operating leverage and financial leverage. The degree of operating leverage (DOL) calculates the magnification effect of a percentage increase in sales quantity on the resulting percentage increase in operating profit (earnings before interest and tax or EBIT). The degree of financial leverage (DFL) calculates the magnification effect of a percentage increase in operating profit on the resulting percentage increase in earnings per share (EPS). Combining the two we get the degree of combined leverage (DCL) of a firm that calculates the magnification effect of a percentage increase in sales quantity on the percentage increase in the earnings per share (Brigham and Ehrhardt 2017).

Second, in corporate finance the objective of a firm is considered to be increasing the earnings per share, and therefore, towards this objective, a firm usually tries to use leveraging. Third, the EPS–EBIT indifference analysis in corporate finance shows that higher financial leveraging can be chosen only by firms with higher levels of operating profits. Below a minimum level of operating profit, financial leveraging will not be effective in ensuring higher earnings per share. So, firms with low levels of operating profits, that is, the smaller firms, do not get the advantage of financial leveraging (Brigham and Ehrhardt 2017).

Now we come to its economic implications. To reap the benefit of operating leverage in the production structure, firms would always prefer to replace the variable labour costs by fixed costs using a more mechanised production process (e.g. fixed lease rental and depreciation charge on machines and related overhead costs of production). The more the fixed costs of production the higher will be the percentage increase in operating profits brought about by percentage increase in sales quantity. So, the fixed costs in the production structure act as the fulcrum of operating leverage – the higher the fixed costs of production the higher will be the DOL. The advantage of operating leverage gives a clear explanation why firms prefer to go for a capital-intensive production process. Rising capital intensity through automation and mechanisation of even clerical works is now a fact seen in the larger companies. For this reason, it would be incorrect to consider that labour intensity or capital intensity of production is merely a matter of technological choice with respect to the relative factor prices. By increasing capital intensity, firms derive financial benefits through operating leverages. This is similar to the proposition of rising organic composition of capital in Marxian terminology.

Next, we notice the benefit of financial leveraging. It works through raising fixed charges in the financial structure by increasing the interest-bearing debt finance in relation to equity finance. Here also, these fixed charges act as the fulcrum of the lever – the higher these fixed interest charges the higher will be the DFL. By this leveraging, a percentage increase in operating profit leads to a magnified effect on percentage increase in earnings per share. Therefore, firms, especially the large ones including financial companies and banks, to reap the benefits in a finance-led growth regime, would increasingly go for leveraging, as seen in recent times.

We look at some misconceptions in the ideas of shareholders value orientation and the corporate objective, especially under the conditions of a finance-led regime. The corporate objective of raising the earnings per share (EPS) needs to be emphasised properly. The effects of financialisation on investment behaviour of firms have been discussed extensively by a number of authors in post-Keynesian models of distribution and growth. It is argued, as a general proposition, that in the process of financialisation, the policies to 'downsize and distribute' are likely to replace the policies to 'retain and invest' (Lazonick and O'Sullivan 2000). Crotty (1990) has considered the 'owner-manager conflict' at the firm level. Stockhammer (2004, 2005–06) underlines the 'growth-profit trade-off': the phenomenon of managements supporting growth (accumulation) and shareholders vying for the short-term profit maximisation (dividend income). Boyer (2000) similarly proposes a model with shareholders imposing a 'financial norm' on management. However, although this general proposition gives us an easy and quick way of explaining the rising share of dividend income, it overlooks a few straightforward facts of corporate decision-making because of the sweeping generalisation that shareholders value orientation works only in terms of higher distributed profits or dividend payout.

Contrary to the sweeping generalisation of shareholders value orientation in terms of dividend payout only, we may mention four facts. First, in shareholders' objectives, especially in situations of finance-led growth, EPS is much more important than dividend per share (DPS). In such situations, investments are made in shares for capital gains, rather than for dividend incomes. Generally higher EPS is expected to be reflected in appreciation of the market price of shares. Moreover, institutional investors are more concerned about the market value of shares rather than pressing for a policy of 'downsize and distribute' to earn higher rates of dividend per share. Second, earnings per share is the accepted yardstick of measuring corporate performance by both the shareholders and the managers – there exists neither any conflict of interest in this regard between them, nor any 'growth-profit trade off' so far as increasing EPS is concerned. With the same DPS/EPS, higher EPS would naturally mean higher DPS. In fact, EPS is more fundamental, as it determines the ability of a firm to pay dividends. The proposed 'growth-profit trade off' may arise only when at the same level of EPS a firm decides to raise the DPS/EPS, which is a case rather unlikely in reality. Third, in shareholders' objective also, the growth of the firm by raising EPS, while maintaining their controlling interest through leveraging, is a cherished goal rather than 'downsize and distribute'. We may mention here that in the case of financial leveraging, that is, debt financing instead of equity financing that brings in new shareholders, the existing shareholders maintain their controlling interest. Moreover, when growth leads to increased EPS, the existing shareholders get higher dividend per share even at the same dividend payout ratio. So, neither 'downsize and distribute' nor 'growth-profit trade off' would be the shareholders' true concern. Fourth, whether lucrative dividends (DPS) are being paid currently or not, the investors in the share market rest their judgement more on the basis of EPS in estimating price-earnings ratios, known as P/E ratio.

Accepting that increasing the earnings per share is the common motive of both the existing shareholders and the management, we may examine the implications of leveraging. Leveraging can be seen as a common process leading to both rising capital intensity and rentier income. First, we notice that operating leverage and financial leverage go hand in hand – one requires the other. As a general principle of corporate finance, long-term debt finance essentially forms permanent capital, which goes for creating fixed assets, rather than being used as working capital. For this reason, financial leveraging would necessarily require increasing the use of machines in the production process, raising the capital intensity of production. On the other hand, a firm desiring operating leverage by introducing mechanisation would require additional financial investments over and above the working capital. This would call for debt financing with financial leveraging, at the given rate of interest, so as to protect the controlling interest of existing shareholders as well as enhancing the EPS. Because of this reason, leveraging in the finance-led growth regime, which we may call leveraged growth, necessarily results in rising capital intensity on one hand and rising debt financing on the other.

Whether increasing debt financing would subsequently tend to raise the interest rate in the capital market would depend on the flow of finance to the capital market. Here, we need not consider the probable subsequent macroeconomic impact, noting that a firm undertakes an investment project only when the rate of operating profit (EBIT) it generates is more than the interest as the cost of capital and corporate taxes. By all such investments, with positive earnings after interest and tax, DOL will necessarily create a magnification effect on EPS.

The second implication is also quite obvious. In the process of leveraging, while wage income declines, dividend income increases as earning per share increases, even with the unchanged dividend payout ratio. Moreover, total interest income also increases with increasing debt in corporate capital structure. Thus, income redistribution with rising share of dividend as well as interest as rentier income, and a declining share of wage income, are natural outcomes of leveraged growth.

The third implication of leveraging, though indirect, can be derived to get a complete structure of a theory of leveraged growth. Leveraging would require rising flow of debt financing to the corporate sector and this becomes possible with rising income inequality in the households' income distribution. The household sector is the ultimate source of providing debt finance. With income redistribution brought about by corporate leveraging, the section of HNIs within the household sector realises growing rentier income. The debt finance required in the process of leveraged growth flows out from the savings of this section of the household sector.

We may mention another aspect of rising capital intensity and income redistribution in the process of leveraged growth. We have already noted that only the large firms with higher levels of operating profits can reap the benefits of leveraging. This explains why we find empirically the phenomenon of rising capital intensity particularly in large-scale units. This phenomenon is not so strong in medium- or small-scale units (Uchikawa 2003). With the benefits of leveraging, the large firms grow faster than the medium or small firms. Leveraged growth thus results in another type of inequality. Side by side with the growing income inequality in the household sector, we see that, in the corporate sector as well, large firms become even larger, creating an increasing inequality in the firm-size distribution in the leveraged growth process.

The circuit design of the global financial economy

We may now consider the circuit design of the global financial economy. Unlike the country-specific open-ended economic circuits with foreign trade we saw in the earlier nascent and matured phases of corporate production, here in the era of globalisation, we have one closed global economic circuit, having intricate linkages in the global web of financial transaction, domestic and outsourced production, and trade. There are of course different layers or segments of the global circuit's spread over different countries with national currencies (other than in the Euro countries) and local economies that are still subject to some local dynamics. But these may be soon taken over by the dynamics of the global circuit.

Virtual money now flows in the circuit in the form of account transfers creating surplus or deficits in the accounts, and the US dollar now continues as the global monetary unit of account only. We can no more distinguish between money and capital markets. The distinction has become obscure. Instead, we have one financial market and the erstwhile distinction of the capital flow and money flow being erased as they are now merged simply into fund flows in the form of receipts and payments in fund accounts.

We should keep a note of an important point here. Globalisation is not complete as yet – there still exist in the developing and less developed countries some large number of dispersed local production and financial transaction economies, not yet linked or integrated with the global circuit. The financial transaction or savings by the individual household in these local economies may look quite petty, but when pulled together they make a sizeable amount of financial fund. We will see later that the prospective growth of the global financial circuit now lies in spreading globalisation in these areas also, linking them to the global financial circuit.

The chart of the circuit is presented in Figure 9.1. We have marked three types of economic agents in three sectors – the corporate sector, the household sector, and the government sector. As before, we have shown them in the diagram in marked rectangles. In the corporate sector now, we have the companies in production activities of the real sector, as well as the banks and financial companies of the financial sector. We show now, not the stock of goods produced, but the composition of output flow as sales. The stock in trade is included in the variable capital of the corporate sector. Further, money, foreign exchange, or gold reserves, which we saw in the earlier circuits, do not appear any longer in a single global digitalised financial circuit, as they, being virtual entities, remain in financial accounts only.

The household sector has two sections – the workers and employees and the HNIs. The HNIs earn most of their personal incomes from the ownership of financial and real estate assets. Their personal incomes and assets, as well as liabilities, are clearly distinguished from those of the companies in the corporate sector. They are marked as HNIs as they have high positive net worth, meaning financial value of their assets is more than the debt liabilities.

Some care must be taken in calculating separately the net worth of the HNI vis-à-vis that of the corporate sector. We deduct from the assets of the HNIs the investments made by them in corporate equity capital, which is included in corporate net worth. This is required to avoid double counting. Further, for the sake of simplicity of understanding, what are shown as the household and government debts are actually the negative net worth (excess of debt liabilities over assets) of these two sectors, not their total debts. Once again it is important to remember that this household sector does not include the HNIs. This we mention particularly because the statistical data on household net worth we get now include also that of the HNIs.

The workers and employees in the household sector depend on wages and salaries as their primary sources of income. They are the

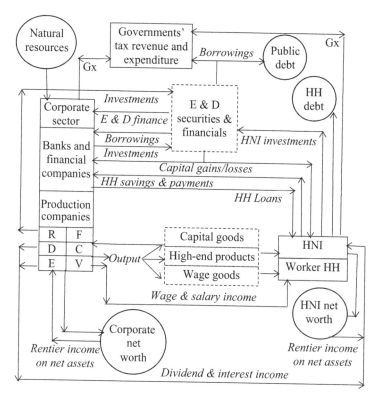

Figure 9.1 The real and financial circuit

Notes: Constructions explained in the text

E = equity capital; D = long-term debt; C = fixed capital assets; R = retained profit; V = working capital; F = financial assets; HNI = high net worth individuals

HH = households; Public debt = accumulated fiscal deficit of governments

Gx = flow of government tax revenue and expenditure

Source: Prepared by the authors

consumers of the wage goods of basic needs produced by the corporate sector. On the other hand, the HNIs in the household sector are the consumers of the high-end products that include luxury items, consumer durables, and five-star services. The primary source of income of the HNIs is rentier income, that is, the rental income from ownership of financial and real estate assets, and dividend income on shareholding. There are, of course, two other components of their income, namely, the salaries and bonuses of the corporate

CEOs, and capital gains arising on marking-to-market of the financial assets, if any.

It is important to note what constitutes rentier income. Usually we focus more on the dividends earned as profit share and interests earned on loans as the sources of rentier incomes. But a far more important source of rentier income is now the flow of rental earnings on real and financial assets held. In the case of assets, held as real estate properties including land and infrastructure as well as natural resources, rent and royalty flow to the asset owners as their incomes. For the financial assets held as securities or some tranches of them, whether asset backed or mortgage backed, the generation of the money flow from these comes to the owners as another source of rent income. The HNIs having net assets over their debts, reflected in their net worth, have the rental earnings on such assets as an important source of their incomes. Similarly the companies in the corporate sector also, besides their usual revenue earnings from the regular lines of business, earn rentier incomes from the net real and financial assets held by them, which are reflected in their net worth.

The government sector operates by collecting various taxes as its revenue from the households and corporate sectors, and incurring expenditure on providing them the public goods and subsidies. The excess of expenditure over its revenue is the fiscal deficit met by borrowing from the financial market against the issue of government securities. This accumulates as the public debt.

How the circuit works – the circuit results

We now look at the transaction flows among these agents in the three sectors in Figure 9.1. As before, we mark the direction of the transaction flows by lines with arrow heads. Arrow heads in both ends of a line indicate two-way flows. For example, the tax revenues flow in and public expenditure and subsidies flow out from the government sector. We note that in the financial market, which is indicated in the diagram by a rectangle of dashed lines as being notional, the equity and debt (E&D) securities and the financials, as well as the loans or borrowings, create supply of securities and investments mean purchase of these securities.

The stream of scheduled repayment of household loans and savings deposits as well as all committed payments to the banks and financial companies create supply of securities via the process of mortgage and asset backed securitisation by the financial companies. Besides this, the government borrowings, the borrowing for leveraging by the financial companies, and the issue of shares and securities by the companies also create supply of securities in the financial market.

The investment or the purchase of securities comes from the financial companies and the HNIs and now, in some cases, also from the public deposit-taking banks. Another source of investment in securities, usually through the SPVs, generates from the retained earnings of the corporate sector. As mentioned earlier, the investors get the cash flows from the securities as their rental income. Besides that, the capital gains, which may arise from appreciation of price of the securities due to buying pressure in the market, also accrue to the investors, that is, to the companies in the corporate sector and the HNIs in the household sector. These capital gains or losses on financial assets accrue on a daily marking-to-market basis to the investors' margin accounts held in the trading exchanges.

The output of the production companies is now shown as segregated into the capital goods that go to the corporate sector as fixed assets, the high-end products for HNI consumption, and the wage goods for basic consumption of the low-income group households, namely the workers and employees. There are two income flows generating from the production activities. These are the wages and salaries going to the workers, and the dividend and interests going to the HNIs. Over and above these, the HNIs have further sources of income from rentals earned on net assets held and capital gains.

The circuit design as shown in the diagram in Figure 9.1 has three distinct parts. The upper part of the diagram shows the circuit design of the financial sector and the central part shows that of the real sector. In the lower part, we have the rental income flows from the net assets held by the corporate sector and the HNIs.

Creation of asset price bubble

The first two parts of the circuit design, the real and the financial circuits, do have links, but the financial circuit has an avenue for spiralling up its own activities, independent of the real sector. This avenue is financial leveraging by the banks and financial companies, that is, to invest in financial commodities using borrowed funds. The companies in the corporate sector and the HNIs invest on (buy) securities and derivatives to make speculative capital gains by buying cheaper and reaping the benefit on a marking-to-market basis in situations of rising prices of these commodities. In such situations, the more the fund invested in buying the financial commodities, the more is the gain. This leveraged fund can come from borrowing from the security market itself by issuing (supplying) new securities and investing the fund obtained again on buying securities with expected price appreciation. Evidently, leveraged investments create, on one hand, supply of new securities and, on the other hand, investments in these securities that creates buying pressures that lead to price appreciation and opportunities for further leveraging. Thus, it spirals up the prices of financial assets, leading to creation of an asset price bubble. But there is a simple condition for this to happen – funds flow into the particular financial market must keep on growing so that, on one hand, borrowing of funds for leveraging becomes possible and, on the other, buying pressure appreciates the price of the financial assets. Continuously growing the flow of funds in a financial market would lead to continuous general appreciation of price in that financial market, which will ensure net capital gains for all investors there. Otherwise, without a continuous pouring of funds, capital gains would be cancelled out by capital losses, making net capital gains of all the investors in the financial market equal to zero in that market. We discuss this in more detail in the Appendix. This is in fact what we see today in financial market segments. Time and again we have seen asset price bubbles in different segments of financial markets; for example, the Asian financial crisis of 1997, and the worst being the US housing bubble of 2007.

Growth of high-end products but stagnation in the real sector

As discussed earlier, companies, especially the larger ones, always tend to leverage their production and capital structure for raising earnings per share. The operating leverage, increasing the capital intensity, squeezes the wage and salary incomes, while financial leverage blows up the interest and dividend incomes. Further, wages and salaries are spent mostly on consumption of basic wage goods and high-end products are mostly purchased by dividend incomes. As a consequence of the demand signals that generate in the market, the composition of output of the production circuit, so as to match the demands for the types of products, tilts towards high-end products and capital goods.

By the same line of argument, we come to another important conclusion – leveraging in a finance-led growth regime necessarily creates demand depression in the real sector. The demand for capital goods is generated only as a derived demand. The only sources of final demand are the demand for wage goods for mass consumption by the workers and employees and the demand for high-end products for consumption by the HNIs. However, the increase in mass consumption demand cannot create sufficient demand for output since wages and salaries do not increase proportionately with output due to operational leveraging. The dividend and interest incomes of the HNIs from production activities do increase due to financial leveraging. But due to the meagre number of the HNIs in the total population as well as due to their higher propensity to save, demand for high-end products alone cannot create sufficient demand for boosting up the real sector production activities.

Grow with growing indebtedness

We now take up the question of the paradox of profit in the production circuit. We saw in the earlier phases of nascent and matured corporate production that income generation within the production circuit could never be sufficient for realisation of profit through the sale of the surplus production. For realisation of profits, additional money values must flow into the production circuit from outside. In the earlier phases of nascent and matured corporate production we had country-specific open-ended circuits trading with the rest of the world, and saw that the production circuit of a country could realise monetary profits and grow only through net exports outside, implying growing indebtedness of the rest of the world. At the matured phase, we had, in addition, for the realisation of monetary profits within the circuit, the growing indebtedness of the households and the governments. But now we have a single global circuit built by the financial economy, which appears to be closed, having no rest of the world national economies other than some scattered local economies not linked to it. Naturally, we may ask how this global economic circuit tackles the problem of the paradox of profit in it.

The global economic circuit overcomes the paradox of profit creating additional money values (receipts) now flowing into the circuit from different sources. First is the fiscal deficit of the governments. Governments, spending more than their revenue incomes, with public debt from the financial sector, generate additional flow of income or receipts in the circuit. Next is the household debt. When the current consumption spending of the households exceeds their current income, as met by loans taken from the financial sector, additional flow of receipts takes place in the circuit for realisation of corporate profits.

The household and government debts, when amortised, create a further flow of rental income (receipts) on the debt security assets in the financial market that goes to the corporate sector and the HNIs. So, apparently, we have a third source from which additional money values may flow into the circuit generating corporate receipts for realisation of profits in the real sector. The rental incomes of the HNIs from the net assets owned by them, to the extent they go for purchasing high-end products, create this additional flow of money values from the financial circuit into the production circuit. But again, we notice that increase in the flow of rental incomes from financial securities comes, in fact, from the growing indebtedness of the household and the government sector that generates the necessary additional flow of funds into the financial circuit. Thus, ultimately the paradox of profit is overcome here also by growing indebtedness as before – the households and the governments must become more and more indebted in the circuit.

Our next conclusion is that the global financial circuit can continue to operate only when it grows. The realised flow of profits in the production sector as before, and the rental incomes flow from the net assets held by the corporate sector and the HNIs, add to the accumulation of financial capital, which needs to be invested again. A part of it would go to the production sector for expanding output of the high-end products and another part to the financial sector for financing the household loans and government borrowings, as well as for purchasing real estate assets and other contracts having future cash flow. The sequence repeats. In this sequential growth, household indebtedness grows and they fall into a debt trap, with increasing portions of their current incomes now going for amortised loan repayments. This growth process of the global financial circuit, with continuously growing future contracts and virtual money, seems to follow the Hicks–Lindahl sequence economy as developed later by Hahn (1965, 1973) and Radner (1972).

The growing public and household debts create cash flow-generating financial assets, which keep on flowing into the global financial circuit. This keeps it operating and growing. The current global scenario of rising public and household debts corroborates our finding that the global financial circuit grows only with growing indebtedness. On the other hand, the outcome of the growth process is growing accumulation of wealth of the corporate sector and the HNIs, as well as rising income inequality between the wage and salary earners and the rentier income earners. The simultaneous accumulations of debt and wealth are reflected in the stock positions in the global financial circuit. All inflows add to stocks and all outflows deplete them. In the diagram of Figure 9.1 we have encircled the five types of stocks. The stock of natural resource is given as a gift of nature. It depletes with the outflows of extractions made for production activities. However, we do not assign economic values to this stock, so it remains outside the economic calculations of gains or losses.

The other four stocks – namely the net worth of the corporate sector, net worth of the HNIs in their personal accounts, the debts of the governments, and the debts of the households (other than HNIs) – keep on accumulating with the growth of the global financial economy. Theoretically, if it were possible to calculate and construct a balance sheet of the global financial economy, these four stocks would have been balanced – net public debt and household debts as liability would balance the net worth of the corporate sector and the HNIs as assets. These assets and liabilities keep on accumulating in the continuous process of the growth of the financial economy. Thus, in our circuit framework the concept of endogenous economic growth appears to be a myth, since within the global financial circuit economic growth necessarily means simultaneous growth of indebtedness, making creation of wealth just a fictitious construct for the privileged.

The present treading upon the future

How do we interpret the functioning of the global financial circuit? It functions by treading upon its own future. Every debt means a commitment to repay from the future income. In other words, debt means we are financing our current spending from the future income. So, the growing public and household debts in the global circuit means it thrives on its future income. If future income flows can be brought into the present as financial assets, which it does by securitisation, the opportunities for growth of financial capital can be made limitless, provided the future growth is everlasting.

The corporate sector and the HNIs with accumulated high positive net worth now hold absolute power over the economic future of the others. In all debt agreement the debtor sells his economic future to the creditor. We show in Chapter 2 that the corporate giants with their accumulated net worth have dwarfed many of the low- and middle-income national economies. Looking at the accumulated net worth of the corporate sector vis-à-vis the accumulated debts of the governments and the households, would it be too drastic to say that the governments and common households in these economies have committed their economic future to the corporate sector and the HNIs? This appears to be the philosophical undercurrent of the economic structure of the global financial economy.

In a nutshell, this is the ultimate meaning of leveraged growth – we are borrowing from our future to achieve our current growth. The households and the governments borrow from their future earnings to leverage their current spending on corporate products and the corporate sector gets the leveraged growth of their net worth. Any future income stream is now being converted to an asset of the present and owned by the corporate or the HNIs. The financial engineering of securitisation follows a basic stratagem of bringing the future income streams to the present. The whole complexity of financial markets is built on the expectations of future growth in income, which must materialise to sustain this structure. Economic growth is the mantra of our time. We must keep on attaining it. The system is thus treading upon its own future to cater to its present activities and growth. But, could the household and government debts extend limitlessly, or the future economic activities keep on growing limitlessly in a finite world to ensure an everlasting future growth and make us live happily ever after in this global financial economy?

A cause of worry

In the current economic structure no one should be allowed to go bankrupt, as that would cause devastation. When such possibility arises, more loans would be given to keep the wheels moving. Any significant or persistent failure to attain the expected future growth, for whatever reason, may have an unimaginable effect on the circuit. In that case it will no more be a crisis, rather an economic devastation. The economic circuit that has now evolved is possibly the Final Circuit. With this Final Circuit the corporate economic system that stemmed out in the 1850s in the West is perhaps now reaching the end of its evolutionary path.

However, possibilities of failure to attain the future growth are not imminent. Financialisation, as we mention at the beginning of this chapter, is not complete yet. We see the reflections of its further integration in the current process of financialisation in developing countries like India. The global economic circuit still has some scope for its expansion in these economies. Through the process of financialisation some more funds could be squeezed from them by integrating with the global circuit their local production activities and small savings that are still taking place outside the global economic circuit. Even the apparently small insignificant savings would be brought into the global circuit. We may mention a simple reason. A savings of two dollars per day of a person is apparently an insignificant amount, having almost no financial importance. But when this insignificant amount of savings per day by five billion people, presently isolated and scattered in different corners of the world, are pooled into a single kitty, it makes a sizeable financial fund. Similarly, apparently ignorable service charges on all digital transactions of money (which were not there in cash transactions) and the daily unspent balances in the millions of e-wallets of the payment banks, create a huge fund for the financial market of money at call and short notice.

In the context of money-hungriness of the circuit, we mention in Chapter 7 that the entire money in the circuit must always be in circulation. It cannot be allowed to stay anywhere for long. At this final stage, we see money is not even allowed to stay out of circulation for a split second. Holding a few dollars in currency notes at your home or in your pocket for a day just for petty purchases means those few dollars are out of circulation for the day. Transactions by digitalised money overcome this possibility, as all money now stays not in currency notes, but in digitalised accounts. Digitalised money drives out the currency money. This is the economics of digitalisation. In this digitalised world many of our earlier notions become obsolete – even the Keynesian idea of money holding for transaction and speculation purposes, which lies at the foundation of our economic analysis, appears a pre-historic one. Further, in this world, financialisation of household consumption – financing current consumption from the expected future earnings – makes expected future earnings a more important determining factor. We can neither say the current disposable income alone determines consumption demand (Keynesian consumption function), nor say demands (as desires especially for durable goods, items available on credit purchases, and services, like education and health) are determined by the current prices only (neoclassical demand functions). What matters more now are the expected future earnings.

Our economic existence is now being digitalised and thereby becoming a virtual one in a digitalised global financial web. Would it be rather drastic to comment that even a temporary breakdown of this digitalised global financial web might cause an economic devastation affecting all of us?

10 Concluding note

The present as the future

It appears now apt to borrow this title from Galbraith's (1987) book *A History of Economics: The Past as the Present*, where the final chapter is named, 'The Present as the Future'. After traversing a vast canvas of economic evolutions of the corporate financial economy since the 1850s, we have reached at present and find that it is now the future that determines the present. We are mounting debts on our future to inflate our present activities. So our future is lost in the present, as our present debts must be repaid ultimately out of our future earnings.

The corporate wealth is growing and, with it, the household and public debts are growing at alarming rates in our present economic system. The circuit analysis here establishes a link between the two – the gains the corporate sector is realising in their net worth are coming through the loss of the public by the operation of the financial circuit. The circuit uses a simple fact – every gain is at the same time a loss, every inflow also means an outflow, and hence no one can gain unless someone else loses.

By the same rule, that there is a paradox of profit within an economic system or circuit cannot be denied. In economic systems of manufacturing, trade, and financial exchanges, profits are simply a matter of economic construct; it cannot really exist on the whole in economic systems. By the construct of charging profits over the cost of production (or the money outlay in production), surplus production accumulates with the corporate sector, which they convert into monetary gains (profits) by making the households and the governments, whether within or outside the circuit, monetarily indebted in providing the additional money flow into the circuit.

The French economists of the 18th century, referred to as the physiocrats, were quite candid in their conclusion, which they reached with circuit formulations, that there is no *produit net* in the economic circuit of manufacturing, trade, or financial activity (Galbraith 1987: 52).

We have reached the same conclusion with the qualification that a circuit may realise monetary profits by creating indebtedness inside or outside through net exports. Otherwise, there are really no monetary profits. However, the modern circuit theorists, in their formulations of the theory of monetary circuit, are not so candid. In spite of the fact that their monetary circuits also reveal the same fact that profit cannot emerge from within a circuit, they make attempts to solve an insoluble riddle, which they call the paradox of profit. Interestingly, not only with profit, the same problem is revealed by circuit formulation in respect of the other economic constructs like charging interest and depreciation in the cost of production. Also, household savings accentuate the same paradox. So, something must have blurred the vision of the modern circuit theorists – they could not believe to have seen what the physiocrats could see and accept centuries ago with the help of their circuit formulations. The problem the monetary circuit theorists face in the circuit formulation is perhaps due to the classical or neoclassical legacy in their economic ideas and conceptions.

Economics as a discipline took birth in the milieu of economic development in the West with large-scale modern industries, following the industrial revolution and colonial conquests and trade. In this backdrop, capital as a means of production embodying the new industrial technology and entrepreneurial profits were seen as the key factors of economic development – the mantras of the time. The classical and neoclassical economic thinkers, therefore, tended to see capital as a produced means of production that was essential for modern industrialisation, rather than as a monetary fund. Following this tradition, even today a student of economics defines capital as means of production, although the dictionary meaning of capital is monetary fund. The problem with the economic definition, that it does not include working capital, which is necessarily a monetary fund circulating in the production process, did surface off and on, but was ignored as a matter of lesser importance.

The elusive concept of capital as a means of production created a further problem in economic literature – interest and profit got mixed up in the earlier classical and neoclassical theories as, during their time, there were the shadows of the age-old canonical taboos on taking interest on money loans and on buying cheaper and selling dearer. Perhaps for this reason the classical and the neoclassical thinkers of the time were apathetic towards viewing and bringing out theories of interest as a usury charge on monetary funds, and, more so, they did not consider capital to be a monetary fund. The essence of capitalism is buying and selling capital as a monetary fund, but it was lost from their analysis. Moreover, following the Ricardian tradition of tri-partite division of factors of production, interest and profit got muddled in the early neoclassical writings as the remuneration to capital as a means of production and, so, confusions brewed in spelling out whether interest was a cost of capital or a return to capital.

Entrepreneurial profit is the mantra of capitalism and our present economic system is institutionally built to ensure it. Yet, it would not be incorrect to say that there is no theory of profit in economic literature, except an early attempt by Frank Knight (1921) to justify profits as the return to the entrepreneurs for taking risks. Our understanding of the element of profit in production has been quite hazy. Textbook theories of firms proclaim that 'normal profit' is included in the cost of production. But they do not explain what determines its rate, as they do in the case of other elements of costs of production like wage, rent, and interest. How can profit, if it is 'normal' as an element of cost, be maximised by the rational behaviour of the firms? Moreover, this treatment of profit as an element of cost puts a haze over the fact that the profit element (so also depreciation) in entrepreneurial production activity is a charge to be obtained as inflow and not an outlay of money or outflow as we see for the other elements of the cost of production. So inflow and outflow get mixed up in this conception of profit.

In our circuit formulation of production economy, we have included a mark-up over the cost of production as the entrepreneurial profit, which is in fact the practice. In reality, the corporate sector does make profits and accumulate further monetary capital out of the undistributed profits. Our primary question is then how does it become possible when the profit paradox exists in a circulating economy? In a circulating economy as a whole, economic gains or profits in production, trade, and monetary transaction may emerge only by buying cheaper and selling dearer, the difference being the economic gain. But this is not possible unless the reciprocal loss accumulates somewhere – inside or outside the economy.

By the construct of charging profits we have introduced in the economic system an element of a crisis – how to realise monetary profits. We have seen in the circuit formulation that surplus production may be created by the construct of profits, but monetising it into realised monetary profits is not possible within the production circuit. This has put the economic system in crisis time and again.

We have traced the evolutionary path of the corporate economic circuit since its beginning in the 1850s in the West in three phases – the nascent corporate production (1850–1930), the matured corporate production with creditisation (1945–70), and the financial economy since the 1990s. In the nascent stage, it could flourish in the West, under the Gold Standard money, with colonial trade with the rest of the world rescuing the circuit from its profit paradox. Nevertheless, with the decline in this opportunity for trading in terms of gold, the Gold Standard money became golden fetters, and in the 1930s came the crisis. From the crisis of the 1930s evolved the next phase of development of the corporate production economy where it reached its maturity with the endogenous creation of credit money. Then by the end of the 1960s another crisis came due to stagnation in industrial production with its consumption demand getting saturated and downturn in labour productivity. The next phase of evolution began through the ICT revolution of the late 1980s. Since the 1990s, through a process of globalisation and introduction of various financial commodities, this evolution is now integrating the world in a global financial circuit.

We may now summarise our findings. Several important conclusions have emerged from our analysis of economic circuits in these three phases of evolution. First, we have seen that since its birth the corporate production circuit is money-hungry because of its problems of monetising the surplus production created by the construct of profits – for realising monetary profits it must get more money flowing into the circuit than what it starts with in every production cycle. But the irony is that the more money flow it gets towards realisation of monetary profits, the more its money-hungriness becomes and a process of financial accumulation starts for which the circuit must continue to expand.

The circuit analysis reveals an important fact about the well-known debate between the Monetarist and Keynesian schools. What should be the policy in a situation of depression when monetary profits cannot be realised: raising the money supply by the government or raising the government expenditure to create income generation that will boost up the demand for the goods produced within the economic circuit? We find both are simultaneously needed, as one cannot work without the other.

The trade pattern we find from the circuit analysis also gives an explanation to the Leontief paradox that contradicts the neoclassical theory of trade based on the Hekscher-Ohlin theorem. Our circuit analysis shows that the corporate production circuit of the West specialises in exporting the goods of the production circuit with a higher labour–capital ratio than the importing economies in the rest of the world. The importing economies in the rest of the world are forced to specialise in exporting material-intensive primary goods of their production circuits employing less labour per unit of capital.

The circuit formulation helps us distinguish between exogenous growth, endogenous growth, and endogenous dynamics or adjustments. In the case of the nascent corporate production circuit we have seen that without money flow coming from outside, as a source of exogenous growth, the circuit cannot expand on its own. Interestingly, we have seen peculiar endogenous dynamics that start with household savings that create a liquidity crisis for the corporate production sector. A kind of Keynesian paradox of thrift occurs here and, in addition, we get income redistribution effects favouring rentier income over wage income, when there is no opportunity for the circuit to expand through net exports to the rest of the world. When there is such opportunity, then also income redistribution effects would take place, although we may not see in the circuit the liquidity crisis or paradox of thrift as such.

In the case of the corporate production circuit at its maturity phase with credit money, household savings creates more peculiar dynamics, depending on whether household savings are deposited in banks creating new bank deposits, or go to the share market for speculative trading. Here the flow balance of the corporate production circuit becomes quite fragile – a slight change in the quantum and direction of money flow arising from household savings may lead to liquidity crisis in the system.

Dividend income also creates different endogenous dynamics in the circuit, depending upon whether it is saved or consumed. If it is saved in bank deposits, then the banking sector faces the problem of excess liquidity, which cannot be absorbed in new money loans, unless the corporate sector expands production. On the other hand, if the dividend income, as distributed from the monetary profit realised through the sale of the stock of goods, goes for consumption expenditure, it leads to inflationary rise in prices, giving signals to the corporate sector to increase production. The outcome would of course depend on the quantum of dividends paid and undistributed profit retained.

Since the time of the matured corporate production circuit with credit money, government fiscal deficits and balance of payments deficits have been seen. An important corollary of the operation and expansion of the corporate production circuit with credit money in the West is that the rest of the world realises growing balance of payment deficits as well as fiscal deficits. Similarly, we see a feature of inducing the wage income earners in the circuit to spend more than they earn by taking bank credits, creating household indebtedness.

Our circuit analysis here brings out a simple, yet important, puzzle of the mainstream economic theory – should an economy save more or consume more for achieving economic growth? The classical and neo-classical conclusion was to save more, whereas the Keynesian prescription was to consume more. Saving more is necessary to create capital formation that may be invested as increased money capital to expand production, and more consumption is necessary to create the demand for the goods produced. But both cannot take place simultaneously. The circuit analysis gives a simple answer – the wage income earners should consume more to ensure that the revolving money capital flows back from the sale of output. The more the better, when they spend more than their current income by taking loans, as this will create additional money flow in the system. But the dividend income earners should save more to ensure capital formation. This solves the puzzle.

Coming to the phase of financial circuit, we have dealt with corporate leveraging, an aspect essentially seen in the operation of the financial economy. We have found three aspects of leveraging in the corporate production sector. First, financial and operating leverages go hand in hand, as one requires the other. Second, income redistribution with a rising share of dividends and interest as rentier income, and a declining share of wage income, are the natural outcomes of leveraged growth. This again helps corporate leveraging further by providing for the debt financing out of the savings by the rentier income earners. Third, leveraged growth results in another type of inequality. Only the large firms having higher levels of operating profits can reap the benefits of leveraging. This explains why we find empirically the phenomenon of rising capital intensity particularly in large units. We see that, in the corporate sector, the large firms become even larger, creating an increasing inequality in firm-size distribution in the leveraged growth process as a natural consequence of leveraging.

The analysis of the financial circuit brings out several conclusions. We may list them as:

i) As a consequence of leveraging that raises capital intensity and favours rentier incomes of HNIs, the composition of output, so as to match the demands for the products, tilts towards high-end products and capital goods;
ii) leveraging in a finance-led growth regime necessarily creates demand depression in the real sector;
iii) households and governments in the global financial circuit must become more and more indebted;
iv) the global financial circuit can operate only when it grows;

v) in the sequential growth over time, households become more indebted and they fall into a debt trap, with increasing portions of their current incomes going for amortised loan repayments;

vi) the outcome of the growth process is growing accumulation of wealth of the corporate sector and the HNIs and rising income inequality between the wage earners and the rentier income earners;

vii) if it were possible to calculate and construct a balance sheet of the global financial economy, these four stocks would have balanced – public debt and household debts as liability would have balanced the net worth of the corporate sector and the HNIs as assets in the global balance sheet;

viii) within the global financial circuit economic growth necessarily means simultaneous growth of indebtedness; and

ix) by the leveraging, we are actually borrowing from our future to achieve our current growth.

The evolutionary path of the corporate economy marks occurrence of crises, one after another, and the evolutions that stem out of the necessity the crises create. We saw three different phases of growth followed by crisis – the nascent production circuit faced the Great Depression of the 1930s, then the matured production circuit was trapped into the real sector depression of the 1970s, and finally the global financial circuit has registered the financial crisis of 2008.

The global financial crisis of 2008 originated with the declaration of financial bankruptcy of an US investment company, spreading panic of further bankruptcy, as we see in a house of cards. It could be somehow managed by bailout packages of the states, with the lesson that no one should be allowed to declare bankruptcy and default, whatever be one's burden of debts. The same reality is revealed in the sovereign debt crisis of Greece. So, all creditors must come together to rescue and re-finance the debtors so that the ball could keep on rolling. This is the principle of a credit economy and it is concealing the loss by keeping the asset value intact in the books.

We inflate our economic activities by financial transactions. Nevertheless, however inflated the financial sector could be, at the foundation remains the real sector. There is now the danger of growing depression in the real sector. The growing disparity in income distribution has a depressing effect on the consumption demand in the real sector. Stagnation in the real sector has been a global phenomenon for the last few decades. The growth in the emerging economies is also coming mostly through the financial sector activities. Our circuit analysis has established that growing the financial sector necessarily leads to real sector stagnation. But the stagnation in the real sector will ultimately hit back on the financial sector when many of the future financial claims on the real sector activities fail to materialise in the future. What is of utmost importance now to survive in the present is to have everlasting future growth. Would it be possible in a finite world?

The corporate economic circuit, in its present phase of financial circuit, has possibly reached the end of its evolutionary path. So, we call it the Final Circuit. Now it would be no more at the edge of a crisis, but perhaps at the edge of devastation when globalisation completes, leaving no income generation or financial savings outside the circuit for its required re-capitalisation or expansion. In a digitalised global circuit, all money, held even in the smallest savings or for the pettiest transactions, are now being squeezed. Digitalisation of money is making money a virtual entity, not staying anywhere in currency notes, but in records of digitalised accounts of banks, or in e-wallets of payment banks. This is the financial aspect of the economics of digitalisation, now an emerging area of studies covering also the impacts of digitalisation. The Final Circuit, for its money-hungriness, cannot allow any money to stay out of circulation as being held in currency notes for even a split second. In this process, our economic existence remains no more real but becomes a virtual one in the intricate linkages of a digitalised global financial web. Any operational failure arising at any corner of the web may put all of us hopelessly entangled in an economic devastation.

Growing accumulation and concentration of wealth and inequality have been established by Piketty as a statistical fact by analysing voluminous statistical data. We give the logical explanation for this phenomenon – why it necessarily arises as a systemic phenomenon in the capitalist economic structure. In view of this global phenomenon, Piketty has recommended imposing a progressive global tax on capital or wealth and far higher marginal tax rates on top incomes (Piketty 2014). These recommendations may appear quite bold but a little unrealistic. However, since the growing accumulation of wealth of the corporate sector and HNIs matched by growing government and household debts is a systemic phenomenon, even the bold policy recommendations of Piketty may not work to restrain it. What would be the outcome of such policies? They will only temporarily reduce the inequality with no lasting effect. Within a short while, accommodating for taxes by the governments, inequality as a systemic phenomenon will continue to grow again. Moreover, as an outcome of such policies, government revenue income will rise. What would the governments do with it – hold it just for accumulating idle national wealth with no economic function? This is not likely. And when the governments spend it for whatever purpose, say for the welfare of common people, we would be brought back much faster to the same square. Therefore, if anything is to be done, it must be eliminating the cause at its root in the economic systems. Only through some revolutionary changes in its structural construct at the foundation, say in charging profit, interest-bearing debt financing, and retaining undistributed profits by the companies, may the economic system avoid economic devastation.

We highlight the need for a structural transformation at the foundation – if not elimination all together, at least some restrictions on charging profits, leveraging through debt financing, and retaining undistributed profits by the corporate sector. This might appear bolder than Piketty's. But is it unrealistic too? Only about four hundred years ago charging interest on money loans and making profits through buying cheaper and selling dearer came in human society as matters of economic constructs of the mercantile period. French physiocrats were quite sceptical about mercantilism (Galbraith 1987: 55–6). Before that, over thousands of years, these were not in practice in human society.

With our present as the future, a structural transformation has now become necessary since, contrary to the justification attempted by a misquote of Keynes saying that in the longer run we are all dead, our present concern is: if we are all dead in the longer run, our economic structures would not survive in the present either.

Appendix
Notes on some financial aspects

1. New-generation financial commodities

Since the mid-1960s the growing financial capital could not be fully absorbed in financing only the industrial production activities, whose growth has been stagnating. Therefore, a frantic search has begun for alternative ways of gainfully investing the financial capital. The alternative that has emerged is growing investment in speculative trading in a new generation of financial commodities known as derivatives and securities, which have been evolving in the global financial economy.

Emergence

Forward contracts, or agreements to buy or sell an underlying asset on a future date at a specified (future) price, are nothing new. They existed even in the ancient commodity trade. Speculative trading on forward contracts was seen as early as the Tulip Mania of 1637. During the golden period of industrial growth of the corporate production economy, trading on forward contracts remained dormant and linked mostly with ensuring flow of raw material over time for industrial production and trading, especially to and from distant places having no specified market. With the beginning of stagnation in the growth of industrial production activities in the late 1960s, speculative trading in forward contracts started to soar up with increasing investment of financial capital. But trading remained mostly as OTC agreements made directly by the reciprocating investors. However, in the United States, there was already an organisation named the CBOT, supposedly established as early as 1848, working as an exchange for such trading. In the early 1970s investment on exchange traded forward contracts, called the futures contract, recorded a very rapid growth. CBOT recorded trading on another type of such contract in 1973, called the options. The largest exchanges in which futures contracts are now traded are the CBOT and the CME. As a regulating authority the CFTC was established in the United States in 1974, followed by the formation of the National Futures Association in 1982. Other bodies, like the SEC, were also established (Hull 2001). We now see similar exchanges and regulatory bodies in almost all the developed and developing countries. They act to create confidence in speculative activities, ensuring checks against fraudulent activities, defaults, or dishonours, as well excessive speculative buying or selling pressures in the markets.

Mechanism of speculation

The mechanism of speculation is quite simple. Till the time of maturity of a contract, speculative gains may occur to the holder of a contract to buy (or sell) the underlying asset. Such gains arise when, in the course of further trading on similar contracts by other speculators, the future price of the contract goes above (or falls below) the specified future price at which the contract has been made between the holders. In trading exchanges, the gains or losses to the holders of the contracts are now calculated on an everyday basis, marking to the market the value of each contract at the future price on the day. The gains and losses are set off among speculators on an everyday basis. Further, a holder of a contract has the option to opt out simply by taking the opposite position on the contract at the going market future price – that is, the holder of a contract to buy the asset may close out by entering into another offsetting contract to sell the asset, and vice versa. This gives an opportunity to quick profit taking (or restricting loss). Trading and profit taking continue in a continuous chain of investments through buying and selling by speculators. Ultimately, all speculators on the contract usually close out, meaning that there would be no actual buying or selling of the underlying asset in reality. The only result would be that, on that contract, for some speculators there would be gains matched by an equal amount of loss by some others. It is simply like gambling in a casino.

Speculative gains for all?

If all individual gains are set off by individual losses of speculators, then how could there be net gain on the whole for all from speculations in a financial market? We mention a condition for creation of such a situation where all the speculators may realise speculative gains in a particular financial market. This has a significant implication in our circuit analysis. As explained earlier in the Appendix, the gains are set off by an equal amount of loss when we consider a particular transaction on a single contract. But when we consider a financial market as a whole with many such contracts on which buying and selling by speculators take place in a continuous chain, all speculators may gain in situations when prices of all contracts continuously spiral up, or have an overall upward trend with some short-term fluctuations. This spiral over time ensures that the losses incurred today will get recovered in the subsequent transactions tomorrow. So, here we are considering a dynamic case of sequential states, not simply a static particular state.

This can happen in a particular financial market as an isolated phenomenon when more and more financial capital continues to flow into it for a period of time. But again, when we consider all financial markets together, that is the financial economy; by the same logic, all gains and losses would cancel out each other. So, here net gain can occur in the dynamic sequential states of a spiral, which requires continuous additional pumping of funds into the financial economy from outside. We discuss this phenomenon in more detail in the section on 'Concern over leveraging and economic bubbles'.

Derivatives and financial architecture

The group of the new-generation financial commodities, primarily used for speculation and risk hedging, is now termed derivatives. Beside the forward and futures contracts, as well as option contracts, another major type is over-the-counter swaps contracts. Other than these there can also be more complex and specialised derivatives. Derivatives are also called contingent claim and can be contingent on any underlying variable, from 'the price of hogs to the amount of snow falling at a ski resort' (Hull 2001: 1). The rate of return on investment a speculator may realise from derivatives is significantly higher than the spot market speculation because the initial cash payments required in derivative contracts are usually negligible compared to the value of the asset. For futures contracts, exchange requires some deposits in a margin account and for options contract it specifies the cost per option. But for forward or swap contracts between parties usually there are no initial payments.

Evolution of derivative trading opened up a new avenue for financial investment for individual investors as well as institutions. Side by side, we see another evolution at the level of financial institutions –

that is, the evolution of the process of securitisation and creation of structured securities. A more detailed discussion on these structured securities as the 'new financial architecture' (NFA) and their implications may be found in Crotty (2008).

Securitisation and rental income

Securitisation by the financial institutions of its financial assets, both mortgage backed securities (MBS) and asset backed securities (ABS), was initially developed in the United States in the early 1970s and has demonstrated remarkable growth ever since, with almost all forms of debt obligations and receivables generating future cash flow being securitised now. In the case of mortgage loans, as amortised, the future cash flow generates from the repayment instalments of the loan with interest. Future cash flow also generates from other sources receivables as assets, which include various types of rentals, insurance premiums, committed contributions to pension funds, credit card receivables, telephone receivables, royalty receivables, and so on, which are securitised as financial assets promising future flow of incomes.

The future cash flows, whether generating from mortgage loans or from an asset-creating agreement, are clearly financial incomes in the form of rental to the holder of the contract. The receivers, at the beginning of it, are the initiators who initially finance the mortgage loan and receive the cash flow under an agreement. But as such these are illiquid assets to them. To the mortgage initiators this creates a problem. When their proprietary funds get exhausted in financing mortgage loans, apparently they would not have liquidity any more to finance any further mortgage loan. Securitisation allows them to overcome this problem, providing a way for leveraging. They can raise more funds against the fund flows assured in the existing mortgage loans they have given and now held as apparently non-liquid assets in the form of a number of contractual loan agreements. By securitisation they can simply sell these agreements as cash flow-generating assets in the financial market and raise further funds.

Securitisation further represents the pooling of cash flow, producing illiquid assets and issuing claims on the cash flow of combined assets in the form of a marketable security at a price. It implies that a large number of similar future cash flows (in terms of income streams, maturity, credit, and interest rate risks) are bundled together and sold as structured securities on a formal market (Heffernan 2005: 44–5; Gomez 2008: 450; Schlosser 2011: 25–6). In the process of pooling or bundling, which is now called financial architecture, the overall future stream of cash flow is often split into parts, usually four, to allow multiple investors investing on different parts of the cash flow generating from the same structured security. That is, after being pooled and turned into a security, the cash flows of the combined assets in the security are split into different investment classes or security tranches. This is known as tranching. In that case, collateralised debt obligations (CDOs) are created for the multiple investors. Other CDOs include collateralised bond obligation (CBOs) and collateralised loan obligation (CLOs), which involve collateralised pools of corporate loans or other credit facilities. CLOs originated in the 1990s and consist of a pool of investment-grade revolving/term loans, standby letters of credit, and even derivatives. All of these complex instruments in effect allow illiquid loans to become liquid tradable securities (Heffernan 2005: 46–8; Schlosser 2011: 26–7).

Special purpose vehicle

There is also an organisational evolution in the process of securitisation. Usually the institution securitising its future cash flow-generating assets does not itself pool the securities and directly sell them to the market. They create another organisation, a subsidiary, called the SPV for this purpose. The securities, containing assets which are naturally exposed to varied credit risks, are sold to the SPV. The SPV in turn refinances by pooling the securities and selling the pooled security as a tradable security in the financial market.

There are two advantages of creating SPVs in the securitisation process. First is that they are bankruptcy remote. In case of credit defaults in the future cash flow, no direct reflection comes to the originator. Second, in the process of securitisation with the SPVs, the original assets move out of the balance sheets of the originator, while the incomes generated by selling them to the SPVs are shown as income in their financial accounts. It becomes possible to move illiquid assets from the balance sheet so that the actual leveraging of the originator is concealed. This is now known as off-balance sheet transactions. The credit and other risks associated with the pool of assets are thus transferred from the originator to the SPV. Moreover, the SPVs also buy several other future cash flow-generating assets from the market and pool them in different ways according to the riskiness and perceived profitability to create the tradable structured securities.

Claims on the future

We may now notice a common characteristic of the new-generation financial commodities. Both derivatives and structured securities deal with the future. They are the instruments that make the future growth to be realised in current gains. Derivatives are contingent claims on the future and structured securities give assured claims, associated with some risks of default. In both cases, current gains occur only when the future grows as expected. But there is now a 'trap of bubbles' creation – the future growth, brought to the present, capitalises the future flow and creates newer financial assets, which generate current speculative gains. Therefore, investments of such gains, in turn, would require further future growth. The process becomes more intense with leveraging, that is, investment with borrowed funds.

2. Corporate restructuring

A crucial factor in the growth of the giant corporation that we see today in the global financial economy is the continuous 'merger and acquisition' (M&A) process since the 1980s. The 1980s became an era when the mergers and acquisitions got huge momentum with sophisticated financing structures, with hostile M&A and litigation being freely used. The stagnation in the real sector since the late 1960s made many of the corporate units non-viable, especially the small- and middle-sized ones by their capital base and in the traditional lines of business, and some of them were at the verge of bankruptcy. On the other hand, accumulation of financial capital, which could not be gainfully engaged otherwise, financed the creation of private equity funds by the large companies. There were raids by the private equity fund to take over the small companies, either by straight acquisition or through mergers, to make the large companies even larger.

The second half of the 1980s saw some of the largest transactions globally, which included the Kohlberg Kravis & Robert's $25 billion-leveraged buy-out of RJR Nabisco, the largest leveraged buy-out ever; Gulf Oil's $13 billion acquisition of Chevron; and Kraft's $13 billion acquisition of Philip Morris. Leveraged buy-outs were further encouraged with the advent of the junk bond market in the 1980s. The United States Tax Reform Act of 1986 facilitated corporate restructurings, resulting in numerous restructurings of companies in tax-free transactions. Many of these were hostile acquisitions of companies by the so-called corporate raiders leading the charge (Hunt 2009: iii–vi).

Corporate acquisitions were financed by substantial amounts of leverage with the use of the increasingly popular junk bonds or high-yield
debt. In the United States, the investment bank Drexel Burnham Lam-
bert was credited with invention of the modern junk bond market in
the 1980s. Michael Milken, the firm's West Coast chief, was heralded
as the 'junk bond king' propelling the corporate raider activity of the
1980s. This frantic acquisition process, however, came to an end with
Milken being charged later for securities fraud and the winding up of
Drexel Burnham, but not before contributing hugely to the savings and
loan crises of the late 1980s. The pace of acquisitions quickened in the
1990s with a booming stock market, relaxation of regulatory norms,
international competition, and abundance of financial capital. With the
globalisation drive since the late 1990s, the global mergers continued to
rise with a flurry of restructuring activity. With the expectation of a consequent rise in the shareholder value, 'merger and acquisition' became
a prime strategy for enhancing shareholder value (Hunt 2009: *Ibid.*).

3. Emergence of Euro-dollar and changing role of banks

The stagnation in the real sector in the 1960s had an immediate reflection on rising deposit liabilities of the banking sector. There were several other developments too. The need to recycle OPEC (Organisation
of the Petroleum Exporting Countries) surpluses contributed greatly
to an increase in Eurocurrency deposit liabilities in the early 1970s.
This proved instrumental in the surge of debt flow to developing countries and the financial asset proliferation that followed.

One of the origins of the Eurocurrency market could be traced
back to 1957 when the Russians, having acquired US dollars through
exports, were wary of holding these with US banks. They held the
account with a French bank in Paris, leading to the creation of the first
Euro-dollars (Eatwell and Taylor 2000: 36–8; Pilbeam 2006: 306–07).
Further, in 1958, with the abolition of the European Payments Union
and restoration of the convertibility of the European currencies, European banks could hold US dollars without being forced to convert
them to domestic currencies. The other important factor contributing to the growth of the Euro-dollar market came from the increased
regulation of domestic banking activities by US authorities. Two regulations could be underlined here. First, the introduction of Regulation
Q which imposed a 5.25 percent ceiling on the rate of interest that US
banks could pay on savings and time-deposit accounts. Given that the
regulation did not apply to the off-shore banks, many US banks set up

subsidiaries abroad in centres such as London. Second, with the interest equalisation tax (IET) introduced in the same year, the cost of borrowing to foreigners in the United States went up substantially, leading them to borrow on the Euro-dollar market. These regulations led many domestic banks in the United States to resort to Euro-banking activities to circumvent the effect of these controls with foreign branches and subsidiaries were set up to escape banking regulations (Pilbeam 2006).

Another aspect of rising deposit liabilities was that, following the oil price hikes, OPEC deposited large amounts of surplus dollars in the Euromarkets, which were then used to fund the deficits of oil-importing countries. With stagnation in the real sector in Western countries, these deposits were used in giving massive loans to developing countries, especially in Latin America. However, with the Mexican default of 1982 and the following 'developing countries debt crises', the deposits began to be channelled to the financial markets in developed and subsequently in developing countries, leading to explosive growth in these markets. As Eatwell and Taylor (2000: 36–8) put it, 'the international financial flood of the past twenty-five years rose from a tiny spring – the Eurodollar (later Eurocurrency) markets in the 1990s'.

The changing role of banks

In the evolution of the financial economy, we see the traditional roles of banks are changing. Securitisation of assets naturally has an impact on changing the role of the traditional banks, as it provides an easy route for raising liquidity. Theoretically, banks can directly issue a bond with the pooled assets acting as collateral. But it faces some disadvantages there. First, the credit rating of the bank gets assigned to this security. Second, the proceeds of the bond are subject to reserve requirements. And third, the assets remain included in the computation of the bank's capital ratio. These constraints are avoided if a bank establishes a SPV. The bank transfers its assets to the SPV, which pays back to the bank for the assets from the proceeds of the sale of securities pooled. In the process, securitisation reduces the number of assets on the balance sheet and gives a boost to the bank's risk–asset ratio or Basel capital ratio, as the credit risk is passed onto a third party. It raises also the liquidity because it frees up the funding tied to the existing loans. In this process, the assets become marketable, as they can now be traded on secondary markets, unlike assets on a bank's balance sheet that cannot be traded.

From the early 1980s, there were several changes in the domain of banking activities in the industrialised countries. The US economy, worried by falling profitability of commercial banks, saw a host of 'deregulation' measures. Starting in the mid-1980s, there had been a gradual removal of the earlier regulations imposed on the US financial system under the Glass–Steagall Act of 1933. The US commercial banks' share in the financial assets held by all financial institutions fell dramatically from around 50 percent in the 1950s to around 25 percent in the 1990s. This was because the banks suffered competition for both deposit business (coming from thrifts and non-regulated money market accounts) and for commercial and industrial loan business (coming from commercial papers). The Glass–Steagall Act of 1933 had restricted commercial banks from entering into the potentially profitable capital market activities, such as the sale and management of trust and investment funds. However, in a series of rulings in the 1980s, this Act was revised to allow banks to form affiliates to engage in these activities, if the earnings they generated did not surpass specified limits. Thus, it was deemed acceptable for a bank as a holding company to form a subsidiary that conducted permissible activities that were sufficiently large to be considered its principal activity. This gave an opportunity to indirectly engage, in some lesser proportion, in otherwise prohibited activities in which it was considered not to be 'principally' engaged (Kregel 2007: 15). This enabled commercial lenders such as Citigroup, which was in 1999 the largest US bank by assets, to underwrite trade instruments such as mortgage backed securities and collateralised debt obligations through structured investment vehicles (SIVs). This development allowed commercial lenders to foray into underwriting derivatives through SIVs.

The commercial banks, thus, began to shift their activities to relatively riskier areas, like real estate loans, off-balance sheet activities, and lending for corporate takeovers, as well as leveraged buyouts in an attempt to maintain profitability. This led to an increase in the back-up lines of credit and guarantees, which gained at the expense of actual lending. The credit derivatives came to constitute a major share of banks' off-balance sheet activities (Barth et al. 2000: 191–204; Özgür and Ertürk 2008: 6).

Since the 1980s banks in the major developed nations were no longer servicing business lending only or dependent primarily on net interest margins for its income. Instead, their income depended on the ability of their proprietary trading desks to generate profits and affiliates to produce fee and commission income. Ben Bernanke, the chairman of the Board of Governors of the Federal Reserve, indicated in a speech in 2007 that while banks did continue to play a central role in credit markets, because of the rapidly increasing market for loan sales, they created considerably more loans than they kept on their books (Kregel 2007: 16; Bernanke 2007).

Banks have now become more of 'arrangers', creating financial assets that they then sell to a subsidiary who in turn sells them in the financial market. The business of banking has changed, from being one of holding assets to generate income from interest rate spreads to one of moving assets, which is known to be the traditional activity of brokers and investment banks. This changing role of banks is often seen as being responsible for much of the instability generated in financial markets (Kregel *Ibid.* 2007: 17–18).

The changing role of the banks has been vindicated by some studies. Ertürk (2006) has shown that the statistical link between bank credit and total broad money has become tenuous after the mid-1990s. He contends that this is because of the changing role of banks in the last twenty years – the rising importance of non-deposit liabilities of banks, the easing of reserve requirements, and the increased ability to securitise assets. Due to falling core deposits in the era of financial liberalisation, the depository institutions are forced to engage increasingly in liability management, independent of deposits in their balance sheets. On one hand, with the drastic easing of reserve requirements by the mid-1990s, the constraints on extending bank credit by deposits are relaxed, and on the other, new layers of intermediation have emerged, expanded, and multiplied through asset securitisation. As these are not reflected in banks' balance sheets, the constraints imposed by their capital base can now be sidestepped. Thus, extension of bank lending no longer necessarily leads solely to the creation of new deposits. It is now increasingly being directed towards financing of debt instruments by other financial institutions. Thus, the connection between bank lending and deposits is much weakened. Quite expectedly, in the non-depository component of M3, the share of money market mutual funds soared up. The rapid increase of money market mutual funds in broad money supply (M3) after 1995, reaching almost 30 percent by 2001, shows the magnitude of non-bank financial intermediation (Özgür and Ertürk 2008: 8–12).

4. Concern over leveraging and economic bubbles

With the innovations of derivatives and structured securities, and leveraged investments on these, a peculiar development has taken place – both the supply of and demand for financial assets now can grow hand in hand, creating financial bubbles of continuously appreciating prices of financial assets. In the situations of spiralling growth, the speculative demand for financial assets increases continuously, leading to appreciation of the price of the asset. The resulting flow of financial gains in turn, invested further in financing loans, leads to creation of newer financial assets, adding to the stream of supply. The financial capital, revolving in a continuous chain of buying and selling, also gets inflated through leveraged investments – speculators now borrow and invest to make even more speculative gains. This becomes similar to the Ponzi scheme. A bubble, once established, gets inflated more by the joining of more speculators and squeezing of the finance flowing from other sectors or segments of financial markets. In this situation of asset price bubble, speculators usually follow herd behaviour – one follows the other – and everyone assumes that there exists a greater fool who will buy the asset from him at a higher price.

The continuous growth of financial capital and its investment in the financial economy may lead to creation of economic bubbles in segments but impacting on the whole economy. Kindleberger defines a bubble as 'an upward price movement over an extended range that then implodes' (Kindleberger 1978: 16). Some neoclassical economists, who allow the existence of bubbles, usually define it as a situation where an asset's price exceeds the 'fundamental' value of the asset. The 'fundamental' value is the expected value of all dividends the asset yields over its lifetime, properly discounted to reflect the present-day value of the dividends paid at future dates (Barlevy 2007: 46).

In this context, Minsky (1982) has pointed out that the capitalist structure is inherently subject to booms, crisis, and depressions. The process, Minsky has outlined in his financial instability hypothesis (FIH), begins with initial profitability of investment activity and builds up households and business leverage, but ultimately ends with unrealistically high asset prices. When asset prices collapse, the negative wealth effect on aggregate demand is heightened because of the financial accelerator, the falling aggregate demand aggravating the sharp fall in credit. Undoubtedly, the withdrawal of credit from an overleveraged private sector can result in a severe economic decline (Auerback et al. 2010: 119).

Minsky has pointed out that stability in economic systems begins to generate a behaviour that produces fragility. The longer benign conditions are present, the more risk the borrowers will take. The resultant rise in financial fragility makes the system more prone to an unstable outcome as adverse changes in financial circumstances impact negatively on the return on investment projects. Minsky underlines that the declining margin or cushion of safety in financial transactions is amplified by the reckless use of financial leverage. The Minsky moment represents a point in the credit cycle when rising debt caused by financing speculative instruments burden investors with cash flow constraints. When cash flows fail to meet the expectations, and as debt charges become less bearable, investors begin to question the valuation strategies used and a major sell-off begins. As the perception spreads of a reversal of the previous asset price trends, prospective buyers turn cautious and uncertainty grows, leading to a sudden collapse in the market, clearing asset prices.

5. The move to economic bubbles and the onset of crises

The financial economy that has been evolving since the 1990s achieved rapid economic growth globally during the 1990s with consolidation and freeing of the flow of global finance capital. The economic growth, however, was noticed to have come mostly from the appreciation of the value of financial assets and consequent rise in the rentier incomes, with no marked reflection in the production activity and income generation in the real sector, other than in real estate. Soon after, within the first few years of the new century, the scenario changed. The global financial economy was hit by the global economic crisis in 2008 that started with the collapse of the US housing bubble in November 2006. It was not just a usual phase of cyclical recession postulated in economic business cycle theory – it was apprehended as a crisis that might have brought down the entire global financial economy like a house of cards, creating the worst-ever crisis in human history.

The global financial economy was rescued from the immediate effects of the crisis of 2008. It came through the direct bail-out packages given to the global corporate sector, by the respective governments in the countries having their headquarters, for recapitalising them with new finance and taking over their loss-generating toxic financial assets. In other countries, the national governments took indirect measures of various tax reliefs and subsidies as well as issues of fresh infrastructure bonds to help the corporate sector recapitalise and hold more risk-free government assets.

The true magnitude of the corporate losses globally from the crisis could not be assessed. A large portion of the losses remained concealed in the corporate off-balance sheet transactions. Some international agencies, like the IMF, tried to estimate the accumulating loss at the beginning of the crisis. But their estimates kept on being continuously revised upward in every subsequent estimate; finally reaching over some trillion dollars, they stopped making further estimates. The accumulated loss seems to be unfathomable.

One can guess that the burden of corporate loss taken over by the national governments all over the world, through the bailout packages and other measures, runs over several trillion dollars. A question remains. The government interventions helped the corporate sector wipe out their accumulated corporate losses from their books. But did it erase the accumulated losses from the global financial economy as a whole, making it start afresh on a clean slate? Is it not a fact that the burden of those unfathomable corporate losses still remains within the system as imposed on some other sectors, for example, on the government or the household debts within the financial economy? Economic reflections of it may not be registered as yet in the financial economy. But that does not prove that it is not there or will not cause problems in the future.

The government intervention could only water down the crisis by the relief measures but could not remove or solve it. Since the crisis of 2008, crises in different forms kept on flaring up sporadically at different segments of the global financial economy. There were European debt crises leading to the sovereign debt crisis of Greece, the Russian financial crisis with falling value of Russian rouble, slowing down of the growth rate in China and the Chinese stock market crash, and so on.

There is now a vast literature that has investigated different aspects of the global economic crisis of 2008 – how and why the US housing bubble was created and collapsed, how and why the sub-prime mortgage crisis in the US house financing could spread like a wildfire into a global financial crisis. Unfortunately, the standard explanations of the crisis, what we usually find, focus on many probable reasons for it, but at the surface level only. We now have a long list crowded with many such reasons – the rampant speculation by financial institutions; the reckless lending by loan initiators lowering lending standards and encouraging predatory lending by taking advantage of securitisation; the off-balance sheet transactions with SPVs concealing loss; the architecture of structured securities concealing credit risks; the CDOs and derivatives like CDSs spreading the loss to multiple investors; the marking-to-market system of accounting for the financial assets that generate windfall booking profits on market capitalisation on a daily basis; the leveraged investments that amplify loss by working in the reverse direction in the case loss; and above all, the failure of the government regulatory authorities to effectively control these trends (as if these were otherwise quite natural in the financial economy).

If so many problems keep on surfacing and the government authorities are to keep a check on them to avoid such crisis, it necessarily indicates that there are some structural problems inherent in the financial economy. Underneath the superficial trends describing the crisis, we need to probe the operational structure of the financial economy to locate the real cause of its persistent occurrence. Whether or not the development of such devastating economic crisis in some segment and its subsequent global spread could be checked in the future by effective government regulations is not really the question. In fact, the current crisis has shown that government regulations cannot really stop its occurrence. In the crisis of 2008 the governments could at best only bail out. But there is no guarantee that they would always be able to do so in the future. The recent sovereign debt crisis has shown that even the governments may go bankrupt. Who will then bail out whom? The real question is whether or not a structural imbalance necessarily grows in the system, which puts the financial economy at the edge of crisis.

6. Financialisation in the Indian economy

The global financial circuit is now expanding to bring in more finance. More finance is required to boost up the financial activities as well as to recapitalise the loss that might have been generating within the circuit. Hence, the production, financial activities, and financial savings in the developing economies, which so far have remained outside the purview of the global circuit, are now being brought into it through a process of globalisation and financialisation. These economies, especially the so-called emerging economies of the East, namely, China and India, are being integrated with the global financial circuit. The process of it is now reflected in the financialisation of these economies. We may mention in this context a remarkable feature of both China and India – they have high household savings. Prior to globalisation, the household net assets were also significantly high in these two countries. However, in recent times, a steep rise in inequality in household income and wealth distribution is being witnessed, especially with the sudden rise in the number of billionaires in China and India. Alongside this, now the household debts are also apprehended to be on the rise. However, these are some general observations on the possible causes and consequences of financial integration of these economies with the global circuit. Establishing these by empirical evidence is outside the scope of this book. We would rather focus here on the financialisation aspect as such – is there empirical evidence of financialisation in these countries? We will present here some empirical evidence of financialisation in the Indian economy as found in a study by Roy (2009).

Concepts and evidence of financialisation

The notion of financialisation could be viewed from different angles and so its reflections as an essential feature of the growing financial economy may be seen in many ways. These may be seen in the impact of financialisation on corporate governance with increased dominance of shareholders over management, corporate restructuring and shift in management priorities, inequality in wage income, shifts in the balance of power to the owners of financial capital in the corporate world etc. Two major aspects of financialisation in the major developed economies indicated in several studies are the slowdown in accumulation of physical assets and the rise in rentier incomes (Eatwell and Taylor 2000; Power et al. 2003; Epstein and Power 2003; Stockhammer 2004; Van Treeck 2009).

In the last two decades, investments in physical assets by non-financial businesses have been slowing down. They also tend to increase financial investments, causing this slowdown of their investments in physical assets. There is also evidence that the shareholder revolution has indeed curbed management's scope to accumulate physical capital. First, a strong positive correlation exists between the availability of internal sources of finance and investment in physical assets. So, the increase in firms' dividend payout ratio reduces the internal generation of funds and causes a consequent decline in investments in physical assets. Second, there has been a declining role of the stock market for providing investment finance to firms (Van Treeck 2009: 3–4). In the real sector, investments have also been restrained by low profit rates and excess capacity. In the major advanced economies, especially in Germany, France, the United Kingdom, and the United States, the investment–profit ratio shows a declining trend. It is also seen that the gross fixed capital formation as percentage of GDP in the major industrialised countries has been falling since the late 1970s (Navarro et al. 2004; Stockhammer 2008).

Financialisation has been found to cause increasing rentier share in national income (Hein and Van Treeck 2007). Estimates of the rentier share of income in twenty-nine OECD countries over the period 1960–2000 show that the rentier share of income has increased in most of these countries between the 1960s and 1970s, and the trend has continued in the 1980s and 1990s (Power et al. 2003). Several other studies have established that financialisation has increased the rentier motivations of industrial firms (Dumenil and Lévy 2000; Krippner 2005; Epstein 2003).

Indication of financialisation in the Indian economy

In the Indian economy, the period since the 1990s has been marked by globalisation and privatisation drives resulting in changed economic structures in the post-1990s period. At a glance, this period shows a significant increase in GDP and per capita income. But at the same time the impact of globalisation and privatisation on the real and financial sector have been reflected in the changing composition of income generation in India, which is indicative of a process of financialisation following the global trend.

An indirect way to consider financialisation is to look at the physical capital formation vis-à-vis the capital formation through savings in the economy. The global scenario of financialisation in developed countries since the late 1970s shows evidence of not only the slowing down of physical asset accumulation, but also the falling investment–profit ratio and gross fixed capital formation as percentage of GDP (Stockhammer 2004, 2008; Navarro et al. 2004). However, financialisation at the economy level is expected to have a direct reflection on the rentier income shares in the GDP. Another way to get an indication of financialisation is to examine the distribution of income. We may compare the pattern of growth in wages and profits in the manufacturing sector with the growth in rentier shares. The increasing gap between the two could be an indicator of financialisation. We examine these two aspects of financialisation in India in the remaining sections of this Appendix.

Rentier income shares in the Indian economy

We calculate rentier shares for the Indian economy over the period 1980–2015, somewhat modifying and broadening the definition of rentier income used by Power et al. (2003). Using the CSO National Accounts Statistics (NAS) and RBI data, two alternative measures of rentier income shares, R1 and R2, are calculated to accommodate the different ways of defining rentier income, as well as the data availability problems. The estimate R1 calculates rentier income with only operating surplus of the financial sector. In our second measure of rentier income, R2, we include along with the components of R1 the profit income accruing to the owners of landed property, shown as operating surplus and mixed income of the real estate, ownership of dwellings, and business services sector.

The two estimates of rentier income in India, R1 and R2, are as follows:

R1 = Operating surplus of the financial sector
R2 = Operating surplus of the financial sector + operating surplus and mixed income of the real estate sector

Based on these two estimates (R1 and R2) of rentier income, we get two measures of rentier shares, R1* and R2*, expressing rentier income as percentage of GDP at factor cost. Both factor incomes and GDP at factor cost are calculated at current prices (2015–16), as CSO (2017) data on factor incomes is available at current prices only. The old series (period 1980–2010) is therefore converted to current prices to maintain conformity. Using these two measures the picture we see for the Indian economy over the period 1980–81 to 2015–16 is presented in Table A.1.

It can be seen that R1* has increased steadily during this period. The rate of increase picked up after 1990–91, recording a significant rise during 2000–01 to 2004–05, when it reached 3.66 percent. Thereafter it has remained at that level. Alongside this, when we put the estimates obtained by R2*, we see a phenomenal increase in the rentier income share and a steep jump in the mid-1990s. The later period (late 1990s to early 2000) saw R2* falling a little, after which it once again increased from 2005–06 onwards. Evidently, the inclusion of income from ownership of landed property in the definition of rentier income

Table A.1 Rentier income share in GDP in India, 1981–2016

(Average annual percent)

Period	R1*	R2*
1980–81 to 1984–85	1.45	0.69
1985–86 to 1989–90	1.59	1.23
1990–91 to 1994–95	2.50	6.42
1995–96 to 1999–00	3.23	4.93
2000–01 to 2004–05	3.66	5.88
2005–06 to 2009–10	3.52	6.61
2010–11 to 2015–16	3.60	7.17

Notes: Calculated on the basis of data from CSO national accounts and RBI database

R1* and R2* are rentier income shares as explained in the text helps underline the drastic rise in rentier shares since the late 1990s in India.

Share of income – gap between productive and rentier income

Growth of rentier income alone may not be conclusive proof of financialisation. But financialisation, as conceptualised in current economic literature, could be conclusive when it leads to growing rentier incomes at a much faster rate than productive incomes. We now examine this aspect in the context of the Indian economy during the period 1980–81 to 2015–16.

The productive income in an economy is best reflected in the wages and profits in the manufacturing sector. So, to get conclusive evidence of financialisaton in India, we compare the appropriation of incomes by the rentier class with that by the wage earners and profit income of the firms in the manufacturing sector as share of GDP. For the rentier share we use the estimate (R2*), which we have obtained earlier. The wage and profit incomes are taken as the compensations and the operating surplus in the manufacturing sector and their shares are obtained as percentage of GDP.

The data for calculating operating surplus and compensations in the manufacturing sector as percentages of GDP at factor cost are taken from CSO (2017) National Income Accounts and RBI database (2017). The data are at current prices, as explained earlier. The results we have obtained are presented in Table A.2.

Table A.2 Manufacturing sector and rentier incomes as percentage of GDP in India, 1981–2016

(Annual average)

Period	Share of manufacturing sector		Share of rentier income
	Compensation	Operating surplus	
1980–81 to 1984–85	5.22	10.66	0.69
1985–86 to 1989–90	5.08	10.30	1.23
1990–91 to 1994–95	4.67	10.12	6.42
1995–96 to 1999–00	4.21	10.82	4.93
2000–01 to 2004–05	4.06	9.30	5.88
2005–06 to 2009–10	3.82	10.33	6.61
2010–11 to 2015–16	3.76	9.05	7.17

Source: Calculated on the basis of data from CSO national accounts (2017) and RBI database (2017), as explained in the text

There is clear evidence that rentier shares in GDP have grown at a much faster pace since the late 1990s compared to that of the compensations and operating surplus in the manufacturing sector in India. Compensation in the manufacturing sector as share of GDP at factor cost has steadily declined over this period. In fact, the rise in rentier share compared to that in wage and profit shares is quite significant, particularly since the early 1990s. While wage incomes or compensations as percentage of GDP have fallen over this period, profits as reflected in operating surplus as percentage of GDP have recorded marginal increase with some fluctuations. Thus, we may conclude that there is a definite evidence of financialisation with a rising trend in the Indian economy since the 1990s.

Bibliography

Abiad, A. and Mody, A. (2005). Financial reform, what shakes it? What shapes it? *The American Economic Review*, 95 (1), 66–88.

Acemoglu, D. and Zilibotti, F. (1997). Was Prometheus unbound by chance? Risk, diversification and growth. *Journal of Political Economy*, 105, 709–75.

Aerni, V., Juniac, C., Holley, B. and Tang, T. (2008). A wealth of opportunities in turbulent times. *Boston consulting group report*. USA: Boston Consulting Group.

Ahluwalia, I. J. (1992). *Productivity and growth in Indian manufacturing*. Delhi: Oxford University Press.

Ahmad, S. (1991). *Capital in economic theory: Neoclassical, Cambridge, and chaos*. Cheltenham, UK: Edward Elgar.

Allain, O. (2007). *Monetary circulation, the paradox of profits, and the velocity of money*. Proceedings of International Conference on Principles of Post-Keynesian Economic Policies. CEMF, Université de Bourgogne, Dijon, France, November 30 – December 1, 1–15. Retrieved 10 September 2008 from http://ideas.repec.org/p/hal/cesptp/halshs-00196485.html

Allen, F. and Gale, D. (1997). Financial markets, intermediaries, and intertemporal smoothing. *Journal of Political Economy*, 105, 523–46.

Andersen, T. and Trap, F. (2003). Financial liberalisation, financial development and economic growth in LDCs. *Journal of International Development*, 15 (2), 189–209.

Andresen, T. (1996). Economic black holes – the dynamics and consequences of accumulation. *Nonlinear Dynamics, Psychology, and Life Sciences*, 3 (2), 161–96.

Arestis, P. and Demetriades, P. (1996). Financial development and economic growth: Assessing the evidence. *The Economic Journal*, 107 (May), 783–99.

Argitis, G. and Pitelis, C. (2001). Monetary policy and the distribution of income: Evidence for the United States and the United Kingdom. *Journal of Post Keynesian Economics*, 23, 617–38.

Argitis, G. and Pitelis, C. (2006). Global finance, income distribution and capital accumulation. *Contributions to Political Economy*, 25, 63–81.

Argy, V. (1981). *The post-war international monetary crisis: An analysis.* Great Britain: Routledge.

Arnsperger, C. and Varoufakis, Y. (2006). What is neoclassical economics? The three axioms responsible for its theoretical oeuvre, practical irrelevance and, thus, discursive power. *Post-Autistic Economics Review, 38* (1). Retrieved 2 February 2010 from www.paecon.net/PAEReview/. . ./Arnsperger Varoufakis38.htm

Auerback, M., McCulley, P. and Parenteau, R. W. (2010). What would Minsky do? In D. B. Papadimitriou and R. L. Wray (Eds.), *The Elgar companion to Hyman Minsky*, pp. 117–33. Cheltenham, UK: Edward Elgar Publishing Limited.

Bagnoli, P., Goeschl, T. and Kovács, E. (2008). *People and biodiversity policies: Impacts, issues and strategies for policy action.* Paris: OECD Publishing.

Baily, M. N. and Elliott, D. J. (2011). The causes of financial crisis and the impact of raising capital requirements. In A. Demirguc-Kunt, D. D. Evanoff and G. G. Kaufman (Eds.), *The international financial crisis: Have the rules of finance changed?* United Kingdom: World Scientific Press.

Bakaert, G., Harvey, C. R. and Lundblad, C. (2005). Does financial liberalisation spur growth? *Journal of Financial Economics, 77*, 3–55.

Bank for International Settlements. (2009). Amounts outstanding of over-the-counter (OTC) derivatives by risk category and instrument. *BIS quarterly review.* Retrieved 28 April 2010 from http://www.bis.org/statistics/derstats.htm

Banta, M. (1993). *Taylored lives: Narrative production in the age of Taylor, Veblen, and Ford.* Chicago: University of Chicago Press.

Barbon, N. (1690[1905]). *A discourse of trade.* Jacob H. Hollander (ed.). Library of Economics and Liberty. Retrieved 29 May 2017 from www.econlib.org/library/YPDBooks/Barbon/brbnDT0.html

Bardhan, P. (2010). *Awakening giants, feet of clay: Assessing the economic rise of China and India.* Princeton, UK: Princeton University Press.

Barlevy, G. (2007). Economic theory and asset bubbles. *Economic perspectives*, Federal Reserve Bank of Chicago, 3Q, 44–59.

Barlow, A. (2003). *Between Fear and Hope: Globalization and Race in the United States.* Oxford, UK: Rowman & Littlefield Publishers.

Barth, J. R., Brumbaugh, R. D. and Wilcox, J. A. (2000). Policy watch: The repeal of Glass-Steagall and the advent of broad banking. *Journal of Economic Perspectives, 14* (2), Spring, 191–204.

Baumol, W. J. (1967). Macroeconomics of unbalanced growth: The anatomy of urban crisis. *American Economic Review, 57* (3), 415–26.

Baumol, W. J. (2001). Paradox of services: Exploding costs, persistent demand. In Ten-Raa and R. Schettkat (Eds.), *The growth of service industries: The paradox of exploding costs and persistent demand*, pp. 3–28. Cheltenham, UK and Northampton, MA: Elgar.

Beck, T., Demirguc-Kunt, A. and Levine, R. (2004). *Finance, inequality, and poverty: Cross-country evidence.* Policy Research Working Paper Series.

The World Bank, No. 3338, pp. 1–36. Retrieved 22 March 2009 from http// ideas.repec.org.p.nbr.nberwo.10979. html

Bellofiore, R., Davanzati, G. F. and Realfonzo, R. (2000). Marx inside the circuit: Discipline device, wage bargaining and unemployment in a sequential monetary economy. *Review of Political Economy, 12,* 403–17.

Bencivenga, V. R. and Smith, B. D. (1991). Financial intermediation and endogenous growth. *Review of Economics Studies, 58,* 195–209.

Bernanke, B. (2007). Remarks. *Federal Reserve Bank of Atlanta's (2007) Financial Markets Conference.* Sea Island, Georgia.

Bhaduri, A. and Marglin, S. (1990). Unemployment and the real wage: The economic basis for contesting political ideologies. *Cambridge Journal of Economics, 14,* 375–93.

Bianconi, M. (2013). *Financial economics, risk and information* (2nd ed.). Singapore: World Scientific.

Birner, J. (2002). *The Cambridge controversies in capital theory: A study in the logic of theory of development.* London: Routledge.

Blackburn, K. and Hung, V. T. Y. (1998). A theory of growth, financial development, and trade. *Economica, 65,* 107–24.

Blaug, M. (1996). *Economic theory in retrospect* (5th ed.). Cambridge, UK: Cambridge University Press.

Bliss, C. J. (1975). *Capital theory and the distribution of income.* Oxford: North-Holland Publishing.

Böhm-Bawerk, E. (1890). *Capital and interest: A critical history of economic theory* (Tr. by W. A. Smart). London: Palgrave Macmillan.

Bordo, M. D. (1993). The Bretton Woods international monetary system: A historical overview. In M. D. Bordo and B. Eichengreen (Eds.), *A retrospective on the Bretton Woods system: Lessons for international monetary reforms,* pp. 1–108. London: The University of Chicago Press.

Bordo, M., Eichegreen, B., Kingebiel, D. and Martinez-Peria, M. S. (2001). Is the crisis problem growing more severe? *Economic Policy, 16* (32), 51–82.

Bossone, B. (2003). Thinking of the economy as a Circuit. In L. P. Rochon and S. Santos, Rossi (Eds.), *Modern theories of money: The nature and the role of money in capitalist economy.* Cheltenham, UK: Edward Elgar.

Bosworth, B. and Triplett, J. (2007). The early 21st century U.S. productivity expansion is still in services. *International Productivity Monitor, 14* (Spring), 3–19. Retrieved 13 March 2009 www.ideas.repec.org/a/sls/ipmsls/ v14y20071.html

Boyer, R. (2000). Is a finance-led growth regime a viable alternative to Fordism? A preliminary analysis. *Economy and Society, 29,* 111–45.

Brazier, G. (1996). *Insider dealing: Law and regulation.* London, UK: Cavendish Publishing Limited.

Brewer, A. (2005). *Cantillon, Quesnay and the Tableau Economique.* Discussion Paper No. 05/577, Department of Economics, University of Bristol.

Brigham, E. F. and Ehrhardt, M. C. (2017). *Financial management: Theory and practice* (15th ed.). Boston, MA: Cengage Learning.

Calomiris, C. W. (1993). Financial factors in the Great Depression. *Journal of Economic Perspectives, 7* (2), 61–85.

Cantillon, R. (1755 [1959]). *Essaisur la nature du commerce in Général (Essay on the nature of trade in general)*. Henry Higgs (ed. and trans.). Library of Economics and Liberty. Retrieved 29 May 2017 from www.econlib.org/library/NPDBooks/Cantillon/cntNT.html

Case, K.E & Fair, R.C. (2007). *Principles of economics*. 8th Edition. New Delhi:Pearson Education Inc.

Central Statistical Organisation (2009). *National accounts statistics, factor incomes (Base Year 1999–2000: 1980–81, 1999–2000)*. Ministry of Statistics and Programme Implementation, Government of India. Retrieved 14 July 2009 from www.mospi.gov.in

Central Statistical Organisation (2014). *National accounts statistics*. Ministry of Statistics and Programme Implementation, Government of India. Retrieved 4 April 2016 from www.mospi.gov.in

Chang, H. and Yoo, C. (2002). The triumph of the rentiers? The (1997) Korean crisis in a historical perspective. In J. Eatwell and L. Taylor (Eds.), *International capital markets: Systems in transition*, pp. 369–90. New York: Oxford University Press.

Clark, J. B. (1899). *The distribution of wealth: A theory of wages, interest and profits*. New York: The Macmillan Company.

Cohen, A. J. and Harcourt, G. C. (2003). Retrospectives: Whatever happened to the Cambridge capital theory controversies? *Journal of Economic Perspectives*, *17* (1), 199–214.

Cohen, A. J. and Harcourt, G. C. (2005). Capital theory controversy: Scarcity, production equilibrium and time. In C. Bliss, A. J. Cohen and G. C. Harcourt (Eds.), *Capital theory: Volume I*, pp. xxvii–lx. Cheltenham, UK: Edward Elgar Publishing Limited.

Cohen, B J. *The international monetary system: diffusion and ambiguity. International Affairs*, 84 (3), 455–470.

Colander, D. (2000). The death of neoclassical economics. *Journal of the History of Economic Thought*, 22 (2), 127–43.

Conard, J. W. (1959). *Introduction to the theory of interest*. Los Angeles, CA: University of California Press.

Cottrell, A. (1994). Post Keynesian monetary economics: A critical survey. *Cambridge Journal of Economics*, *18*, 587–605.

Crotty, J. (1990). Owner-manager conflict and financial theories of investment instability – a critical assessment of Keynes, Tobin, and Minsky. *Journal of Post Keynesian Economics*, *12* (4), 519–42.

Crotty, J. (2000). *Slow growth, destructive competition, and low road labor relations: A Keynes-Marx-Schumpeter analysis of neoliberal globalization*. Working Papers, no. 6. Political Economy Research Institute, University of Massachusetts, Amherst. Retrieved 1 March 2009 from www.papers. ssrn. com/sol3/papers.cfm?abstract_id=332220

Crotty, J. (2007). *If financial market competition is so intense, why are financial firms profits so high? Reflections on the current 'Golden Age' of finance'*. Working Paper Series, no. 134, Political Economy Research Institute, University of Massachusetts, Amherst. Retrieved 9 July 2009 from www.peri.umass. edu/fileadmin/pdf/working_papers/working_papers_101–150/WP134.pdf

Crotty, J. (2008). *Structural causes of the global financial crisis: A critical assessment of the 'New Financial Architecture'*. Economics Department Working Paper Series, no. 16. University of Massachusetts, Amherst. Retrieved 9 July 2016 from http://scholarworks.umass.edu/econ_workingpaper/16

Crouznet, F. (1972). Introduction. In F. Crouznet (Ed.), *Capital formation in the industrial revolution*, pp. 1–69. New York: Harper and Row Publishers, Inc.

Cullison, W. E. (1989). The U.S. productivity slowdown: What the experts say. *Economic Review*, July/August, 10–21.

Dean, P. (1972). Capital formation in Britain before the railway age. In F. Crouznet (Ed.), *Capital formation in the industrial revolution*, pp. 94–118. New York: Harper and Row Publishers, Inc.

Debelle, G. (2004). *Macroeconomic implications of rising household debt*. BIS Working Papers, no. 153, pp. 1–40. Monetary and Economic Department, Bank for International Settlements (BIS). Retrieved 11 October 2010 from www.bis.org/publ/work153.htm

Demir, F. (2009). Private investment and cash flow relationship revisited: Capital market imperfections and financialisation of real sectors in emerging markets. *World Development*, 37 (5), 953–64.

Demirgüç-Kunt, A. and Detragiache, E. (1999). Financial liberalisation and financial fragility. In B. Pleskovic and J. Stiglitz (Eds.), *Annual world bank conference on development economics 1998*, pp. 303–31. Washington, DC: The World Bank.

Demirgüç-Kunt, A. and Levine, R. (1995). *Stock market development and financial intermediaries: Stylized facts*. Policy Research Working Paper Series, no. 1462, pp. 1–52. The World Bank. Retrieved 27 March 2009 from http://www.wds.worldbank.org.servlet.WDSContentServer.WDSP.IB. (1995).05.01.000009265_3961019111757.Rendered.PDF.multi_page.pdf

Dodd, R. (2003). The role of derivatives in the East Asian financial crises. In J. Eatwell and L. Taylor (Eds.), *International capital markets: Systems in transition*, pp. 447–73. New York: Oxford University Press.

Dos Santos, C. H. (2004). *A stock-flow consistent general framework for formal Minskyan analyses of closed economies*. Working Paper, no. 403, pp. 1–30. The Levy Economics Institute. Retrieved 9 July 2009 from http://ideas.repec.org/p/lev/wrkpap/403.html

Dowd, K. and Hutchinson, M (2010). *Alchemists of Loss: How Modern Finance and Government Intervention Crashed the Financial System*. UK: Wiley.

Dowrick, S. (1995). The determinants of long-run growth. In P. Andersen, J. Dwyer and D. Gruen (Eds.), *Productivity and growth*, pp. 7–47. Reserve Bank of Australia. Retrieved 29 November 2008 from www.rba.gov.au/PublicationsAndResearch/Conferences/1995/Dowrick.pdf

Dumenil, G. and Levy, D. (2004). The real and financial components of profitability (USA 1948–2000). *Review of Radical Political Economy*, 36, 82–110.

Dumenil, G. and Lévy, D. (2001). Costs and benefits of neoliberalism: A class analysis. *Review of International Political Economy*, 8 (4), 578–607.

Dutt, R. C. (2003). Labour market – social institution, economic reforms and social cost. In S. Uchikawa (Ed.), *Labour market and institution in India: 1990s and beyond*. Delhi: Manohar.

Eatwell, J. and Taylor, L.(2000). *Global finance at risk*. Cambridge, UK: Polity Press.

Eichengreen, B. J. (1992). *Golden fetters: The gold standard and the great depression, 1919–1939*. New York: Oxford University Press.

Epstein, G. (2003). Introduction: Financialization and the world economy. In G. Epstein (Eds.), *Financialization and the world economy*. Cheltenham, UK: Edward Elgar Publishing Ltd.

Epstein, G. A. and Jayadev, A. (2005). The rise of rentier incomes in OECD countries: Financialization, central bank policy and labor solidarity. In G. A. Epstein. (Ed.), *Financialisation and the world economy*, pp. 46–74. Cheltenham, UK: Edward Elgar.

Epstein, G. A. and Power D. (2003). *Rentier incomes and financial crises: An empirical examination of trends and cycles in some OECD countries*. Working Paper Series, no. 57, Political Economy Research Institute, University of Massachusetts: Amherst.

Ertürk, K. A. (2006). *Speculation, liquidity preference, and monetary circulation*. Working Paper, no. 435, pp. 1–25. The Levy Economics Institute of Bard College. Retrieved 23 August 2010 from www.levyinstitute.org/files/download.php?file=wp_435.Pdfandpubid

Fabozzi, F. J., Neave, E. H. and Zhou, G. (2011). *Financial economics*. Hoboken, NJ: Wiley.

Fetter, F. A. (1977). Capital, interest, and rent: Essays in the theory of distribution. In M. N. Rothbard (Ed.), *Library of economics and liberty*. Retrieved 13 June 2009 from www.econlib.org/library/NPDBooks/Fetter/ftCIR17.html

Field, A. J. (1984). Asset exchanges and transactions demand for money, 1919–1929. *American Economic Review*, 74 (1), 43–59.

Fisher, I. (1906). *The nature of capital and income*. New York: Palgrave Macmillan.

Fisher, I. (1911[1922]). *The purchasing power of money* (2nd ed.). New York: Palgrave Macmillan.

Fisher, I. (1930). *The theory of interest*. New York: The Macmillan Company. Retrieved 21 February 2008 from www.econlib.org/library/NPDBooks/Fisher/ftCIR.html

Forbes (2006–2011). The world's leading companies. In S. De Carlo. (Ed.), *Special report*. Retrieved 23 December 2011 from www.forbes.com/global2000/list

Friedman, M. and Schwartz, A. J. (1963). *Monetary history of the United States 1867–1960*. Princeton: Princeton University Press.

Galbraith, J. K. (1987). *A history of economics: The past as the future*. London: Hamish Hamilton.

Ghosh, A. K. (1994). Employment in organised manufacturing in India. *The Indian Journal of Labour Economics*, 37 (2), April–June, 141–62.

Girouard, N., Kennedy, M. and André, C. (2006). *Has the rise in debt made households more vulnerable?* OECD Economics Department Working Papers, no. 535. OECD Publishing. Retrieved 04 January 2009 from http://www.oecd.org/LongAbstract; doi:10.1787/352035704305

Gkamas, D. (2006). Banking. In N. Wilson (Eds.), *Encyclopaedia of ancient Greece.* New York: Routledge.

Gnos, C. (2003). Circuit theory as an explanation of the complex real world. In L. P. Rochon and S. Rossi (Eds.), *Modern theories of money: The nature and the role of money in capitalist economy,* pp. 322–38. Cheltenham, UK: Edward Elgar.

Gnos, C. (2006). French circuit theory. In P. Arestis. and M. Sawyer (Eds.), *A handbook of alternative monetary economics,* (pp. 87–104). Cheltenham, UK: Edward Elgar.

Goldstein, M. et al. (1993). *International capital markets: Exchange rate management and international capital flows.* New York: International Monetary Fund.

Gomez, C. (2008). *Financial markets, institutions and financial services.* New Delhi: Prentice-Hall of India, Pvt. Ltd.

Goodhart, C. A. E. (2005). Review of credit and state theories of money: The contributions of A. Mitchell Innes. *History of Political Economy, 37* (4), Winter, 759–61.

Gordon, R. J. (1995). Problems in the measurement and performance of service-sector productivity in the United States. In A. Palle, J. Dwyer and D. Gruen (Eds.), *Productivity and growth,* pp. 139–66. Proceedings of RBA Annual Conference Volume, Economic Group, Reserve Bank of Australia. Retrieved 29 November 2008 from http://ideas.repec.org/p/nbr/nberwo/5519.html

Gordon, R. J. (2002). *Saving and investment in the rise and fall of the new economy.* Keynote address at 2002 Forum Risparmio, Milan, Italy, January 23, 2002. Retrieved 29 November 2008 from http://faculty web.at.northwestern.edu/economics/Gordon/LINSavEng.pdf

Gourinchas, P. O. and Jeanne, O. (2006). The elusive gains from international financial integration. *Review of Economic Studies, 73* (3), 715–41.

Graziani, A. (1989). *The theory of the monetary circuit.* Thames Papers in Political Economy, Spring: 1–26. Reprinted in Musella, M. and Panico, C. (Eds.) (1995). *The money supply in the economic process.* Aldershot: Edward Elgar.

Graziani, A. (2003). *The monetary theory of production.* Cambridge, UK: Cambridge University Press.

Greenwood, J. (1997).*The third industrial revolution: Technology, productivity, and income inequality.* Washington, DC: American Enterprise Institute for Public Policy Research.

Greenwood, J. and Jovanovic, B. (1990). Financial development, growth, and the distribution of income. *Journal of Political Economy, 98,* 1076–107.

Griliches, Z. (1994). Productivity, R and D, and the data constraint. *American Economic Review, 84* (1), (March), 1–23.

Group of Ten. (2001). *Consolidation in the financial sector.* Summary report. IMF. Retrieved 17 March 2011 from http://www.imf.org/external/np/g10/(2001)/01/eng/index.htm

Guiso, L., Jappelli, T., Padula, M. and Pagano M. (2004). Financial market integration and economic growth in the EU. *Economic Policy, 19* (40), 523–77.

Hahn, F. H. (1965). On some problems of proving the existence of an equilibrium in a monetary economy. In F. H. Hahn and F. P. R. Brechling (Eds.), *Theory of interest rates.* London: Palgrave Macmillan and New York: St Martin's Press.

Hahn, F. H. (1973). On transactions costs, essential sequence economics and money. *Review of Economic Studies, 40* (4), October.

Harcourt, G. C. (1972). *Some Cambridge controversies in the theory of capital.* London, UK: Penguin.

Harvey, R. (2005). *Comparison of household saving ratios: Euro area/US/Japan.* Statistical Brief. OECD, 8 June. Retrieved 15 February 2009 from www.oecd.org/dataoecd/53/48/32023442.pdf

Heffernan, S. (2005). *Modern banking.* West Sussex, UK: John Wiley and Sons.

Hein, E. (2006). Interest, debt and capital accumulation – a Kaleckian approach. *International Review of Applied Economics, 20,* 337–52.

Hein, E. (2007). Interest rate, debt, distribution and capital accumulation in a post-Kaleckian model. *Metroeconomica, 58* (2), 310–39.

Hein, E. and Van Treeck, T. (2007). *Financialisation in Kaleckian, post-Kaleckian models of distribution and growth.* IMK Working Paper, no.07–2007, pp. 1–33. IMK at the Hans Boeckler Foundation, Macroeconomic Policy Institute. Retrieved 9 July 2009 from http://ideas.repec.org.p.imk.wpaper.07–2007.html

Hennings, K. H. (1987). Capital as a factor of production. In J. Eatwell, M. Milgate and P. Newman (Eds.), *New Palgrave: A dictionary of economics* (Vol. 1, pp. 327–33). London: The Macmillan Press Limited.

Henwood, D. (1998). *Wall street: How it works and for whom.* New York, London: Verso.

Hicks, J. R. (1933). Gleichgewicht und Konjunktur. *Zeitschrift für National-ökonomie,* IV (June): 441–55. [Trans.1980]. Equilibrium and the trade cycle. *Economic Inquiry, 18,* 523–34.

Hicks, J. R. (1965). *Capital and growth.* Oxford: The University Press.

Hicks, J. R. (1973). *Capital and time.* Oxford: The University Press.

Hicks, J. R. (1980). *IS-LM: An explanation. Journal of Post Keynesian Economics, 3* (2), 139–54.

Hilferding, R. (1910[1981]). *Finance capital. A study of the latest phase of capitalist development* (Tom Bottomore, Ed.). London: Routledge & Kegan Paul.

Hobsbawm, E. (1975). *The age of capital: 1848–1875.* London: Abacus.

Homer, S. and Sylla, R. (1963). *A history of interest rates.* Trenton, NJ: John Wiley and Sons Inc.

Hosseini, H. (1990). The archaic, the obsolete and the mythical in neoclassical economics: Problems with the rational and optimizing assumptions of the Jevons-Marshallian system. *American Journal of Economics and Sociology*, *49* (1).

Hughes, T. P. (2004). *American genesis: A century of invention and technological enthusiasm, 1870–1970*. Chicago: The University of Chicago Press.

Hull, J. C. (2001). *Options, futures, and other derivatives* (3rd ed.). New Delhi: Prentice-Hall.

Hume, M. S. (2008). *Importance of measuring household liability details and net worth*. Working Party on Financial Statistics, OECD, Paris, France October 13, (2008). Retrieved 15 February 2009 from www.oecd.org/dataoecd/23/32/41514228.t

Hunt, P. A. (2009). *Structuring mergers and acquisitions: A guide to creating shareholder value* (4th ed.). New York: Aspen Publishers.

Inklaar, R., Timmer, M. P. and Van Ark, B. (2007). *Mind the gap! International comparisons of productivity in services and goods production*. Hi-Stat Discussion Paper Series, d06–175, pp. 1–30. Institute of Economic Research, Hitotsubashi University. Retrieved 9 July 2009 from http://ideas.repec.org/p/dgr/rugggd/gd-89.html

Innes, A. M. (1913). What is money? *The Banking Law Journal*, May, 377–408.

International Monetary Fund (2009). *World economic outlook update*. Retrieved 19 December 2011 from www.imf.org/external/np/sec/mds/1996/mds9613.htm

Ivo, W. (2014). *Corporate finance* (3rd ed.). Marina del Rey: Printing Source.

Kalecki, M. (1954). *Theory of economic dynamics: An essay on cyclical and long-run changes in the capitalist economy*. London: George Allen and Unwin.

Kerry, E. B. (2010). *Asset pricing and portfolio choice theory*. New York: Oxford University Press.

Keynes, J. M. (1930[1973]). A treatise on money. In J. M. Keynes (Ed.), *The collected writings*. London: Palgrave Macmillan. Retrieved 1 August 2008 from http://ideas.repec.org/p/lev/wrkpap/wp

Keynes, J. M. (1932). *Essays in persuasion*. New York: Harcourt Brace. Retrieved 1 August 2015 from http://www.questia.com/. . ./essays-in-persuasion-by-john-maynard-keynes.jsp

Keynes, J. M. (1936). *General theory of interest, employment and money*. New York: Harcourt, Brace.

Kindleberger, C. P. (1973). *The world in depression, 1929–1939*. London: University of California Press.

Kindleberger, C. P. (1978). *Manias, panics and crashes*. New York: Basic.

Kindleberger, C. P. (1984). *A financial history of Western Europe*. Crows Nest: George Allen and Unwin Publishers Ltd.

King, R. G. and Levine, R. (1993). Finance and growth: Schumpeter might be right. *Quarterly Journal of Economics*, *108* (3), 717–37.

Kirzner, I. M. (1976). Ludwig von Mises and the theory of capital and interest. In L. S. Moss (Ed.), *The economics of Ludwig von Mises: Toward a critical reappraisal*. Kansas City: Sheen and Ward, Inc. Retrieved 26 January 2008 from http://oll.libertyfund.org/title/109/30537

Knight, F. (1921). *Risk, uncertainty, and profit*. Boston, MA: Houghton Mifflin. Retrieved 19 December 2011 from www.econlib.org/library/Knight/knRUP.html

Knight, F. (1936). The quantity of capital and the rate of interest. *Journal of Political Economy* (reproduced in 1999, I).

Knight, F. (1938). On the theory of capital: In reply to Mr. Kaldor. *Econometrica*, 6 (1), 63–82.

Kornai, J. (1971). *Anti-equilibrium: On economic systems theory and the tasks of research*. New York: American Elsevier.

Kornai, J. (2007). *By force of thought: Irregular memoirs of an intellectual journey*. Cambridge, MA: MIT Press.

Kozicki, S. (1997). The productivity growth slowdown: Diverging trends in the manufacturing and service sectors. *Economic Review*. Federal Reserve Bank of Kansas City, Q I, 31–46.

Kregel, J. (2007). *The natural instability of financial markets*. Economics Working Paper Archive, no. 523, 1–28. Levy Economics Institute. Retrieved 25 August 2010 from www.levyinstitute.org/pubs/wp_523.pdf

Krippner, G. (2005). The financialization of the American economy. *Socio-Economic Review*, 3, 173–208.

Krizner, I. M. (1976). Ludwig von Mises and the theory of capital and interest. In L. A. Moss. (Ed.), *The economics of Ludwig von Mises: Toward a critical reappraisal*. Kansas City: Sheed Andrews and McMeel Inc. Retrieved 21 February 2008 from www.econlib.org/library/NPDBooks

Lavoie, M. (1985). Credit and money: the dynamic circuit, overdraft economics and post-Keynesian economics, in M. Jarsulic Ed. *Money and Macro Policy*, as cited in Cottrell, A. (1994). Post Keynesian monetary economics: A critical survey. *Cambridge Journal of Economics*, 18, 587–605.

Lavoie, M. (1992). *Foundations of post-Keynesian economics*. Aldershot: Edward Elgar.

Lavoie, M. (2009). Cadrisme within a post-Keynesian model of growth and distribution. *Review of Political Economy*, 21 (3), 369–91.

Lavoie, M. and Godley, W. (2001–2002). Kaleckian models of growth in a coherent stock-flow monetary framework: A Kaldorian view. *Journal of Post Keynesian Economics*, 24 (2), 277–311.

Lazonick, W. and O'Sullivan, M. (2000). Maximizing shareholder value: A new ideology for corporate governance. *Economy and Society*, 29 (1), 13–35.

Lewin, P. (1999). *Capital in disequilibrium: The role of capital in changing world*. London: Routledge.

Maclean, D. (1997). *Lagging productivity growth in the service sector: Mismeasurement, mismanagement or misinformation?* Working Paper, no.

97–6, Bank of Canada. Retrieved 27 September 2010 from http://www.bankofcanada.ca/en/res/wp/(1997)/wp97–6.pdf

MacLean, L. C. and Ziemba, W. T. (2013). *Handbook of the fundamentals of financial decision making*. Singapore: World Scientific Publishing Company.

Maddison, A. (2001). *The world economy: A millennial perspective*. Paris: OECD.

Maddison, A. (2006). *The world economy (Volume 1: A millennial perspective, Volume 2: Historical perspective)*. New Delhi: Academic Foundation.

Marshall, A. (1890 [1920]). *Principles of economics* (8th ed.). London: Macmillan and Co. Ltd.

Marx, K. (1867 [1906]). *Capital, a critique of political economy (Das Kapital)* (Engels, F., Untermann, E. Eds. and Moore, S., Aveling, E., trans.). Library of Economics and Liberty. Retrieved 29 May 2017 from www.econlib.org/library/YPDBooks/Marx/mrxCpContents.html

Meissner, C. M. (2010). Surplus reversals in large nations: The cases of France and Great Britain in the interwar period. In S. Claessens, S. Evenett and B. Hoekman (Eds.), *Rebalancing the global economy: A primer for policymaking*. London: Centre for Economic Policy Research.

Menger, C. (1871). *Principles of economics*. Online version by the Ludwig von Mises Institute, Auburn, Alabama. Retrieved 27 September 2010 from www.mises.org

Menger, C. (1892). On the origin of money (trans. Caroline A. Foley). *Economic Journal*, 2, 239–55.

Messori, M. and Zazzaro, A. (2005). Single period analysis: Financial markets, firms' failures and the closure of the monetary circuit. In G. Fontana and R. Bellofiore (Eds.), *The monetary theory of production: Tradition and perspectives*. London: Palgrave Macmillan.

Milanovic, B. (2011). More or less. *Finance and Development*, 48 (30), September. Retrieved 19 March 2011 from http://www.imf.org/external/pubs/ft/fandd/(2011)/09/milanovic.htm

Mill, J. S. (1848[1909]). *Principles of political economy with some of their applications to social philosophy* (William J. Ashley, Ed.). London: Longmans, Green and Co.

Minsky, H. P. (1982). The financial instability hypothesis: A restatement. In H. P. Minsky (Ed.). *Can 'It' happen again? Essays on instability and finance*. Armonk, New York: M. E. Sharpe.

Mises, L. (1949). *Human action: A treatise on economics*. Irvington-on-Hudson, NY: The Foundation for Economic Education. Retrieved 21 March 2008 from www.econlib.org/library/NPDBooks/Fisher/ftCIR0.html

Moore, B. (1988). *Horizontalists and Verticalists: The macroeconomics of credit money*, CUP: Cambridge, *as cited in* Cottrell, A. (1994). Post Keynesian monetary economics: A critical survey. *Cambridge Journal of Economics*, 18, 587–605.

Munro, J. (2008). *Basic principles of Marxian economics*. Lecture Notes, University of Toronto. Retrieved 24 June 2007 from www.economics.utoronto. ca/munro5

Munro, J. (2009). *Coinage and monetary in Burgundian Flanders during the late-medieval bullion famines 1384–1482*. Working Paper, no. 361, pp. 1–43. University of Toronto. Retrieved 14 July 2010 from www.economics. utoronto.ca/index.php/research/WorkingPaperDetails/361

Navarro, V., Schmitt, J. and Astudillo, J. (2004). Is globalisation undermining the welfare state? *Cambridge Journal of Economics*, 28, 133–52.

Neill, T. P. (1949). The physiocrat's concept of economics. *The Quarterly Journal of Economics*, 63 (4), 532–53.

Nell, E. J. (2002). On realizing profits in money. *Review of Political Economy*, 14 (6), 519–30.

Nitzan, J. and Bichler, S. (2000). Capital accumulation: Breaking the dualism of 'economics' and 'politics'. In R. Palan (Ed.), *Global political economy: Contemporary theories*, pp. 67–88. New York and London: Routledge.

Nordhaus, W. (1982). Economic policy in the face of declining productivity. *European Economic Review*, May/June, 131–57.

Nordhaus, W. (2004). *A retrospective on the postwar productivity slowdown*. Cowles Foundation Discussion Papers No. 1494. Cowles Foundation for Research in Economics, Yale University. Retrieved 24 July 2008 from www. ideas.repec.org/p/cwl/cwld/1494.html

OECD (2008). *Growing unequal? Income distribution and poverty in OECD countries*. OECD. Retrieved 19 December 2011 from www.oecd.org/ dataoecd/45/42/41527936.pdf

OECD (2016). *Inequality update figures*. Retrieved 27 April 2017 from www. oecd.org/social/OECD2016-Income-Inequality-Update.pdf

OECD (2017). *OECD data*. Retrieved 27 April 2017 from https://data.oecd.org

O'Mahony, M. and Van Ark, B. (Eds.). (2003). *EU productivity and competitiveness: An industry perspective can Europe resume the catching-up process?* Luxembourg: Office for Official Publications of the European Communities. Retrieved 13 March 2009 from www.enterprise.europe. network.sk/docs/NB5503035ENC

Omay, T. and Atasü, R. (2004). *Rethinking the equilibrium concept in mainstream economics*. 6th Graduate Conference in Erlangen: Border Crossings Culture-Media- Economy, University of Erlangen, Nuremberg, Germany, November.

Orhangazi, Ö. (2008). Financialisation and capital accumulation in the non-financial corporate sector: A theoretical and empirical investigation on the US economy: 1973–2003. *Cambridge Journal of Economics*, 32, 863–86.

Özgür, G. and Ertürk, K. A. (2008). *Endogenous money in the age of financial liberalization*. Working Paper, The IDEAs working paper series no.05/2008, 1–18. Retrieved 1 December 2010 from www.networkideas.org/working/ aug2008/05_(2008).pdf

Palley, T. (2006). Class conflict and the Cambridge theory of income distribution. In E. Hein, A. Heise and A. Truger (Eds.), *Wages, employment, distribution and growth: International perspectives*, pp. 223–46. Basingstoke: Palgrave Macmillan.

Panchmukhi, V. R. (2000). Five recent paradoxes and anomalies of economics. *Asia- Pacific Development Journal, 7* (2), 1–31.

Parguez, A. (1975). *Monnaie et macroéconomie*. Paris: Economica.

Perez, C. (2002). *Technological revolutions and 'financial capital': The dynamics of bubbles and golden ages*. Northampton, MA: Edward Elgar Publishing Inc.

Phelps, E. S. (2007). Foreword. In R. Frydman and M. D. Goldberg (Eds.), *Imperfect knowledge economics: Exchange rates and risk*, pp. xiii–xx. Princeton, NJ: Princeton University Press.

Pieterse, J. N. (2002). Global inequality: Bringing politics back in. *Third World Quarterly, 23* (6), 1–24.

Piketty, T. (2014). *Capital in the twenty-first century* (A. Goldhamme, trans.). Cambridge, MA: The Belknap Press of Harvard University Press.

Piketty, T. and Saez, E. (2003). Income inequality in the United States, 1913–1998. *Quarterly Journal of Economics, 118* (1), 1–39.

Pilbeam, K. (2006). *International finance* (3rd ed.). New York: Palgrave Macmillan.

Pineault (2001). *Finance capital and the institutional foundations of capitalist finance: Theoretical elements from Marx to Minsky*. Retrieved 5 May 2011 from https://depot.erudit.org/retrieve/774/000267.pdf

Poulon, F. (1982). *Macroéconomie approfondie, equilibre, déséquilibre, circuit*. Paris: Cujas.

Power, D., Epstein, G. and Abrena, M. (2003). *Trends in rentier income share in OECD countries, 1960–2000*. Working Paper Series, no. 58a, pp. 1–77. Political Economy Research Institute, University of Massachusetts Amherst. Retrieved 30 June 2008 from www.peri.umass.edu/fileadmin/pdf/working_papers/working_papers_51–100/WP58a.pdf

Quesnay, F. (1759). Tableau économique. 3d ed. Reprint. Edited by M. Kuczynski and R. Meek. London: Macmillan, *as cited in* The Concise Encyclopedia of Economics (2008). *François Quesnay*. Library of Economics and Liberty. Retrieved January 8, 2018 from http://www.econlib.org/library/Enc/bios/Quesnay.html

Radner, R. (1972). Existence of equilibrium of plans, prices and price expectations in a sequence of markets. *Econometrica, 40* (2), 289–303.

Rajan, R. G. and Zingales, L. (1998). Financial dependence and growth. *American Economic Review, 88* (3), 559–86.

Ramsay, I. M. (1998). Models of corporate regulation: The mandatory/enabling debate. In C. Rickett and R. Grantham (Eds.), *Corporate personality in the 20th century*, pp. 215–70. Oxford: Hart Publishing.

Reserve Bank of India (2009). *Real-time handbook of statistics on the Indian economy*. Database on the Indian Economy: RBI Data Warehouse. Retrieved 7 July 2009 from https://dbie.rbi.org.in

Robinson, J. (1952). The generalization of the general theory. In *The rate of interest and other essays*. London: Palgrave Macmillan.

Robinson, J. (1953–1954). The production function and the theory of capital. *Review of Economic Studies, 21* (2), 81–106. Reprinted in Robinson J. (1960). *Collected Economic Papers*. Vol 2. Oxford: Blackwell.

Rochon, L. P. (1999). *Credit, money and production: An alternative post-Keynesian approach*. Cheltenham, UK: Edward Elgar.

Rochon, L. P. (2005). The existence of monetary profits within the monetary circuit. In G. Fontana and R. Realfonzo (Eds.), *The monetary theory of production: Tradition and perspectives*, pp. 125–36. London: Palgrave Macmillan.

Rogers, C. (1989). *Money, Interest and Capital*, CUP: Cambridge, as cited in Cottrell, A. (1994). Post Keynesian monetary economics: A critical survey. *Cambridge Journal of Economics, 18*, 587–605.

Romer, C D. (1992). What Ended the Great Depression? *The Journal of Economic History, 52* (4), 757–784.

Rose, A. K. and Wieladek, T. (2014). Financial protectionism? First evidence. *Journal of Finance, 69* (5), 2127–149.

Rowthorn, R. E. (1995). Capital formation and unemployment. *Oxford Review of Economic Policy, 11* (1), 26–39.

Rowthorn, R. E. (1999). Unemployment, wage bargaining and capital-labour substitution. *Cambridge Journal of Economics, 23*, 413–25.

Rowthorn, R. and Ramaswamy, R. (1997). Deindustrialization – its causes and implications. *Economic issues*, International Monetary Fund, *10*, 1–12.

Roy, S. (2009). Growing rentier shares in the Indian economy: A study. *Research Journal Social Sciences*. Panjab University, *17* (1), 50–64.

Roy, S. (2011). The growing dichotomy between real and financial sectors. *Matrix Business Review, 1* (2), 27–38.

Roy, S. (2013). Financialisation and accumulation: A firm-level study in the Indian context. In *Shaping the Future of Business and Society*. Symbiosis Institute of Management Studies, Annual Research Conference, 2013. Retrieved 30 June 2014 from www.sciencedirect.com/science/article/pii/S221256711400203

Ryan, C. K. (2002). Capital and interest theories. *American Journal of Economics and Sociology, 61* (5), 27–46.

Schlösser, A. (2011). *Pricing and risk management of synthetic CDOs*. New York: Springer.

Schmidt, V. A. (2002). *The futures of European capitalism*. New York: Oxford University Press.

Schmitt, B. (1972). *Macroeconomic theory: A fundamental revision*. [Trans. Benvenuta Bras] Albeuve: Castella.

Schnabel, I. and Seckinger, C. (2015). *Financial fragmentation and economic growth in Europe*. Retrieved 19 May 2017 from www.econstor.eu/bitstream/10419/112864/1/VfS_2015_pid_616.pdf

Schumpeter, J. A. (1934). *The theory of economic development*. Trenton, NJ: Transaction Publishers.

Schumpeter, J. A. (1954). *History of economic analysis*. Taylor and Francis e-Library. Retrieved 5 March 2011 from www.books.google.co.in/books?isbn=0415108888

Seager, Henry R. (1913). *Principles of Economics*. New York: Henry Holt.

Seccareccia, M. (2003). Pricing, investment and the financing of production within the framework of the monetary circuit: Some preliminary evidence. In L. P. Rochon and S. Santos, Rossi (Eds.), *Modern theories of money: The nature and the role of money in capitalist economy*. Cheltenham, UK: Edward Elgar.

Sihag, B. S. (2008). Kautilya on risk-return trade-off and diversification. *Indian journal of economics and business*. December, 1–13. Retrieved 29 December 2010 from http://findarticles. com/p/articles/mi_m1TSD/is_2_7/ai_n31524543

Skott, P. and Ryoo, S. (2007). Macroeconomic implications of financialisation. *Cambridge Journal of Economics*, 32, 827–62.

Skousen, M. (2014). *Economic Logic*. Washington DC: Capital Press.

Smith, A. (1776[1904]). *An inquiry into the nature and causes of the wealth of nations* (Cannan, E., Ed.). London: Methuen & Co. Ltd.

Smithin, J. (1994). *Controversies in Monetary Economics: Ideas, Issues and Policy*. Aldershot, UK: Edward Elgar.

Snowdown, B. and Vane, H. R. (2002). Gold standard. In *An encyclopaedia of macroeconomics*. pp. 293–296. Cheltenham, UK: Edward Elgar Publishing Ltd.

Solow, R. M. (1987). We'd better watch out. *New York Times*. July 12, Book Review. p. 36.

Solow, R. M. (1997). How did economics get that way and what way did it get? *Daedalus*, 126 (Winter).

Spooner, F. C. (1972). *The international economy and monetary movements in France 1493–1725*. London: Oxford University Press.

Stefania, V., Glattfelder, J. B. and Battiston, S. (2011). *The network of global corporate control*. Cornell University Library. Retrieved 19 May 2017 from https://arxiv.org/pdf/1107.5728.pdf

Stiglitz, J. E. (1985). Credit markets and the control of capital. *Journal of Money, Credit and Banking*, 17, 133–52.

Stockhammer, E. (2004). Financialisation and the slowdown of accumulation. *Cambridge Journal of Economics*, 28 (5), 719–41.

Stockhammer, E. (2006). Shareholder value orientation and the investment-profit puzzle. *Journal of Post Keynesian Economics*, 28, 193–215.

Stockhammer, E. (2008). Some stylized facts on the finance-dominated accumulation regime. *Competition and Change*, 12 (2), 189–207.

Taylor, F. W. (1911). *The principles of scientific management*. Retrieved 1 December 2010 from www.forgottenbook.org

Taylor, L. D. (2000). *Capital, accumulation, and money: An integration of capital, growth, and monetary policy*. Boston, MA, New York: Kluwer Academic Publishers.

Timmer M. P., O'Mahony, M. and Van Ark, B. (2007). Growth and productivity accounts: An overview. *International Productivity Monitor, 14* (Spring), 71–85. Retrieved 29 November 2009 from http://ideas.repec.org/a/sls/ipmsls/v14y20075.html

Triffin, R. (1960). *Gold and the dollar crisis.* New Haven, CT: Yale University Press.

Triplett, J. E. (1999). The Solow productivity paradox: What do computers do to productivity? *Canadian Journal of Economics, 32* (2), 309–34.

Turgot, A. R. J. (1774). *Reflections on the formation and distribution of wealth* (trans. Condorcet). London: E. Spragg. Library of Economics and Liberty. Retrieved 21 March 2008 from www.econlib.org/library/Essays/trgRfl1.html

Turner, M. S. (1989). *Joan Robinson and the Americans.* New York: M. E. Sharpe.

Tymiogne, É. and Wray, R. L. (2006). Money: An alternative story. In P. Arestis and M. Sawyer (Eds.), *A handbook of alternative monetary economics,* pp. 1–16. Cheltenham, UK: Edward Elgar.

Uchikawa, S. (2003). Employment in manufacturing organised sector in India: The rise of medium scale units. In S. Uchikawa (Ed.), *Labour market and institution in India: 1990s and beyond.* Delhi: Manohar.

UNDP (2011). *Human development report. Sustainability and equity: A better future for all.* UN Plaza, New York: UNDP.

United Nations (2009). *The current global crises and their impact on social development.* Commission for Social Development. Forty-seventh session. Retrieved 23 February 2009 from www.un.org/esa/socdev/csd/2009/documents/crp2.pdf

Van Treeck, T. (2007). *Reconsidering the investment-profit nexus in finance-led economies: An ARDL-based approach.* IMK Working Paper, no. 1/ (2007), Duesseldorf: Macroeconomic Policy Institute.

Van Treeck, T. (2009). A synthetic, sock-flow consistent macroeconomic model of financialisation. *Cambridge Journal of Economics, 33* (3), 467–93.

Vaughn, K. I. (1976). Critical discussion of the four papers. In L. S. Moss (Ed.), *The economics of Ludwig von Mises: Toward a critical reappraisal.* Kansas City: Sheen and Ward, Inc.

Veblen, T. (1900). The Preconceptions of Economic Science. *The Quarterly Journal of Economics, 14* (2), 240–269.

Walras, L. (1874). *Elements of pure economics or the theory of social wealth* (trans. W. Jaffé 1954). London: George Allen & Unwin Ltd.

Walsh, V. and Gram, H. (1980). *Classical and neoclassical theories of general equilibrium: Origins and mathematical structure.* New York: Oxford University Press.

Wheelock, D. C. (1990). Member bank borrowing and the Fed's contractionary monetary policy during the Great Depression. *Journal of Money, Credit and Banking, 22,* 409–26.

Wheelock, D. C. (1992). Monetary policy in the Great Depression: What the Fed did and why. *Federal Reserve Bank of St. Louis Review, 74,* 3–28.

Wicksell, K. (1893). *Value, capital and rent* (trans. S. H. Frowein). London: Allen and Unwin, 1954. Reprint (1970). New York: Augustus M. Kelley.

Wicksell, K. (1898[1936]). *Interest and prices.* London: Macmillan and Co. Ltd.

Wicksell, K. (1901[1934]). *Lectures on political economy.* Vol. 1 (trans. E. Classen). London: Routledge and Kegan Paul.

Wilson, J. F. (1995). *British business history 1720–1994.* Manchester: Manchester University Press.

Wolff, E. N. (1997). *The productivity paradox: Evidence from indirect indicators of service sector productivity growth.* Working Paper, no. 97–39. C.V. Starr Center for Applied Economics, New York University. Retrieved 23 February 2009 from http://ideas.repec.org/p/cvs/starer/97–39.html

World Bank (2010). Financial markets. In *Global economic prospects 2010,* January. Retrieved 5 April 2010 from www.worldbank.org

World Bank (2011). *World development indicators database.* Retrieved 23 December 2011 from http://data.worldbank.org

World Bank (2017). *World development indicators.* Retrieved 27 April 2017 from http://data.worldbank.org

Wray, L. R. (1990). *Money and credit in capitalist economies: The endogenous money approach.* Aldershot: Edward Elgar.

Wray, L. R. (1998). *Understanding modern money: The key to full employment and price stability.* Cheltenham, UK: Edward Elgar.

Wray, L. R. (Ed.) (2004). *Credit and state theories of money: The contributions of A. Mitchell Innes.* Cheltenham, UK: Edward Elgar.

Wray, L. R. (2006). *Banking, finance, and money: A socioeconomics approach.* Working Paper, no. 459. The Levy Economics Institute of Bard College University of Missouri.

Zazzaro, A. (2003). How heterodox is the heterodoxy of monetary circuit theory? The nature of money and the microeconomics of the circuit. In L. P. Rochon and S. Rossi (Eds.), *Modern theories of money: The nature and the role of money in capitalist economy,* pp. 219–45. Cheltenham, UK: Edward Elgar.

Zezza, G. (2004). *Some simple, consistent models of the monetary circuit.* Working Paper, no. 405. University of Cassino, Italy, and The Levy Economics Institute. Retrieved 1 December 2010 from www.econstor.eu/dspace/bitstream/10419/316411/504002392.pdf

Index

Note: Page numbers in **bold** denote tables and in *italics* denote figures.

abstinence theory of interest 49
abstract capital: fund 52
accountancy 31
accounting 7, 41, 68, 107–9, 112, 121, 183; entry 36, 42, 96; procedures, rules 86, 89
accumulated values 31, 32
accumulation: of financial capital 1–6, 30, 37, 38, 62, 63, 65, 72, 102, 115–17, 119, 124, 127, 145, 158, 176; of nominal reserves **105**, 115, 117, 119; physical capital 25, 26, 185, 186; rate of 122; stock of goods 90, **105**, 108, 115, 119; of wealth 1, 2, 11, 19–21, 63–5, 81, 84, 102, 158, 168, 169
advances 31, 32, 73, 86, 113, 114
Age of Capital x, 5, 30, 82, 93
agio 53
agricultural production (produce) 32, 39, 73
amortised loan repayments 158, 168, 174
annuities 46
Arthashastra 44, 45
artisans 32, 73, 102
asset-backed securities (ABS) 174
asset price bubble 155–6, 181
assets 1, 4, 7, 8, 19, **20**, 22, 23, 26–8, 31, 34, 37, 38, 40, 42, 65, 86, 89, 93, 94, 96, 104, 106, 109–11, 117, 130, 144, 150, 152–9, 168, 174–6, 178–85
Australia **18**, **19**, 21, **25**, 28

Austrian theory of interest 53
automation 148
average period of production 50, 51, 53, 54

bailout packages 168, 183
balance of payments 91, 131, 140, 141; deficits 6, 129, 136, 166
balance sheet: corporate **105**, 111–13; sectoral 109–11, 113–14
bank: credit 77, 79, 97, 126, 133–5, 137, 166, 180; deposit 91, 93, 103, 105, 110, **110**, 121, 126, 130, 135, 139, 166; deposit interest 110, **110**; dividend income **110**; equity investment **110**; failures 91, 123; loan, loan finance 81, 97, 99, 105, 108, 111, **111**, 112, 117, 118, 120, 122, 131, 136, 138, 139
banking sector 77, 78, 96, 97, 102–5, **105**, **106**, 107, 113–14, 117, 118, 120, 126, 130, 132, 135, 166, 177
Bank of England 85, 88, 125
Bank of International settlements (BIS) 23, 91
bankruptcy ix, 9, 168, 175, 176
barter 40, 68
Belgium 28
bills of exchange 39, 40, 46
bimetallism 88
Böhm-Bawerk 36, 48–55, 60
bonds: junk 176, 177
book debt 85, 88, 89

book keeping transaction 35
boom 127, 181
Brazil 22, 84, 144
Bretton Woods conference 128
broad money supply (M3) 180
bullion famines 83
business: accounting norms 7;
    dividend income **110**; equity
    investment **110**; process
    outsourcing 6, 145

cadrisme 147
Calvinism 47
Cambridge capital controversy 65
Canada **18, 19,** 28
canonical prohibition 55–7
canon law 46, 47
capacity utilisation 147
capital: abstract 52; abstract concept
    of 36; Austrian theory 53;
    circulating 85, 86; circulation of
    74, 75; consumption allowance
    55; cost of 43, 54, 150, 164;
    fixed 25, 32, 41, 42, 185, 186;
    flows 23, 24, 27, 89, 91, 138,
    151, 167; fluid 41; formation 17,
    18, 25, 137, 138, 146, 167, 185,
    186; gains 136, 138, 144, 149,
    154, 155, 156; goods (aggregate
    52); human 21, 36, 37, 42;
    infrastructure 37, 42; intellectual
    37; intensity 8, 145, 146–51, 156,
    167; marginal efficiency of 59;
    non-reproductive 33; paid up 85;
    permanent 150; public 37; share
    40; structure 53, 150, 156; sunk
    41, 42; theory 31, 52, 53, 55, 66;
    twin concept of 30–42; variable
    33, 152; working 32, 34, 41, 54,
    85, 89, 150, 163
capitalism 1, 2, 11, 34, 66, 74, 98,
    100, 101, 126, 163, 164
capitalist 1, 5, 9, 13, 33, 34, 48, 49,
    54, 66, 75, 77, 78, 86, 88, 90,
    126, 127, 131, 169, 181; means
    of production 3, 33, 35, 42, 48,
    163, 164
capital labour substitution 146
cash: balances 57, 58, 69; flow 144,
    155, 158, 174, 175, 182; supply
    of 57, 58

central bank 5, 10, 69, 88, 90, 125,
    126, 132, 139
central bank's monetary
    management 90
Chicago Board of trade (CBOT) 24,
    171, 172
Chicago Mercantile exchange
    (CME) 24, 172
China 13, 21, 89, 144, 183, 184
circuit: analysis 1, 62–81, 97,
    99, 122, 137, 140, 162, 165,
    167, 173; closed 4, 8, 81, 102;
    construct 74, 76–8, 82–100;
    dynamics 73, 121; final 142,
    146, 160, 169; monetary 3, 4,
    75–81, 95, 103, 109, 132, 163;
    production 104; revival of 76;
    rudimentary formulation 97,
    101–23; theory 4, 62, 72–6, 81
circulation of money 73
circulation of money and goods 76
class: mercantile 39, 40; productive
    73; proprietary 73; sterile 73;
    working 75
classical economic thinkers 47, 163
classical political economy 33, 75
coinage 39, 68, 88
collateralised debt obligations
    (CDOs) 175, 183
collateralised loan obligations
    (CLOs) 175
colonial conquests 82, 88, 90, 163
colonies 2, 89, 99, 120
Columbus's voyage 1492 83
commercial banks 27, 28, 93, 94,
    124, 126, 132, 134, 140, 179
Commodities Futures Trading
    Commission (CFTC) 24, 172
company shares 87
compensation 39, 46, 49, 54, 55,
    188, 189
computers 15, 16
concentration of wealth 2, 8, 19, 21,
    145, 169
conglomerates 7
constant return to scale 70
consumer durables 153
consumers 26, 77, 78, 153
consumption: demand for industrial
    goods 130, 141; expenditure 141,
    166; function (Keynesian 161);

future 54, 59; household 26, 161; present 57
contingent claims 173, 176
contractual interest (contract interest) 44, 45, 52
corespective firms 25
corporate: bonds 78, 134; control 28; governance 28–9, 185; havens 7, 21, 144; industrial production 2, 6, 102, 120; production x, 2, 5, 6, 82–125, 127, 130, 132–41, 144, 151, 157, 164–7, 171; restructuring 28, 145, 176–7, 185; taxes 150; wealth 11, 19–21, 65, 162
corporate production circuit 5, 6, 94, 94, 95, 97–100, 117, 118, 120, 122–5, 132–41, 165, 166; country-centric 144; fragility of 118
corporate production economy: with creditisation x, 2, 165; matured 6, 132, 133; nascent 5, 82–101, 105, 106, 120, 132; organisational structure 103
cost of capital 43, 54, 150, 164
cost plus profit 107, 133
country specific circuits 6, 7
credit: crisis 10; default swaps (CDS) 24, 183; mechanisms 86; rationing 69; against the stocks 90; system 34, 39, 44, 46, 90
creditisation x, 2, 6, 100, 101, 123, 124–42, 165
crisis: of 2008 ix, 9, 144, 145, 168, 182–4; banking 28, 92, 117, 118; Brazilian 22; Chilean 22; currency 28; Latin American debt 22; liquidity 83, 98, 118, 121, 123, 124, 134–6, 166; management 29; South East Asian 22; tequila 22
CSO National Account Statistics 186
currency 88–91, 126, 129, 132, 136, 140, 141, 151, 161, 169; convertible 88, 91, 126, 129, 177
current account: deficits 131; surpluses 89

Das Kapital 33
debit 39, 40, 68, 110, **110**, 111, **112, 114**

debt: crises x, 9, 10, 22, 27, 168, 178, 183, 184; finance 4, 148, 150, 151; financing (short-term 79); obligations 174 (long-term 79, 150); trap 158, 168
debtors 8, 39–41, 44, 85, 168
decision theory 38
declining labour productivity 6
default 9, 44, 168, 172, 175, 176
deferred payments 46, 68
deficit financing 127, 128
deflation 122, 123
degree of combined leverage (DCL) 147
degree of financial leverage (DFL) 147, 148
degree of operating leverage (DOL) 147, 148, 150
deposit multiplier 69
depository institutions 180
depreciation 4, 32, 41, 42, 55, 60, 71, 104, **106**, 107, 108, 111, **111**, **112**, 113, 116, 117, 124, 137, 148, 163, 164; charged **106**, 112, **112**, 116; charges 108, 117, 124, 148; reserve 41, **111**, 113, 137
deregulation 179
derivative of marginal desirability 51
derivatives 7, 24, 28, 143, 155, 173–6, 180; credit 179; exchange traded 24; over the counter (OTC) 23, 24
developed countries 10, 17, 24, 91, 127, 132, 172, 186
developing countries 2, 6, 7, 24, 127, 131, 132, 136, 144, 160, 172, 177, 178; debt crisis 178
digitalisation: economics of 161, 169
digitalised 152; accounts 161, 169; financial web 9, 143, 161, 169; money 9, 161
discount of future goods against present goods 53, 54
disembodied 39, 40, 86
disequilibrium analysis 73
distribution 12, 16, 19, 21, 70–2, 77, 112, 147, 148, 151, 167, 168, 184, 186
dividend: rate of 116, 121, 122
dividend income 107, 109, 110, **110**, 135–9, 144, 149, 150, 153, 156, 166, 167

dividend payout 29; ratio 28, 149, 150, 185
dollar liabilities 129
double charge 60
double entry book keeping 86
downsize and distribute 28, 148, 149

earnings 8, 22, 80, 89, 104, 124, 148–50, 154–6; future 26, 59, 160–2
earnings before interest and tax (EBIT) 147, 150
earnings per share (EPS) 147–50
East Asia and Pacific 12, **12**
East India company: British 85; Dutch 85
ecologies 37
economic: accumulation of stocks 62, 72; activities 6–8, 35, 36, 38, 40, 43, 45, 57, 72, 81, 92, 131, 160, 168; bubbles 145, 173, 180–4; circuit (close-ended 4, 8, 151; open-ended 4, 83, 151; rudimentary 5, 101; single 6, 7, 144, 145); crisis 22, 142, 145, 182–4; depreciation 41; flows 4, 62, 68, 70, 72, 93, 95, 105 (endogenous); fragility 28; growth 1, 5, 6, 9, 26–8, 30, 36, 37, 124, 128, 137, 139, 140, 145–7, 159, 160, 167, 168, 182; interest 52, 53; interventions 102; policies (post-Keynesian 62); schools of thought (Austrian 62; Circuitists 62); evolutionary 62; Marxist 62; neo-classical 76); stocks 1, 2, 93; systems x, 1–6, 9, 21, 24, 29, 30, 37, 43, 46, 60–3, 67, 70, 76, 81, 129, 146, 160, 162, 164, 170, 181
economy: stationary 78
edge of crisis 1, 142, 184
education 13, 21, 26, 37, 161
effective demand 75, 80
embodied 34–6, 41, 52
employment 16–18, 29, 48, 60, 80, 125, 128, 132, 140
endogenous credit 5, 101, 123, 134, 136, 141
energy crisis 15

entrepreneur 49, 50, 59, 60, 76, 80, 131, 163, 164
environment economics 37
equilibrium: analysis 65–8, 74, 80; anti 66; assumption of 65; convergence to 74, 77; general 68, 72, 74, 80, 103; market exchange 1, 2, 4; partial 74; rate of interest 56; Walrasian 68, 80, 103
equity 7, 23, 31, 79, 86, 93, **105**, 110, 113, 114, 122, 134–6, 139, 148, 149, 154, 176
equity capital 85, 86, 96, 97, 103, 105, 106, 109, 111, **111**, 113, **113**, 121; corporate 152
Euler's theorem 70
Euro currency market 177
Eurodollar 177–8
European monetary system (EMS) 22
European Payments Union 177
evolutionary stages of Western capitalism 2
evolution of capitalism 3
exchange rate 90, 128, 131, 132; flexible 128; floating 131
exchanges: direct 73; indirect 73
exemptions: direct 46; indirect 46
expectations 36, 59, 66, 67, 69, 77, 160, 177, 182
expenditure: on company products **110**
explorations 81, 83

factor: cost 80, 187, 188, 189; income 187; income shares 71; prices 74, 146, 148; shares 74
federal reserve 92, 125, 180; monetary policies 91
Fetter, F. A. 51–3
fiat currency 126
Final Circuit 142, 146, 160, 169
finance: led growth (regime) 148–50, 156, 167; motive 35, 57; un-invested 35
finance dominated regime 26, 28, 30
financial: accounting 68; accounts 143, 152, 175; architecture 7, 173–5; assets 1, 7, 8, 22, 34, 38, 93, 94, 130, 143, 144, 154–6,

158, 159, 174, 176, 177, 179–83; breeding 43–61; capital (mobility of 41; origin of 105); circuit 5, 7–9, 139, 142–62, 165, 167–9, 184; claims 4, 169; commodities x, 3, 23, 24, 101, 142–4, 155, 165 (new generation 7, 22, 23, 143, 145, 171, 173, 176); decision-making 23; economy ix, x, 1, 7, 8, 11, 22–3, 29, 38, 42, 119, 142, 144–6, 151–4, 157, 159, 160, 162, 165, 167, 168, 171, 173, 176, 178, 181–4, 185; evolutions 1, 82; flows 27, 144; leveraging 145, 147–50, 155–7, 182; liberalisation 29, 180; market (fragmentation 27; integration 26–7); profits 23, 24–5, 96; sector 1, 24, 26, 37, 143, 152, 155, 157, 158, 168, 169, 186, 187; transactions 6–8, 20, 24, 143, 144, 151, 152, 168, 182; web (digitalised 9, 143, 161, 169; global ix, 6, 26, 27, 143, 144)

financial instability hypothesis (FIH) 181

financialisation 2, 7, 11, 22–3, 26, 28, 101, 145–8, 160, 161, 184–6, 188, 189

first industrial revolution 36

fiscal: deficits 6, 137, 139–41, 154, 157, 166; policy 91, 125, 127

Fisher, Irving 34, 49, 51 , 52, 55, 59, 69

flow: account 109–14, **110**, **112**, **114**, 122; cycle 103, 109; of dividend 96; of money 6, 61, 75, 78, 80, 95–8, 100, **105**, 108, 117–19, 121, 124, 132, 135, 136, 138, 139, 143, 144, 151, 154, 158, 162, 165–7; of profits 158; of services 71

follow the leader approach 88

forces of production 2

Fordist era 14, 130

foreign: investment 13, 89; trade 6, 13, 85, 151

foreign exchange reserve 91, 132, 136, 140

foreign institutional investments 7, 29

forward contracts 171; exchange traded 171

fractional reserve system 126, 132

France **18**, **19**, 25, **25**, 28, 76, 84, 88, 89, 91, 185

French physiocrats x, 1, 4, 72, 170

Friedman, Milton 69, 92

fund of pure capital 52

fungibility 41

future: contracts 158; earnings 26, 59, 160, 161, 162; income streams 160; trading exchanges 7

giant corporations 8, 145, 176

Glass–Steagall Act 1933 179

global: corporate (concentration 27–8; financial circuit 5; web 27–8); economic circuit 2, 6–8, 151, 157, 160; financial web ix, 6, 9, 26, 27, 143, 144, 161, 169; tax on capital 9, 169

globalisation 2, 7, 13, 23, 26, 144, 151, 152, 165, 169, 177, 184, 186; of economic activities 6

golden: era 5, 87–9, 100, 140; fetters 5, 90–3, 100, 132, 165

golden age: of finance 24; of modern capitalism 11; of Western capitalism 130

gold reserves 89, 91, 93, 97, 98, 100, 102, 103, 120, 129, 132, 136, 152

Gold Standard 88–92, 100, 102, 117, 119, 123–6, 128, 132, 143

Gold Standard money 5, 83, 93, 97, 98, 100, 102, 103, 120, 122, 132, 134, 136, 139, 165

goods: future 50–4; present 50, 52–4

government: borrowings 154, 158; expenditure 97, 100, 127, 165; securities 132, 154; tax 7

Great Depression of 1930s 10, 91, 92, 123–5, 127, 168

Greece debt crisis 168, 183

gross domestic investment (GDI) 17, 18

gross domestic product (GDP) 7, 11, 12, **12**, 14, 15, 18, 20, 25, 28, 185–7, **187**, 188, **188**, 189

gross fixed capital formation 25, **25**, 185, 186; as percentage of GDP 25
gross national product (GNP) 125
growing: concentration of wealth and income 8, 145; indebtedness 8, 137, 139–40, 145, 157–9; unemployment 8, 145
growth: finance led 148, 150, 156, 167; future 55, 60, 61, 159, 160, 169, 176; jobless 11, 17–18, 146; malignant 119; paradox 10–29, 36; rates 11–15, **12**, 17, **25**, 69, 183
growth profit trade off 149

hedge fund 7, 23
Hekscher-Ohlin theorem 99, 165
heterodox economics 58, 69
Hicks, J. R. 58, 69
Hicks Hansen formulation of Keynesian theory 58
Hicks Lindahl sequence economy 158
high-end products 8, 141, 145, 153, 155–8, 167
high net worth individuals (HNIs) 2, 8, 19, 93, 96, 138, 139, 142, 145, 151–60, 167, 168, 169
high positive net worth 152, 159
historical roots of financial evolutions 1, 3
household: consumption 26, 161; debts 8, 18, 19, **19**, 110, 140, 157–9, 168, 169, 183, 184; equity **105**; indebtedness 158, 166; saving rates 18; wealth 19
human capital 21, 36, 37, 42
Human Development Report 21
human impatience 51
human labour 33
human societies 39, 170

ICT (information and communication technology) 6, 14, 15, 17, 24, 37, 142, 143, 165
idle balances 77
illiquid assets 174, 175
impatience 52
implements 32, 39
implicit interest 53

income: current 157, 158, 167, 168; disposable 18, **19**, 26, 161; distribution 12, 16, 21, 70, 147, 151, 168; dividend 107, 109, 110, **110**, 135–9, 144, 149, 150, 153, 156, 166, 167; interest 104, 110, 121, 122, 141, 150, 157; primary source of 153; redistribution 121, 122, 147, 150, 151, 166, 167; streams 160, 174; wage 104, 110, **110**, 121, 122, 134, 135, 137–9, 146, 150, 166, 167, 185, 189
indebtedness growing 158
India 7, 13, 21, 44, 82, 89, 160, 184, 186, 187, **187**, 188, **188**, 189
Indian national income 89
individual: firms 26; rational 64, 70; utility maximising 64
individualistic approach 74, 77
industrial capital 75
industrial revolution 1, 2, 33, 36, 49, 55, 82–7, 90, 99, 163
inequality 2, 10, 11, 13, 17, 21–2, 122, 141, 151, 158, 167–9, 184, 185
inflation 15, 29, 69, 126, 141
information and communication technology (ICT) 6, 14, 15, 17, 24, 37, 142, 143, 165
innovations 2, 6, 35, 119, 120, 140, 180
institutional evolutions 124–5, 132, 140
instruments 39, 45, 68, 175, 176, 179, 180, 182; negotiable 40; transferable 40
intellectual property 37
interbank lending 10
intereo 46
interesse 46
interest: bearing debt 148, 170; contract 44, 45, 52; economic 52, 53; implicit 53; interest equalization tax (IET) 178; monetary theories 48, 55–9; on money 3, 43–61, 82, 163, 170; natural 50
international: agencies 9, 182; bank lending 23; bonds 23; cooperation 88, 89, 91; financial 22, 91, 131,

178; lender of last resort 88, 91; loans 23; Monetary Fund, IMF 128, 131, 182; monetary system 6, 89, 128, 129, 131; reserves 129

International Bank for Reconstruction and Development (IBRD) 128

intertemporal 53

intrinsic values 33, 74

investment: current 41; opportunity 15, 51, 55, 131; past 41

investors 22, 23, 38, 77, 84, 85, 149, 150, 155, 156, 171, 173, 175, 182, 183

IS LM model 58

Italy 28, 76, 85

Japan 12, 13, 15, 17, 18, **18**, **19**, **25**, 28, 128

jobless growth 11, 17–18, 146

joint stock companies 5, 82, 83, 85

Joint Stock Company: Act of 1844 86

Kaleckian models of distribution and growth 147

Kennedy Johnson tax-cut of 1964 128

Keynesian: paradox of thrift 96, 166; prescription (program, policies) 127, 128, 137, 139, 167; theory 57, 58

Keynesianism 6, 76, 125, 127–8, 139, 140

Keynesian liquidity preference theory 56, 58

Keynesians 30, 77

Keynes, John Maynard x, 5, 34, 35, 56–9, 65, 75–7, 90, 92, 170

Kornai, Janos 66

labour: productivity 6, 14, 15, 120, 130, 165; skilled 21; unskilled 21

landed property 187

legal: codes 45; prohibitions 45; tender 44

legitimisation of interest on money 43–61

lender of last resort 88, 91, 126

lending 10, 23, 39, 40, 43, 45, 46, 48, 91, 93, 117, 128, 131, 135, 179, 180, 183

leveraged: buyouts 176, 179; growth 150, 151, 160, 167; system wide 146

leveraging 7, 8, 143–61; financial 145, 147–50, 155, 157

liabilities: limited 5, 83, 84, 86, 87; non-deposit 180; unlimited 84

liberalisation 29, 144, 180

Limited Liability: Act of 1855 86; companies 5, 87

liquid: balances 69, 70, 78, 92; money balances 69; resources 35, 86, 88, 89

liquidity: crisis 83, 98, 118, 121, 123, 124, 134–6, 166; crunches 90; infusion (injections) 10, 85, 86, 127, 128

liquidity injections 10, 127, 128

liquidity preference theory 56, 58

loanable funds theory 56, 58

loan instalments 104

London 84, 85, 178

macroeconomic: aggregation 35; construct 77

macroeconomics 53, 65

management cybernetics and operation research 120

management priorities 28, 185

managerial salaries 147

manna from heaven 70, 80, 103

manufacturing: corporations 34; sector 14, 17, 18, 131, 141, 186, 188, **188**, 189

marginal: analysis 70; desirability 51

marginal productivity: theories of factor remuneration 70; theory of distribution 70

market equilibrium: short-term 56

marking to market 7, 154, 155, 183

Marshall, Alfred 63, 69

Marshall Plan 128, 129

Marx, Karl x, 2, 33, 34, 65, 74–7

matured corporate production circuit 5, 6, 125, 134, 136, 139, 140, 166

mechanisation 148, 150

megamergers 27
Menger, Karl 36, 50, 68
mercantile class 39, 40
merchants 47, 73, 86, 102
mergers and acquisitions 20, 176, 177
methodological: construct 70, 72; individualism 64–5; instrumentalism 64
methodology x, 1, 2, 4, 5, 30, 62–7, 70, 72, 81, 146
Mexican default of 1982 178
Millennium Goals 10
Minsky moment 182
Mises, Ludwig Von 36, 51–4
mixed income 187
model specification 27
monetarist: approach 69; policies 29
monetary: expansion 93, 101, 124, 125, 130; finance 47, 60; flow 4, 75, 76, 80, 81, 123; forces 48, 56; fund 3, 31, 33, 42, 43, 50, 52, 54–7, 60, 61, 163; policy 10, 69 (tight 92); production economy 76; sector 68, 80; units 44, 151; variables 59
monetary circuits 3, 4, 75–81, 95, 103, 109, 132, 163
monetisation 85, 87–90, 98, 123, 124, 136, 137
money: capital (commodified 34; revolving 115–17, 121, 134, 135, 137–9, 167); circulation of 73, 76; commodity 43, 126, 127; credit 5, 6, 86, 90, 101–3, 123–7, 132–6, *133*, 140, 143, 165, 166; digitalisation of 118, 169; endogenous 101, 103, 124, 127, 132, 139; exogenous 101, 102, **105**, 123, 132; fiat 125, 132; flow in the circuit 75, 96, 97, 162; in future 38; growth rates 69; hoarding of 75; hungriness 83, 118, 161, 165, 169; idle 96, 103, 104, 118; income 58, 73, 75, 94, 95, 99, 102, 107, 109, 111, 114, 121, 127, 135, 138; Keynesian approach 69; life-cycle 77; loans 43, 44, 47, 48, 52, 60, 82, 93, 96, 99, 109, 115, 117,
120, 134, 135, 163, 166, 170; market 92, 179 (mutual funds 180); means of exchange 68, 77; means of payment 40, 77; medium of exchange 74; medium of speculation 57; multiplier 92, 126; non neutrality 70; reserves **105**; speculative holding of 134; standard 5, 83, 93, 97, 98, 100, 102, 103, 120, 122, 132, 134, 136, 139, 165; state issued exogenous 102; stock of 57, 79, 103, 115, 118; store of value 40, 60, 68; supply 69, 78, 92, **94**, 97, 100, 125, 126, 132, **133**, 134, 165, 180; supply M1 125; supply M3 180; transferable 40; transfers 38, 102–3, **105**; value of goods consumed **110**; velocity of circulation 73; virtual 6, 9, 151, 158
moneyed capitalists 75
moneylenders 46, 47, 102
mora 46
mortgage 46, 144, 154, 174
mortgage-backed securities (MBS) 174, 179
mortgage loan 144, 174
motives for holding money: finance 35, 57; precautionary 57; speculative 57; transaction 57
mutual funds 23, 180

nascent corporate production circuit 5, *94*, 97, 98, 100, 123, 133, 134, 136, 137, 139, 166
national economies 2, 5, 20, 93, 96–8, 103, 114, 122, 145, 157, 159
National Futures Association 24, 172
nation states 82, 84, 93
natural interest 50
natural resources 37, 81, 93, *94*, 98, *133*, *153*, 154, 158
neoclassical: analysis 1, 63, 67, 69; marginalism 76; theory 49–50, 59, 63–6, 70, 71, 77, 80, 99, 163, 165
net disposable income (NDI) 18, **19**

net exports 6, 97–100, 121, 122, 124, 132, 134, 136, 137, 139, 140, 157, 163, 166
Netherlands 28
net product 72
neutrality of money 69
new classical theory 69
New Deal 127
new economy 14, 16
new financial architecture (NFA) 174
new generation financial commodities 23, 145, 171, 173, 176
new international financial order 22
New Monetary Consensus (NMC) 69
Newtonian mechanics 65, 74
New York 129
non-agricultural production 39
non-financial: businesses 25, 185; sector 26
non-monetary: theories of interest 43, 52, 55
North West Europe 83

OECD (Organisation for Economic Cooperation and Development) 10, 14, 17, 18, 21, 185
off-balance sheet: activities (transactions) 175, 179, 182, 183
oil petroleum exporting countries (OPEC) 131, 177, 178
oil-price shocks 15, 16
open: circuit framework 102; economic circuit 4, 83; market operations 92
operating: profits 147, 148, 150, 151, 167; surplus 186–8, **188**, 189
operational: leveraging 157
options 22, 24, 38, 172, 173
option trading exchanges 7
ordinary prices 51
organisation: evolutions x, 2, 5, 6, 100, 109, 175
organisation and method (O&M) 120
outsourcing 6, 7, 16, 145
over-the-counter (OTC) 23–5, 171

owner manager conflict 149
owner of capital 47–8
ownership 27, 48, 49, 86, 152, 153, 187

paradox of profits 3, 4, 8, 78–9, 81, 95, 117, 157, 158, 162, 163
parity 88, 89, 90
par value system 22
pension funds 23, 174
per capita income 13, 186
permanent fund of capital 52
physical asset accumulation 25, 186
physical capital 3, 4, 29, 31–7, 41, 43, 48, 52, 65, 71, 185, 186; stock of 35
physiocrats x, 1, 4, 32, 47, 72–6, 162, 163, 170
pooled investments 82, 86
Portugal 84, 89
positive: interest rate 4; time preference 50, 52, 59
post-Keynesian: accommodationists 126; models of distribution and growth 147, 148
post-war reconstruction 130, 140
pre-capitalist societies 34
pre-classical 31, 47, 72–4
preferences: driven 64; endogenous 64; exogenous 64
price: accounting 107–9, 112, 121; consumption goods 135; current 26, 109, 161, 187, 188; historical 109; inflationary rise 100, 135, 137, 140, 141, 166; primary commodities 22
primitive society 38
private: capital flows 23
privatisation 144, 186; equity fund 7, 176
produced means of production 3, 36, 41, 42, 48, 163
producer goods 78
product exhaustion theorem 70
production: capital 1, 3, 39, 41, 42, 49; capital primitive form of 39; cycles 32, 89, 95, 96, 102, 104, 108, 115, 135, 137, 138, 165; process 14, 31–3, 35, 36, 39, 43, 47, 50, 70, 80, 85, 88, 89, 148,

150, 163; surplus 96–100, 117, 118, 124, 125, 133–8, 141, 157, 162, 164, 165

productivity: approach 49; decline 15, 16; gains 14, 16; paradox 1, 11–17; slowdown 15, 16; theories of interest 49, 51, 52; unexplained 1, 15

profits: banking sector 104, **106**, 107, 114; entrepreneurial 163, 164; expectations 77 (uncertain 77); mark-up 96, 107, 108, 112, 133, 135; maximisation 71, 116 (short-term 149); maximising 64; monetary 4, 79–81, 102, 104, 107, 133, 135, 140, 157, 163–6; money 4, 5, 79, 81, 97–9, 104, 114, 118, 124, 134, 135, 139; normal 71, 164; operating 147, 148, 150, 151, 167; paradox 164, 165; production sector **106**; rate of 48, 116, 121, 122, 122 , 147, 185; supernormal 24; undistributed retained 99–100, 104, 136, 166, 170

progressive global tax 9, 169

prohibition 45–7, 55–7

prohibition against usury 45, 56

proletarians 77

property rights 39

proprietary funds 174

protestant ethics and spirits 2

psychological theories of interest 52

public debt 139, *153*, 154, 157, 159, 162, 168

public expenditure 91, 154

purchasing power 75

pure closed monetary circuit 4

pure productivity theory of interest 52

Quesnay, Francois 72

rate of interest natural money 56

rational behaviour 71, 164

rational expectations: hypothesis 69; model 66

real: business cycle 66, 67; estate assets 152, 153, 158; gross capital formation 17; minimum wage 16; sector 1, 6, 8, 23–5, 68, 80,

132 (investment activity 17, 29, 185; production activities 157; stagnation 17–18, 24, 130–2, 141, 156–7, 168, 169, 176–8); theory of interest 51

receivables credit card telephone royalty 174

redistribution of income shares 146

Regulation Q 177

regulatory norms 177

regulatory safeguards 28

reimbursement 46

remuneration 70–2, 164

rent 48, 53, 70, 74, 75, 107, 154, 164; on capital 31

rentier: class 29, 188; income 7, 23–5, 72, 121, 122, 138, 145, 146–51, 153, *153*, 154, 166–8, 182, 185–9, **187**

rentier capital flight 29

repayment of loan 46, 81, 104, 107, 108, 158, 168

reproduction schemes 74

research and development 37

reserve: depreciation 41, **111**, 113, 137; requirements 126, 178, 180

reserve (retained profit) 111

rest of the world 5, 6, 81, 90, *94*, 97–100, 102, 103, 106, 114, 118–22, 129, *133*, 134, 136, 137, 139, 140, 157, 165, 166

resurgent Asia 13

retain and invest 28, 149

retained profits 29, 93, *94*, *95*, 100, 104, 106, 107, 112, **112**, 113, 116, 124, *133*, 137

return on capital 43, 71

revenue income 20, 157, 170

revolving fund 35

Ricardo, David 48, 56, 138

risk 22, 38, 45, 59, 143, 146, 164, 173–6, 178, 181, 183

Robinson, Joan 35, 66, 70

roundaboutness of production methods 51, 55

rudimentary economic circuit 5, 101

sale of goods 98, 107, **112**

schools of thought: circuit 62; Keynesian 62; Marxian 62; neoclassical 62

Schumpeter 2, 73
sector: banking 77, 78, 96, 97,
    102–5, **105**, **106**, 107, **113**,
    113–14, **114**, 117, 118, 120,
    126, 130, 132, 135, 166, 177;
    household ix, 19, 93–7, 99, 102,
    105, 107–9, **110**, 110–11, 113,
    120–2, 134, 137–9, 142, 145,
    151–3, 155; production 9, 58,
    94–8, 100, 102, 104, 105, **105**,
    106, 107–17, **111**, **112**, 121, 122,
    130, 133, 134, 136, 137, 158,
    166, 167
sectoral accounts 5
Securities and Exchange Commission
    (SEC) 24, 172
securitisation 7, 8, 22, 144, 145,
    154, 159, 160, 174–5, 178, 180,
    183
seigniorage 103
self breeding 43, 61
sequence economy: Hicks Lindahl
    158
service sector 14, 16, 36, 130, 131,
    141, 142; growth paradox 1, 16
shareholders 26, 28–9, 82–4, 86,
    87, 99, 100, 104, 147–50, 177,
    185
shareholder value revolution 26, 28
Smith, Adam 48, 49, 62, 65, 68, 106
social security system 22
social theory of interest 48
socio-political dimensions 64
Solow productivity paradox 6, 15,
    16
South Asia 12, **12**
sovereign debt crisis x, 9, 10, 27,
    168, 183, 184
Spain 28, 89
special drawing rights (SDR) 131
special purpose vehicle (SPV) 7, 155,
    175, 178, 183
specie 83–4, 88, 97, 102
speculation 28, 57, 129, 143, 161,
    172, 173, 183
speculative: activities 58, 92, 172;
    gains 57, 58, 87, 172–3, 176,
    181; motives 57
speculators 87, 129, 172, 173,
    181
spring of nations 82

stagnation: in real sector 17–18, 24,
    130–2, 141, 156–7, 168, 169,
    176–8
standardisation of monetary units 44
start-ups 80
stationary economy 78
sticky: prices 69; wages 69
stock: exchange 34, 84, 85, 87, *94*,
    133 (London 85); flow 4, 5, 62,
    63, 67, 81, 109, 114; of goods
    31, 33, 39, 87–90, 93, 94, *94*, *95*,
    96, **105**, 106, 108, 109, 111, **111**,
    112, **112**, 113, 115, 117–19, 130,
    133, 135, 152, 166 (accumulated
    106, 111, 113, 115, 118, 119;
    closing 112, **112**; unsold 96,
    98); markets (capitalisation 23;
    medieval 85; modern 85); of
    wealth 34
structural: shift 16; transformations
    x, 9, 170
structured securities 7, 143, 174–6,
    180, 183
subsidy policies 7
subsistence: wage rate 138
subsistence theory 138
super entity 21, 27, 144
surplus: fund 35, 39; production
    96–100, 117, 118, 124, 125,
    133–8, 141, 157, 162, 164, 165;
    value 33, 34, 49, 54, 75, 138
Sweden 28
Switzerland 28
systemic risk 146

Tableau Économique 32, 72
tally 39, 40
taxation 28
tax cuts 127
technical superiority 51, 52
technological innovations 35, 120
technology 6, 14, 16, 30, 35, 37,
    43, 87, 140, 142, 143, 163;
    measurement problems 17, 36, 65
terms of trade 89, 99, 114, 120, 131
theories of monetary circuit 3, 4,
    76–81, 95, 103, 109, 163
theory of capitalisation 53
theory of interest: abstinence 49;
    Keynesian 57; productivity 49, 51,
    52; social 48; use 49, 54

theory of monetary circuit (TMC) 76, 95, 103
theory of rent 53
time: element 53, 103; preference 50–5, 59–61; valuation 50, 51
total factor productivity 14, 130
trade: credit 85, 88, 89; terms of 89, 99, 114, 120, 131
transaction: cost of 68; flow 81, 102, 154; motive 57
transferability of shares 84
transfer of resources: resources 89
transnational corporations (TNC) 21, 27, 144, 145
treading upon the future 4, 38, 159–60
Triffin dilemma 129
tripartite division of factors of production 70, 164
Tulip Mania of 1637 171
Turgot, Anne-Robert-Jacques 32, 47, 48, 54, 72

uncertainty 22, 38, 59, 69, 70, 143, 182
undepreciated portion 41
under-consumption 75
unemployment 8, 17, 18, 69, 123, 127, 145
unidirectional flow 81
United Kingdom 25, 28, 88, 91, 131, 185, xii
United Nations report 10
United States 10, 14–19, 22, 24, 25, 27, 28, 66, 88, 91, 92, 125, 127–9, 131, 171, 172, 174, 176–8, 185; dollars 129, 151, 177; housing bubble 156, 182, 183
'usura' 45
usury 34, 43, 45–8, 52, 55–8, 60, 163
utility 69, 77

value-added production 70, 71
Veblen, Thorstein: negative 63
virtual money flow 6
virtuous circle 21
Volcker's paradox 24

wage: distribution 21; earners 21, 77, 78, 135, 138, 168, 188; goods 8, 145, 153, *153*, 155, 156; income 104, 110, **110**, 121, 122, 134, 135, 137–9, 146, 150, 166, 167, 185, 189; inequality 17, 21; white-collar 21, 147
wealth: creation 2, 84; generation 84
Wealth of Nations 62, 72, 106
Western: capitalism 2, 98, 100, 101, 130; European society 2
why and whence of interest 47
Wicksell, Knut 56, 69, 76
working capital 32, 34, 41, 54, 85, 89, 150, 163
World Bank 10, 12, 17, 128
world economy 11, 129
World Trade Organisation (WTO) 144

For Product Safety Concerns and Information please contact our EU
representative GPSR@taylorandfrancis.com Taylor & Francis Verlag GmbH,
Kaufingerstraße 24, 80331 München, Germany

Printed and bound by CPI Group (UK) Ltd, Croydon, CR0 4YY
01/05/2025
01858414-0002